INDIA-AUSTRALIA

Towards Sustainable Partnership in 21st Century

Edited by
Y. Yagama Reddy

AKANSHA PUBLISHING HOUSE
NEW DELHI • GUWAHATI • VISAKHAPATNAM

AKANSHA PUBLISHING HOUSE
4649-B/21, Ansari Road
Darya Ganj, New Delhi - 110 002
Ph.: 23263193 / 9811582579 / 09435116718
Fax: 011-23263193
Email: ektabooks@yahoo.com
www.akanshapublishinghouse.com

India-Australia: Towards Sustainable Partnership in 21st Century

First Edition, 2012

ISBN 978-81-8370-309-3

PRINTED IN INDIA

Published by Akansha Publishing House, New Delhi and Printed at Harmain Offset Press, Delhi.

Contents

Preface

India-Australia bilateral relationship is a classic case for mixed feelings— a sort of excitement over a set of commonalities and complementarities between them as well as disappointment with their irreconcilable stand on the issues of no significance to their national interests. The bilateral relationship had been a mixture of brief spells of bonhomie and longer periods of hibernation manifesting in estrangement. At the base of this lackluster relationship were the ignorance and negligence coupled with stale impressions of each other country. These impressions of all the more pervasive in nature, though reflected some reality, were also of rhetoric in nature perceptibly echoing an element of contempt and acrimony. Australia is a 'country of cricket players,' for the crazy boys, an exclusive 'habitat of kangaroos' for the biology students, an 'island-continent' for the geography students, 'deputy sheriff' or a 'client state' of the US in the Asia Pacific for the students of international studies and the 'land of Aborigines,' for the anthropologists. But, Indians do have little knowledge about the semblance in certain aspects of physical geography and hardly aware of the human geography of the Aborigines who have ethnic affinities with the tribal communities in peninsular India. On their part, Australians have gained a meagre knowledge of India that it was once a British domain. Besides developing a formidable impression of India as a 'land of dirt and disease', Australians used to deride the multi-faceted diversity in Indian society as being analogous to a tropical jungle. Appallingly, Australia has a very thin memory of the fabulous contribution of the Indian camel drivers and indentured labour to the economic development of Australia in the 19th century. Australia was proud of being identified as the European 'cultural outpost' at the tail-end of Asia; but, about the same time, it was reluctant to develop an understanding of the history, polity, economy and geography of its immediate Asian neighbours. Australia was used to look at India as 'a key player' in South Asian politics, a 'champion' of non-aligned movement, and a 'critic' of the US and a 'proxy' or simply an 'ally' of the Soviet Union during the Cold War period. India simply dismissed Australia as an ally of the US and hence considered it as irrelevant to its interests. Perplexingly, the arguments were much "deeper than the differences" between these two proximate nations to the extent of undermining the immense potentialities for mutual benefit and enduring divergence on matters of no relevance to their bilateral relationship.

The exotic impressions, though altogether unjustifiable, were deeply rooted in the minds of the people that deprived them of the basic knowledge of each other country, even if the people on either side are very much familiar with the facts and figures of the Western world. This was a vacuum which the Australian Prime Minister Gough Whitlam termed as an 'anomaly'. It was simply 'lack of knowledge' and hence 'lack of interest' that perpetuated the attitude of 'indifference' which eventually resulted in 'drift and discord' mind-set. All those lofty propositions envisioned by the statesmen, like Alfred Deakin, H W Hughes, Betram Stevans, Jawaharlal Nehru, Joseph Ben Chifley, H V Evatt, Richard Casey and Gough Whitlam simply remained unfulfilled. Australian White Policy restrictions and the Cold War ideological estrangement had even invalidated the 'gesture' of the Colombo Plan, under which Australia made liberal aid available to India. Similarly, the much qualified support and military aid from Australia in the wake of 1962 Sino-Indian skirmishes and the benevolent neutrality of Australia during the Indo-Pak Wars of 1965 and 1971 did not seem to have contributed to an enhanced bilateral partnership between these two nations. Instead, they suffered a substantial disagreement on the matters concerning the Indian Ocean security; and even the justifiable naval build-up by India had become a source of concern for Australia. It was simply a 'tale of missed opportunities'!

These two Commonwealth nations, which ought to have predisposed to their historical and geographical linkages, had remained in a state of aloofness. The clouds of mistrust began dispersing, when the Australian Standing Committee on Foreign Affairs and Trade ruled out any threat to Australia from the Indian navy. It was the Australian Foreign Affairs Minister Gareth Evans who envisioned the termination of the Cold War tensions and initiated the process of rapprochement between these oft-demurred nations. In pursuit of exploring new avenues of partnership with India, the Australian government began tracing the basic linkages between them. For instance, Australia brought into focus many instances of semblance, like the parallel occurrence of droughts as a result of the El Nino effect, the similarity in 'climatic, geographic and geological conditions' and the complementarities in their economies driven by common elements in history and geography, apart from several other comparable features borne out of their shared colonial past.

In fact, the El Nino effect was recognized by the Indian and Australian meteorologists as far back as in 1879. Even as the Gondwana supercontinent connection was brought to light by the renowned economic geologist V S Dubey, Australia and India have for long paid little or no attention to the incidence of similar mineral wealth in both the countries and to adopting the same techniques that were best suited for mineral prospecting and exploration. Accruing the benefits on account of the shared values of democracy and membership of Commonwealth, besides commonalities in jurisprudence, accountancy and English language, was not altogether a new proposition, given the prospects envisioned by Deakin as early as 1893 and Betram Stevens in 1944.

All said and done, the geo-economic imperatives that gained ascendancy over the geopolitical equations brought in reconciliation in them so much as to embark on vibrant strategies like India's

Look East Policy and Australia-India Council, a commendable Track-II initiative to negate ignorance and negligence of each other country. "*India's Economy at the Mid-night Hour*", an analytical study of Australian DFAT, "*India Today 1994*" festival, simultaneously organized in all the major cities of Australia, and "*Australia-India New Horizons*" campaign bear testimony to the greater degree of importance that Australia had attached to India. Having been fully convinced of India's strategic potential, Australia began relying on Indian surveillance for the security of the commercial ships passing through the Bay of Bengal. The lackluster profile of trade and investment that reigned for over half a century was replaced by a bourgeoning pattern. By all means, it was bonhomie in the India-Australia bilateral relations, as if to be followed by a phase reminiscing of the old rhythm of repulsive behaviour.

A sort of 'underperformance of the bilateral relationship', testifying to a sort of diplomatic chill, is also evident from the Australian high level visits, which were not duly returned by India. The visits to India of six Australian Prime Ministers—Robert Menzies, Gough Whitlam, Malcolm Fraser, Bob Hawke, John Howard and Kevin Rudd— stood no comparison with just two official visits of the Indian Prime Ministers—Indira Gandhi and Rajiv Gandhi. May it be, a host of reasons would have influenced India: its 'strategic mistrust' over Australia in the wake of the Cold War 'geopolitical myopia', its annoyance at the Australia's unbridled alliance with the US, and its resentment of Australia's strident reaction over the May 1998 nuclear explosions as well as of Australia's adamant refusal to supply uranium to India. A spate of attacks on the Indian students in Australia in the recent times is yet another source of annoyance at all levels in India and poses a challenge to the spirit of reciprocity. For all its eloquent appreciation of emerging India as an 'economic giant', Australia's official relationship with India is relatively a 'narrow front' and 'a case of one step forward, two backwards'. Lack of imagination and commitment on both sides turned the strategic and economic outcomes of the official negotiations 'brief and thin', scorning the broader hopes and expectations in the India-Australia relationship. The present experiments in the laboratory of bilateral relationship, being far from realizing the targets naturally expected, could only replicate the results of the past experience.

Lying at the heart of the bilateral relationship are the 'people-to-people contacts' that have proved to be of immense significance to foster mutual understanding and thereby the linkages. 'Second track dialogue' or simply 'second track diplomacy', as a useful adjunct to the formal governmental negotiations, was pertinently expounded by Gareth Evans that 'it is people rather than governments that give content to relationships and drive them forward'. Realization of the full potential of Australia-India relations demands building 'a broad knowledge partnership' and dispelling the ill-conceived notions and misconceptions of each other, besides accommodating the interests and appreciating the attitudes of each other. Should Australia commit itself to adding 'depth and vigour' to its relationship with India, it shall make use of the human resources of about 100,000 Indian students in different Australian institutions and nearly 200,000 Indian-origin citizens in pursuit of building the bridges of friendship and fostering the awareness for future development of the relationship. India, on its part, needs to embark on promoting public awareness of Australia through its academic and cultural institutions, besides revitalizing the much obscured India-Australia Council.

It was against this backdrop, erudite scholars, seasoned diplomats and naval personnel deliberated the issues of vital importance for sustainable India-Australia partnership in the 21st century at the International Seminar organized by my Centre in April 2010. The revised papers, based on the in-depth discussion at the Seminar, have formed the contents of this compendium. The contributors of the papers, besides being entitled to exercise the freedom of expression, are equally responsible for all the viewpoints advanced in their papers.

In the context of history of India-Australia bilateral relationship replete with alternation of cordiality and estrangement, Yagama Reddy finds the two countries getting reconciled to the need for developing a broad and long-term knowledge partnership through broadening the people-to-people links. He further concludes that public diplomacy, besides dispelling the exotic impressions and enhancing the mutual understanding of each other, would become conducive to take the bilateral relationship to the level of strategic partnership and thereby sustaining the spirit of bonhomie.

Tai Wei Lim, while making assessment of the demand for thermal coal in the Indian large scale steel industry and electricity sector, identifies the Australian coal exports to India as one of the key factors of the bilateral trading relationship and further expects them achieving self-sufficiency in the sustainable energy through the collaborative and strategic forums as part of the strategic research fund. Inasmuch as the energy cooperation between India and Australia has taken precedence over the recent proposition of strategic partnership and Australia's inhibitions over the supply of uranium to India, Pankaj Jha looks at the possibilities open for them in forging energy cooperation in such other areas as gas hydrates, coal gasification, solar energy, wind energy and tidal waves energy through technology sharing in power-generation and-transmission, besides examining the India's uranium supply agreements with other countries with no infringement to the nuclear proliferation.

For all the change in the attitude of the Howard Government conforming to the 123 Agreement between the US and India, Uttam Kumar Jamadagni considers the nuclear standoff as a significant issue in the India-Australia bilateral relationship, given the incumbent government's dilemma, whether clinging on to the stance of no sale of uranium to India or falling in line with the other countries having nuclear agreements concluded with India. Vijay Sakhuja calls upon India and Australia to forge defence cooperation, shaped by shared geostrategic perspectives and challenges, for enhancing the stability in the Asia-Pacific region and the growth of trans-regional cooperative mechanisms. The qualitative operational competence of the Indian navy, Sakhuja further underscores, augurs well for a meaningful interaction with the Royal Navy of Australia. India and Australia, though their interests had neither clashed nor converged, are of late looking for strategic partnership. In the context of Australia's recognition of India's growing clout in the global arena and the need for Australia's cooperation for India to increase its presence in the Asia-Pacific and protect sea-lanes of the Indian Ocean region, Subramanyam Raju finds an upward shift in the trajectory of India-Australia relations to a closer engagement and underscores their collaboration for the peace and stability in the Asia-Pacific region. About the same time, as these two leading powers of the Indian Ocean region failed to forge partnerships beyond the regional frameworks, GVC Naidu makes out a case for the creation of a different kind of consultative mechanism for building solid defence links in the Asia-Pacific region.

Gopalji Malviya views that the strategic partnership between India and Australia is a well-intended cooperative approach for promoting regional and global security. Given the track of their engagement and participation in defence-related activities and the threatened strategic environment in the Indian Ocean region, Malviya further identifies the vital areas for shared cooperation between these two beleaguered nations. The growing economic importance and strategic clout of India influenced the Australia's perceptions so much as to promote mutual beneficial initiatives, in which Commodore Vasan finds the commonality of purpose and intent between India and Australia for enhancing constructive maritime cooperation in the Indian Ocean region.

In view of the US-Japan-Australia-India Quadrilateral Initiative being got off with an intention to shape a new international balance in response to the ongoing power shifts to Asia, Surendra Kumar favours India joining this group so much as to strengthen its influence in the Asia-Pacific region to resolve some of the outstanding issues with other partners of this Initiative, as it would be neither a security bloc, nor even an alliance duplicating the existing multilateral arrangements. While India and Australia have a common purpose in working together and with other countries of the Asia-Pacific, Vibhanshu Shekhar perceives the countries as important stakeholders and contributors to the ASEAN-driven multilateral (ADM) institutions which would develop a shared understanding on a gamut of issues concerning the fast-changing politico-strategic landscape of the Asia-Pacific and thereby a stable Asian Order.

Sudhir Kumar Singh calls for an increased cooperation between India and Australia in order to strengthen the security, peace and prosperity of the Asia-Pacific region, now being emerged as a new power house of the international system in the 21st century, besides addressing the issues of common concern to them. Prabhakara examines the possibilities for meaningful triangular partnership among Australia, India and Japan as a means of pursuing prosperity and integration in the Asia-Pacific region, given the strategic partnerships at the bilateral levels among these nations.

Nabeel Mancheri, based on his empirical study, points out absolute advantages out of the Free Trade Agreements between India and Australia by moving beyond the traditional trading relationship, in view of the complementary nature of their economies and the potential human capital and people-to-business in offing.

Chandrakant Yatanoor views a spate of attacks on the Indian students is contrary to the great contribution of the Indian migrants to the growth and development of Australian society and economy over the last two centuries. Cognizant of the tangible contribution of the Indian Diaspora in Australia to enhancing bilateral links, Chandrakant seeks a lasting amicable solution through diplomatic intervention. Prayaga, while tracing the bourgeoning trade and investment patterns between India and Australia in the last two decades, considers the attacks on the Indian students in Australia and the Australia's persistent refusal to supply uranium to India as the most contentious issues impinging on the prospects of bilateral relationship.

It is my pleasure to feel obliged to the sincerity of the scholars for their participation in the Seminar and submission of revised papers that has made this edited volume possible, and to the sustained cooperation of my colleagues in the Centre that has assured me of the expected academic outcome. Deserving all the more appreciation is the sustained commitment of Prof Lakshmana Chetty—former Director of our Centre and former Dean of Faculty of Arts, S.V. University— to the task of editing the papers with meticulous care and precision. Besides the UGC financial assistance to the Centre under Area Studies Programme, I am very much gratified by the Australia-India Council's appreciation of our Centre's research on the Australian Studies and its liberal financial support to organize the April 2010 Seminar. I am rather privileged to avail the benefit of splendid expertise of the seasoned diplomats, like Dr Lakhlan Strahan, Deputy High Commissioner, Australia High Commission in India, New Delhi, Ambassador S. T. Devere, Director General, Indian Council of World Affairs, New Delhi and Mr Le Thanh Hung, Counsellor, Embassy of the Socialist Republic of Vietnam, New Delhi, whose active participation in the deliberations of the Seminar enriched the understanding of the India-Australia relations. M/s Akansha Publishing House, New Delhi, deserves all praise and compliments for its proven expertise and quality-consciousness in bringing out this volume with elegance.

Prof. Y. Yagama Reddy

Our Contributors

Prof Y. Yagama Reddy, Centre for Southeast Asian Studies, Sri Venkateswara University, Tirupati.

Dr. Tai Wei Lim, Assistant Professor, National University of Singapore, Singapore.

Dr. Pankaj K. Jha, Senior Fellow, Institute for Defence & Strategic Studies, New Delhi.

Dr. Uttam Kumar Jamadagni, Associate Professor, Dept. of Defence & Strategic Studies, University of Madras, Chennai.

Dr. Vijay Sakhuja, Research-Director, Indian Council of World Affairs, New Delhi.

Dr. Subramanyam Raju, Associate Professor, Centre for South Asian Studies, Pondicherry University, Puducherry.

Prof. G.V.C. Naidu, School of International Studies, Jawaharlal Nehru University, New Delhi.

Prof. Gopalji Malviya, Dept. of Defence & Strategic Studies, University of Madras, Chennai.

Commodore R. Seshadri Vasan, Center for Asia Studies, Chennai.

Dr. Surendra Kumar, S. Y., Lecturer, Department of Political Science, Jnana Bharathi Campus, Bangalore University, Bangalore.

Dr. Vibhanshu Shekhar, School of International Studies, Jawaharlal Nehru University, New Delhi.

Dr. Sudhir Singh, Department of Political Science, Dyal Singh College, University of Delhi, New Delhi.

Dr. Prabhakar, H. S., School of International Studies, Jawaharlal Nehru University, New Delhi.

Dr. Nabeel Mancheri, Postdoctoral Associate, National Institute of Advanced Studies, Indian Institute of Science (IISC) Campus, Bangalore.

Prof. Chandrakant Yatanoor, Professor of Political Science, Gulbarga University, Gulbarga, Karnataka.

Dr. Prayaga, M., Assistant Professor, Centre for Southeast Asian Studies, Sri Venkateswara University, Tirupati.

1

India-Australia: Need for Knowledge Partnership

Y. Yagama Reddy

India and Australia, on account of their location in the Indian Ocean and their colonial legacy, display definite correspondence based on geography, geology, climate and biotic life as well as history, polity and culture. To the great surprise of many people, both India and Australia together with Antarctica had remained part of the Super-coninent, Gondwana land (Lemuria), until 160 million years ago. Having detached from each other, they drifted away to their present locations on either side of the Equator. Thus, the shared geological past and geomatical location of these Indian Ocean littorals on their side of the Equator conferred on them a broad correspondence in mining and climatic conditions. For all their geographical propinquity, they remained in virtual isolation until late 18th century; thenceforth they had a shared history of British colonization until Australia became a federal state in 1901 and India became an independent nation in 1947. In fact, the commercial contacts began in 1801 with the shipment of Australian coal to Calcutta in lieu of Indian rice to Sydney; and the economic development during the formative phase of British settlement process in Australia owed much to the itinerant Indians who started migrating into Australia since early 19th century. This facet of history made India and Australia emerge "with shared and fundamental commitment to freedom and democracy and with shared membership of Commonwealth," besides commonality in the jurisprudence based on Anglo-American systems and widespread use of English. *Complementarity in their economic outlook and commonalities owing to the British colonial legacy were expected to create an environment conducive to promoting cohesion and integration between these two Commonwealth nations.* These impressive prospects prompted the Australia's renowned historian, Geoffrey Blainey, to remark that "Australia seemed to be a satellite of India as well as a colony of England."

Negated Expectations: On the contrary, there existed feelings of disappointment for the incompatible attitudes of these two countries on the issues that bear no significance to their national interests. A student concerned with the India-Australia relations would be naturally puzzled by certain paradoxes in the pattern of their bilateral relationship. These two littoral states of the Indian Ocean, notwithstanding their geographical proximity, became the victim of tyranny of distance, as if sea is a divisive force rather than a unifying factor. It is although not intended to think about the prospects of bilateral relations on the grounds of mere basic linkages between them owing to their sheer geographical location in the Indian Ocean littoral zone and historical legacy; the fact remains that never did they become susceptible to any accidents of history like border disputes and ethnic tensions.

Perpetuated Exotic Impressions

Obviously, geography and history which ought to have served up the mutual advantage of Australia and India, were scarcely of any significance in promoting mutual understanding of each other country; and as a consequence, the people of both the countries had for long developed the exotic impressions of each other.[1] It is then an expected satirical that the Indians have been constantly cherishing the age-old notion of Australia as a land of kangaroos and cricket players only. It is equally gruesome that Indians are awfully ignorant of the island-continent, as being originally the homeland of Aborigines who bore close resemblance to certain tribal communities in the peninsular India. During my visits to Australia, I was almost astonished to learn that majority of the Indians knew much about the aboriginal art and artifacts, but totally unaware of the history of the Aborigines dating back to some thousands of years, leave alone their diversity in culture, language, polity, economy and ways of life. All that they knew about Australia was that it was a British colony. Evidently, Indians are scantly interested in acquisition of knowledge of the land and people, and security concerns of the country with which they have associated for considerably long period of time. This is a sort of reluctance impinging on their integration with the host communities. For so long a period, Canberra too ignored the value of India's position as a force in the Commonwealth and in Asia as a whole. Instead, Australians who valued much the economic standards felt the need for insulating their territory from the possible clash of cultures.[2] Equally appalling was the Australians' limited knowledge of India and inadequate interest that virtually deprived themselves of the benefit of marked diversity in many facets of India. So much deplorable is that India was totally ignorant of the very geographical location of Australia, abutting the Southeast Asian region with which India sustained contacts for over two millennia. Australia, in the Indian mindset, was 'after all down under' and at the end of any travel line.

Poverty of Knowledge at the base of Lackluster Bilateral Relationship

Despite their tall claims of knowledge in abundance on the world affairs and well-equipped foreign policy-apparatus that ought to have fortified the bilateral relationship, Australia and India have habitually endured lackluster bilateral relationship which obviously owed much to the "lack of knowledge of Australia" in India and "ignorance or neglect of India" in Australia. Though Jawaharlal Nehru in mid-1940s viewed the demographic composition of Australia as a subject of its own discretion, it was dearth of knowledge of the harsh physiography inhibiting uniform economic development and population distribution that made Indians to look at Australia as a vast stretch of barren land with sparse population. It was the same ignorance that would have prompted the Indian High Commissioner in Australia, General Cariappa, later in early 1950s to become critical of Australia's White Policy as being discriminatory to the Indian migrations into Australia.[3] That Australia was preeminently a desert is yet another gloomy impression of Australia shared in the Parliament by Smt. Lakshmi Menon, a member of Indian Parliament.[4] Even as the Colombo Plan had won the frank appreciation of Nehru, the Cold War-related security concerns had widened the gulf between Australia and India, as if to endure divergence on matters of their immediate interest. Their drift and discord attitude was the symptom of ideological estrangement on the lines of Australia's alliance with the US and India's commitment to its self-prophesied non-alignment policy. Despite the Cultural Agreement between the two nations that had been in force since 1971 and reviewed ritually every two years to frame detailed programs, it had not caused any major impact. India considered the Cultural Agreement with Australia as merely one among numerous other agreements with a host of other nations around the world.[5] As the said Indo-Australian Cultural Agreement for mutual cooperation failed to alleviate the poverty of communication links, the former Indian Minister for Information & Broadcasting, I.K. Gujral, on 7 November 1972 at the meeting of the Consultative Committee of the Colombo Plan, emphasized the need for setting up an Asian Agency for the benefit of the countries in the Colombo Plan region, especially *India, which was too ignorant of its neighbours although familiar with the events in the West.*[6] This was a paradoxical situation that prompted the former Australian Prime Minister Gough Whitlam during his visit to India in June 1973 to term

> ***the inability of India and Australia in forging the much expected 'very close relationship' as an anomalous...*** though shared common values in democracy and democratic institutions, links in the commonwealth and their belonging to the geographical region of the Indian Ocean. (Emphasis added).[7]

Divergence in the Estimates and Methods in the Cold War-Security Issues

History amply demonstrates that the erstwhile British colonies had experienced longer periods of estrangement intercepted by inadvertent and brief spells of cordiality in their bilateral relationship. The *relations between them proved to be "indirect rather than direct"- and were "marked by drift and discord" during the* Menzies-Nehru era. The 'disagreement' and thereby estrangement between India and Australia evidently stemmed from differential estimates of potential risks and the best methods of ensuring peace and security in Southeast Asia in the context of Cold War. Their indulgence in all sorts of arguments at various levels had not merely *nullified the good will generated by the Colombo Plan but also exposed their dearth of knowledge of each other's security concerns and responses thereof.* If Nehru was interested in the "changing face of Asia", Menzies dismissed Asia as "irrelevant" and as being "too difficult for any occidental to understand". Their deep-felt convictions had prevented them from transcending the diplomatic gap as well as the cultural and psychological distance between the two nations.[8] They substantially differed in their perceptions of international affairs, and hence displayed open divergence practically on every issue since 1949.

Their superficial understanding of compulsions and indifference to the concerns of the other had merely aggravated their irreconcilable attitude so much as to get drifted further and more from each other. The logical corollary was the disapproval of each other's actions; mention may be made of India's refusal to participate in the Australian proposed regional defence arrangements and Australia's sharp comments on the India's Treaty of Friendship and Cooperation with the Soviet Union. Even there were instances of diametrically opposed policies pursued by the Australian Liberal and Labour Party governments. For instance, the Whitlam government's Asia-oriented policy was totally reversed by the succeeding Fraser Government of Liberal and Country Party which instead overwhelmingly favoured the continuation of the US bases in the Indian Ocean, what it termed as the 'Concept of Balance' to the Soviet intervention in the South Asian region. For over a decade until the middle of the 1980s, Australia remained unconvinced of India's security threat perceptions, and India too was critical of Australia's apprehensive notions of India's naval capabilities. Contrary to the Canberra's deep-rooted perception, Australia of late began gaining confidence in India, thanks to the Report of Senate Standing Committee on Foreign Affairs and Trade (July 1990) that perceived no threat in the Indian Naval built up in the Indian Ocean to Australia at any time in the future. The two nations, oft-demurred on the Cold War security issues that had never fallen within the domain of their bilateral relationship, appeared to have reconciled to the imperatives of globalization. Besides Australia's *eloquent appreciation of India's economic reforms, both the nations pursued the policies duly appreciating the security concerns of each other. Surprisingly, the fast-track bonhomie in their bilateral relationship received a serious setback in the wake of India's nuclear tests at Pokhran in May 1998, to which Australia's reaction was "more strident than the US"*, as evident from a series of sanctions imposed on India. Australia tried in vain to coax ARF into censuring India's nuclear tests; and it had since remained as an indifferent and non-chalant nation for almost two years. Despite its awareness of India's imperatives of nuclear energy for civilian purposes, Australia remained quite adamant in denying the supply of uranium to India. The incessant attacks on the Indian students in Australia betray the claims of having developed proper understanding of each other and tend to erase the spirit of *entente cordiale and* obscure all the benefits of enhanced bilateral partnership.

Australia's Perceived Awareness and Sense of Belonging

Far beyond these undeniable and multitude of instances testifying to shallowness in the levels of mutual understanding and dearth of determination in deepening the partnership, the track of India-Australia bilateral relationship unravels the fact that "the arguments are much deeper than the differences" between these two proximate nations bearing immense potentialities for mutual benefit. Historiography provides the evidences of the perceived awareness in Australia of India's pivotal position in the Indian Ocean with which Australia's security issues were linked. Thanks to their British colonial legacy, these two Commonwealth nations have developed some rudimentary understanding of each other, though failed to reinforce their bilateral relationship. Notwithstanding the exotic impressions such as ignorance, negligence and inattention, there were several instances bearing testimony to the envisioned prospects of Australia-India partnership by the Australian statesmen themselves. Mention may be made of the efforts of Alfred Deakin, W M Huges and Bertram Stevens at developing reciprocal relations between these two Indian Ocean littorals.[9] Much before he became the Prime Minister of Australia (1903-04, 1905-08, 1909-10), Alfred Deakin (in his *Irrigated India,* 1893) envisioned immeasurable potentialities of Indo-Australian relations. It was W H Hughes (1915-23) who got the Reciprocity Act passed for ameliorating the Indian immigrants seeking settlement in Australia. Another Australian Prime Minister Joseph Ben Chifley of Labour Party (1946-49), who considered India as the lynchpin of Asia, envisioned India's role in the post-War international community especially in the affairs of Afro-Asian nations, besides appreciating India's concerns and interests.

Similarly, Jawaharlal Nehru, much before becoming the Prime Minister of independent India, identified Australia "as being nearer to Asia." While extending a warm welcome to the Australian observers attending the Asian Relations Conference at New Delhi in March – April 1947, made a forthright reference to Australia and New Zealand: "*We have* ***many problems in common,*** *especially in the Pacific and in the southeast region of Asia, and we have to cooperate together (to) find solutions.* [10] It was about this time (in 1948) that *The Hindu* in its editorial referred to "a great fund of good will for India in Australia and Indo-Australian cooperation" bearing "a decisive importance in the future of Southeast Asia".[11]

Australia was also well poised to take advantage of its developing links with independent India. In his message on the eve of independence to India, the Australian External Affairs Minister, H V Evatt underscored "the mutuality of interests and a sense of belonging to a shared region" based on their "geographical proximity and common interests in the affairs of Indian Ocean and Southeast Asia...".[12] Like Prime Minister Chifley, the other Australian statesman concurred with Nehru— on matters related to deterring the communist influence on the developing countries— was Evatt who looked upon India as a bulwark against communism. For all the bipartisan commitment to 'White Australia' policy, Australian Labour government joined with India in championing the cause of Indonesia's independence from the Dutch (during 1947-49 period) and Indonesia's admission into the United Nations in September 1950. Other External Affairs Ministers, Spercy Spender (1949-51) and R G Casey (1951-63), got succeeded in persuading Nehru to appreciate Australia's security concerns. Though the relations were 'indirect rather than direct' marked by 'drift and discord' attitude during the Nehru-Menzies era, there were also attempts by the successive Prime Ministers of Liberal Party government at improving the bilateral relationship. Despite India's critical view of Australia's alliance with the US and its involvement in Vietnam War, Australia expected India to play a vibrant role in the Southeast Asian affairs. It was after a lapse of 23 years that the Labour Party government of Gough Whitlam (1972-73) embarked on an Asia-oriented policy at the cost of its traditional alliance with the US. In an effort to remove anomalies rather than to court a complete break with the past, Gough Whitlam of the Labour Party subscribed to the concept of Indian Ocean Zone of Peace (IOZOP) as well as to the Kuala Lumpur Declaration making Southeast Asia a Zone of Peace, Freedom and Neutrality (ZOPFAN).

Mutual Appreciation of Gesture and Sobriety: Though the aid under Colombo Plan was too meagre to serve India's economic development, it had won India's "frank appreciation of the spirit and the humanitarian element of the aid". Even Nehru, who was critical of Australia's alliance with the Western bloc, described the Plan as "remarkable and significant". Equally justifiable appreciation was the Australian response to China's aggression of India's northern borders in 1962 when the Australian public as well identified with India against China's expansionism. The editorials in several Australian newspapers, like *Sydney Morning Herald* (2 November 1962) and *Age* (Melbourne: 24 July 1963), also dealt with the type and quantum of Australian aid that could be offered to India in the light of Chinese aggrandizement. For the entire entire 'drift and discard' attitude between the two, Australia had maintained absolute neutrality during the Indo-Pak war of 1965. Of much appreciation was the Australia's diplomatic support to India on the eve of the Indo-Pak war of 1971 when it became the first Western Bloc country to recognize the newly independent Bangladesh.

Estranged Nations towards Reconciliation

Australia under the Labour Government of James Bob Hawke was quick to perceive the imperative need for reorienting "Australia's approach to the relationship with India" whose relative weight in Asia was set to grow in the context of Cold War receding into history and the cessation of super-power rivalry. In an effort to get the bilateral relationship revitalized after "some years of neglect", the Australian Prime Minister Bob Hawke traced the historic and political ties to their shared colonial past that led to the emergence of shared interests and values[13]. With the annihilation of Cold War irritants, India and Australia began to rediscover each other not only economically as equal partners in trade and investment but also politically and culturally. India's Look East Policy, launched in 1991, was a proactive strategy to refurbish its historical and cultural ties with its eastern neighbours. Australia too embarked on a similar strategy by establishing Australia - India Council (AIC) in 1992 for broadening and deepening the bilateral relations, with an envisaged objective of promoting mutual awareness and understanding that would dispel the long persisting exotic impressions of each other.[14] Worth mentioning initiative for reinforcing the bilateral relationship was the 'India Today' Festival (1994), inaugurated by the Vice-President of India in Sydney on 17th April 1994, a month-long programme simultaneously organized in Australia's four largest cities, Sydney, Melbourne, Brisbane and Perth, for promoting understanding among Australians of India and its people— an understanding of India's enormous potential for rapid economic growth. In his address at the opening of the "India Today 1994", the Australian Minister for Foreign Affairs, Senator Gareth Evans, looked at the 'India Today' as a campaign "to develop a strong and creative economic partnership, to the mutual benefit and prosperity of our countries". While describing the event as a "joint commitment to building closer people-to-people as well as government-to-government ties between Australia and India," Evans was so much exuberant in delineating the purpose as:

> ...an understanding of the human dimensions of your country, as ultimately ***it is people rather than governments that give content to relationships and drive them forward****....* Australia's people and our business sector have the vision and the capacity to take up the challenge of building stronger ties with India.... (T)hrough "India Today", ***many more Australians will come to know about India, and look beyond our immediate neighbours to the potential and opportunities opening up in modern India****....* Australians, like others, are perhaps sometimes guilty of not seeing India for the complex and diverse society that it is, and our perceptions of India are sometimes rooted in traditional and stereotyped images - exotic maybe.... (Emphasis added).[15]

In their quest for a comprehensive understanding of each other, India and Australia sought to focus on complementarities between their economies driven by common elements, by identifying the avenues of cooperation in commerce and trade, transfer of scientific and technical know-how, and investment. The Australian Minister for Trade, Senator Bob McMullan, who led a high profile delegation to New Delhi and Bombay, pertinently mentioned the complementarities between the economies driven by common elements in history, common aspects of our geography and the stages of development [16]. The Indian Minister for Commerce, P. Chidambaram, at the session of Indo-Australian Joint Ministerial Commission and the Indo-Australian Joint Business Council in February 1995, also underscored the existing commonalities between Australia and India in terms of "Anglo-American systems of jurisprudence and accounting" and widespread use of English language" which, he hoped, would "help the business of both countries to do business together [17]. DFAT's study of "India's Economy at the Mid-night Hour" (1994) and "Australia-India New Horizons Campaign (1996) were a few other initiatives of Australia testifying to the perceived need for "expanding the awareness and understanding" of each other country.

Revisited Rhythm of Disagreement and Estrangement Eclipsing Bonhomie: Consequent upon the India's nuclear tests of May 1998, Australia had remained indifferent and non-chalant for almost two years. Despite its awareness of India's imperatives of nuclear energy for civilian purposes, Australia has remained adamant on the supply of uranium to India. Following the high profile visit of the US President Clinton to India in March 2000 that encapsulated US endorsement of India's right to resolve its security concerns through building its own nuclear deterrence, Australia soon shifted its focus on restoring the derelict-wagon of bilateral relationship back onto the track, as was evident from a series of high-level visits of Australian ministers to India which culminated in the visit of Prime Minister John Howard in July 2000. Yet, Australia has been obstinate in its refusal to supply uranium to India's civilian needs, insisting on India sign NPT and CTBT.

People-to-People Diplomacy in Furtherance of Bilateral Partnership: In the process of assisting a wide range of non-governmental entities in conducting diplomatic discourses, people-to-people diplomacy offers the way for engaging the citizens of a country in pursuit of garnering their support for its foreign policy and national interests, imparts a new dimension to international relations. Notwithstanding the rumblings, often noticed in the bilateral relationship at the official level, people-to-people contacts have proved to be of immense significance in dispelling the ill-conceived notions and misconceptions of each other. This was vindicated by the Track –II Conference in September 1998 at Melbourne on the "Security of the Asia-Pacific Region after the South Asian Nuclear Tests". This initiative which represented a classic case of public diplomacy provided a vivid account of both bitterness of Australian government and the appreciation of India's nuclear predicament by the Australian public. To quote Inder Malhotra, a senior Indian journalist who participated in the said-Conference:

> Australia's bitterness against Indian nuclear tests was confined largely to its Government...(An) impressively large number of informed and articulate *Australians even when opposed to nuclear tests anywhere, have shown a keen understanding of (India's) reasons to conduct the tests*...(To them) Canberra has "needlessly over-reacted"....several Australians (at the Conference)...argued that since Australia itself "relied completely" on the US "nuclear umbrella",... it had no right to object to India devising its own nuclear umbrella....*Australian participants insisted on including in the communiqué a plea to their government to end its 'complete disengagement' with India...and to resume 'official contacts and dialogue' with it*...there has not been the slightest whiff of anti-Indian feeling anywhere in Australia either immediately after the Shakti series of tests or later.(Emphasis added).[18]

If the history of the bilateral relationship narrates a regrettable tale of missed opportunities, there is need for India and Australia to get reconciled to the realities of the global order.

Building Knowledge Partnership towards Strategic Partnership

In an effort to take the bilateral relationship to the level of a strategic partnership, the Prime Ministers of India and Australia— Manmohan Singh and Kevin Rudd— acknowledged the need for intensifying their contacts with each other, as can be gleaned from the Joint Statement issued at the end the visit of Prime Minister Kevin Rudd on 12 November 2009 in New Delhi.

> India and Australia are two countries *with shared interests and shared values*. We are both pluralist democracies. We are both global in our outlook, but also closely integrated into the Asian region. .... We have *a shared desire to enhance and maintain peace, stability and prosperity in Asia*. We both value multilateral institutions and recognize the need to reform and renovate them. *Our people-to-people links are broad-based and growing*. (Emphasis added).[19]

The Prime Ministers further recognized the need for building "a broad knowledge partnership, ranging from developing collaborative projects in education from primary school up to university, to conducting joint research in many fields," besides Australia-India Strategic Research Fund" for supporting "large scale research projects" in some frontier areas. The Prime Ministers also agreed that "strengthening these enduring people-to-people links to enhance mutual understanding is vital to the future of the relationship."[20]

That the India-Australia relationship is underpinned by diverse and expanding people-to-people links is further reiterated in a joint ministerial statement made by the Indian Minister for Human Resource Development (HRD) Kapil Sibal and the then Australian Deputy Prime Minister Julia Gillard (who was also Australia's Education Minister) in Melbourne on 8th April 2010, when they said that "India and Australia are at an exciting time in their relationship" and that "people-to-people contacts are at the heart of the bilateral relationship". In the context of a series of attacks on the Indian students in Australia, the education deal signed by the Ministers concerned viewed "the students' role in building bridges of friendship and understanding as a significant resource for future development of the relationship" ("India, Australia sign major deal to expand education partnership", *PTI Daily News Analysis*: Melbourne, 8 April 2010). Both countries are henceforth committed to "the safety and wellbeing of students as they play an important part in the knowledge partnership envisaged between the two countries."[21] The two ministers had also affirmed their pledge to expand collaboration in education, training and research through the Education Exchange Program between Australia and India. Conforming to the Australia and India's broader knowledge partnership, as envisaged earlier in November 2009 by the Prime Ministers of both countries, this integrated programme of research is expected "to create opportunities for Australian researchers and students for enhancing the intellectual and cultural enrichment of Australian university students and staff."[22]

Australia-India Strategic Research Fund: The Round Table discussion on the development of a long-term "Knowledge Partnership" between Australia and India, participated by representatives of the Go8, Universities of Australia, the Australia-India Institute and the federal government, in April 2010 at the University of New South Wales, was well-timed. The discussions, according to the UNSW Pro-Vice-Chancellor (International) Jennie Lang, would contribute to "a much more strategic framework for Australia to engage with India" in education. In his response, the Indian HRD Minister Kapil Sibal strongly favoured the Australia-India Strategic Research Fund, proposed by the two Prime Ministers earlier in November 2009.[23] While expecting the Australia-India Strategic Research Fund to accomplish the knowledge partnership, Kapil Sibal reiterated India's commitment to contributing $100 million; Australia on its part pledged $10 million per year for the next five years.[24] The commitment of the two countries to creating a broad and strong knowledge partnership is amply evident from several collaborative projects undertaken at various levels.

Cultural and educational institutions, whose activities can be described as 'cultural diplomacy, encompass' the exchange of ideas, information, art and other aspects of culture among nations and their peoples in order to foster mutual understanding'. The effective tools for public diplomacy campaigns are tourism and culture, trade and commerce, economic development and education, capable of influencing the public opinion. Educational exchanges, as a form of public diplomacy, are one of the best ways to build stronger links between nations as well as to enhance the understanding of the ideals, values and aspirations of a nation-state.

The sad part of the story is that the state of ignorance or negligence of each other country is persisting in the absence of academic courses being offered in educational institutions. Of some solace is the sustained commitment of Australia-India Council to promoting knowledge in India and Australia of each other's society and culture that would dispel the long persisting exotic impressions of each other; and thereby deepening and strengthening of relations between the two countries. Apart from the regular annual feature, like "Australian Studies Fellowship" programme, the other programmes deserving appreciation are the Australia's "Endeavour Awards" and "Leadership Awards" which are playing an important role in strengthening knowledge links between the two countries. I was an awardee of the covetous AIC fellowship in 2005 that facilitated my visit to a consortium of Australian Universities and Institutions in different cities, when I had the unique opportunity of interacting with the academia and students, besides the overseas students in the University campuses and the general public including the Indian Diaspora. Unlike the overseas Chinese in Australia, the Indian community is far below the expected level in developing the links between India and Australia, as the Indian community is yet to transcend the barriers of language, religion and region which they had inherited whilst they were in India. On the contrary, Australians' "sense of humour," and "spirit of friendliness" make a visitor develop a proper grasp of the Australian society, polity and ways of life.

While underlining "the importance of strong bonds for enduring shared interests", Stephen Smith Australian Minister for Foreign Affairs and S M Krishna Indian Minister for External Affairs in a joint statement issued at the conclusion of the Second Foreign Minister's Framework Dialogue in New Delhi on 13 October 2009 looked upon the 250,000 people of Indian community in Australia as a valuable input to building Australian society and to enhancing bilateral links. [25]

The growing awareness and understanding of Australia among the Indians has become a contributing factor to the bourgeoning relationship, as evident from the substantial increase in the investment flows, transfer of scientific and technical know-how, phenomenal increase in the volume of bilateral trade and the flow of Indian immigrants into Australia either for pursuing higher education or in quest of green pastures. It is largely believed that the upsurge in the Indians' settlement would continue; and this trend would have its impact on the spread of social networks which in turn would facilitate the pursuit of further strengthening India-Australia partnership.

It all depends more on the political will than on any other parameter in the given socio-cultural environment, conducive to *the integration of these two communities in the spirit of accommodating the interests and appreciating the attitudes of each other*. All said and done, there has existed a sort of lopsided political relationship at the highest level. Six Australian Prime Ministers – Robert Menzies, Gough Whitlam, Malcom Fraser, Robert James Hawke, John Howard and Kevin Rudd—visited India in the last 60 years, even some of them more than once or twice, while there were only two official visits to Australia by the Indian Prime Ministers—Indira Gandhi (1969) and Rajiv Gandhi (1986). May it be, it was the ideological estrangement all through the Cold War period that inhibited the Indian leaders to think of Australia, or the Australia's overstepping reaction to India's nuclear explosions in 1998 that made India disenchanted with Australia; and the irritants like Australia's refusal to supply uranium and attacks on Indian students that made India to look at Australia with disdain. The sum total of this predicament, apparently testifying to trust-deficit, is quite reminiscent of the drift and discard attitude they endured during the Cold War period. It is high time India and Australia put in sincere efforts to widen their knowledge partnership, in the context of prevailing supporting environment manifesting in a host of commonalities and complementarities based on geological past (super-continent connection), geographical proximity (as Indian Ocean littoral states), historical semblance (British colonization) and shared perceptions of the global issues—for erasing the exotic impressions so much as to sustain the spirit of bonhomie in their bilateral relationship in the globalized era.

REFERENCES

1. *Asian Recorder* (hereafter *AR*), 17 (47), 19-25 January 1973, p. 11679.
2. *Age,* (Melbourne), Extract from editorial, 24 July 1963.
3. Lead Report, *Courier Mail,* (Brisbane), 22 June 1954, p.1.
4. Lakshmi Menon, *Lok Sabha Debates,* Vol.15, No.41-50, 9 April 1958.
5. Jim Masselos, "Imperatives in Cultural Exchange between India and Australia," in Marika Vicziany and Kenneth McPherson (eds.), *Australia and Southeast Asia...,* National Centre for South Asian Studies, Melbourne: 1994.
6. *Indian & Foreign Review,* 10 (3), 15 November 1972, pp.7-9.
7. *Asian Recorder,* 19 (20), 16-22 July 1973, p. 11392.
8. Meg Gurry, "Leadership and Bilateral Relations: Menzies and Nehru, Australia and India, 1949-1964," *Pacific Affairs,* 65 (4), 1992-93, pp.510-527.
9. For full details of this aspect, see Senate Standing Committee on Foreign Affairs, Defence and Trade, *Australia-India Relations: Trade and Security,* (Canberra, 1990), p.10; Also see A.J. Yardwood, *Asian Migration to Australia,* (Melbourne, 1964), pp.130-140; and also Gardon Greenwood and Norman Harper (eds.), *Australia in World Affairs, 1950-55 and 1956 -1960,* Vols. 1 and 2, (Melbourne, 1957 and 1963.
10. *Selected Works of Jawaharlal Nehru,* 2nd Series, Vol.2, (New Delhi, 1984), p.505.
11. *The Hindu,* 14 December 1948.
12. Quoted in Meg Gurry, *India: Australia's Neglected Neighbour?...,* *n.2,* p.5.
13. *Australia News,* 3 (11), 15 March 1988, p.2.
14. *News from Australia* (hereafter *NFA*), 7 (12), 28 June 1992, pp.1-2. Gareth Evans, who launched AIC at Melbourne in June 1992,

announced Canberra's decision to establish AIC during his visit to New Delhi in September 1991. *IDSA News Review*, 23 (10), October 1991, p.566.

15. Evans, Gareth (1994), *Notes for an address.... at the opening of the "India Today 1994" Festival, Sydney, 17 April 1994,* available at http://www.gevans. org/ speeches/ old/ 1994/170494_fm_ausandindia.pdf
16. *News from Australia*, 1995, 10 (2), pp.1-2.
17. *Indian Recorder*, 2 (13), 26 March -1 April 1995, p.1029
18. *The Hindu*, 30 September 1998, p.12.
19. *file:///I:/Australia India Knowledge %20partnership/India's% 20Trader% 20 Partner% 20% 20Australia%20overview.htm).* Also see "Joint Statement Released by Prime Ministers," *Australia-India Focus*, December 2009, p. 4.
20. "India, Australia take steps to initiate a knowledge partnership", *Asian News International*, 13 November 2009, at http://www.thefreelibrary.com/ India,+Australia+ take+steps+ to+initiate+a+ knowledge+ partnership-a0212009092. See "Joint Statement Released by Prime Ministers," *Australia-India Focus*, December 2009, p. 4.
21. P. S. Suryanarayana, Priority for student safety in knowledge ties, *The Hindu* (Singapore), 9 April 2010.
22. A New India Australia Partnership - Address by Dr Kiran Martin, 15/03/2011, at http://www.asha-india.org/news-and-information/recent-news/kiran-martin-partnership-address.
23. "Partners in knowledge", 13th April 2010, at http://www.unsw.edu.au/ news/ pad /articles/2010/apr/India visit.html.
24. *"India-Australia meet discuss climate change"*, India Climate Watch, November 2009 (8th Issue), at http://www.indiaclimateportal.org/india-climate-watch-november-2009. Also see "Joint Statement Released by Prime Ministers," *Australia-India Focus*, December 2009, p. 4.
25. *Foreign Ministers' Framework Dialogue*, Media release from the Australian High Commission, New Delhi, *13 October 2009, PA/45/09,* http://www.india.embassy.gov.au/ndli/pa4509.html. Also see *Asian News International*; 21 October 2009, at http://www.thefreelibrary.com/ India, Australia+FMs+underline+importance+ of+ strong+ bonds,enduring+...-a0210194169).

2

Energy Cooperation between India and Australia

Tai Wei Lim

Introduction

The main Australian exports to India have so far been minerals and energy commodities.[1] In its 2008 Submission to the Committee, the Australian Department of Resources, Energy and Tourism, summarized the increasing importance of India as an energy market for Australia: India is the world's fifth largest energy consumer with energy needs increasingly in line with a growth rate of approximately 8 percent per annum during the period 2000-2007.[2] Despite the growth in all avenues of trade with India, mineral exports still dominate Australia-India trade statistics and India is one of Australia's fastest growing mineral export markets accounting for eight percent of total mineral exports in 2005-06; Australian coal exports to India were also valued at AUD$687 million.[3]

Strategic forums: Underlining the importance of the energy trade, the Australian Government is actively engaging Indian companies and government over issues in the energy and minerals sector through a number of collaborative and strategic forums, for example, in 2000 the India-Australia Joint Working Group on

Energy and Minerals (JWG) was established to "address trade and investment issues in the energy and minerals sector, to exchange information on policy developments and to identify possible commercial opportunities" and a key outcome of the JWG had been the Australia-India Coal and Mining Forum, held in New Delhi in early 2006; key issues discussed at the Forum included: regulatory frameworks on mining; prospects for mining technology services and equipment; etc. The Australia-India Resources Strategy proposal was endorsed by Trade Ministers at the February 2007 Joint Ministerial Commission Meeting to provide a framework for long term collaboration on key resources issues which were identified by the Australia-India Joint Working Group on Minerals and Energy.[4]

In 2007, Austrade initiated cooperation and collaboration between mining companies in Australia, India and Indonesia through a first-of-its-kind seminar held in Kolkata (India) on Thursday, 22 November 2007 to showcase Australian expertise in mining technology and services directly to industry leaders from India and Indonesia including the world's largest coal producer – Coal India and drive best practice in mine efficiency, safety standards and environmental management, and explore avenues for collaboration.[5] At the seminar, Austrade's then New Delhi-based Senior Trade Commissioner, Michael Moignard said similarities between the Indian and Indonesian mining sectors and a specific interest in investment from Australia prompted Austrade to organize the seminar:

> Both India and Indonesia are resource rich and they have the need for innovative mining expertise... Australian companies have been very successful in supporting the Indonesian mining industry and we wanted to share that experience with an Indian audience...India's dynamic growth was driving the change in the mining sector and creating opportunities for Australian businesses...The reality is: to improve or even maintain a GDP growth of around eight to nine

> per cent, India needs more electricity, more cement, more steel, more building products, more roads, and more rail and port capacity. To do this, India must produce more coal and more iron ore; to do that, India has to run more efficient and more productive mines...By 2012, India anticipates a shortfall in coal production of around 100 million tons. In reality, this figure could be even higher as the estimated production figures are ambitious.[6]

Attended by Former President of Newmont Mining (Indonesia), Mr Noke Kiroyan; Chairman of Hindustan Copper, Mr SC Gupta; CEO of Rio Tinto India, Mr Nik Senapati; Managing Director of Tata Power Trading Company, Mr Amulya Charan; Chairman of Gujarat NRE Resources, Mr Arun Jagatramka; and Former Director of Indian School of Mines, Professor A K Ghose and a 14-member Australian business delegation, the Trilateral Mining Seminar was followed by the Global Steel Conference 2007 organized by the Indian Chamber of Commerce. Participants in the latter conference include senior representatives from the Indian Ministry of Steel, Ministry of Railways, Department of Road Transport and Highways, and mining companies such as China Coal and Coke Holdings (China), Aditya Birla Group (India), Tata Iron and Steel (India) and McCloskey Group (UK).[7]

In the same year, the world's largest coal producer, Coal India Limited, was among the major international buyers invited by Austrade to Asia-Pacific's International Mining Exhibition (AIMEX) 2007 held in Sydney; Coal India Limited is wholly owned by the Government of India, Coal India, boasts a production capacity of over 360 million tons per year and the company's raw coal production saw an increase of 5.1 per cent in 2006-07, from 2005-2006; the Chairman of Coal India, PS Bhattacharyya, led a 44-member high-level Indian mining delegation – the largest ever to attend AIMEX, including key players from the public and private sectors from India: TATA Steel, Hindustan Copper Ltd, SREI Infrastructure and Finance, Essel India (a part of the Aditya Birla Group) and Emami Limited.[8]

Austrade's Senior Export Adviser Craig Senger said Australia's reputation as a global leader in mining operations, technology and services attracted many major league players to AIMEX in 2007 adding: "The Indian delegation is looking to source mining technology and services from Australia and are also seeking investment opportunities in coking coal mines around the country"; Chairman of Coal India Mr Bhattacharyya also noted the importance of energy mining: "Mining is one of the most important economic activities to sustain the kind of growth India has reported recently. Coal mining is also at the centre of India's energy security".[9] According to Mr Bhattacharyya, the Australian mining industry is well-positioned to support India's dynamic economic growth because he argued:

> India has strong capabilities in open-cast mining. However, we lack the technology for the development of large underground mines and Australia has done excellent work in this field...The Indian Government now allows up to 74 per cent FDI (foreign direct investment) in the coal mining sector. So we're looking at working together with Australian companies on a reciprocal basis, from investing in mines to the sharing of technological capabilities...We'd also like to put in place long-term agreements to import coal to India and set up joint ventures that will help to enhance efficiency and maximize coal production.[10]

Coal India also has plans to invest in mines around the world to sustain India's ongoing energy needs and the delegation visited mines near Mackay (QLD) and in the Hunter region (NSW) to see Australian mining operations first-hand.[11]

Other than business forums, both countries have also initiated scientific exchanges in the field of energy. At the Amity Institute of Renewable and Alternative Energy-sponsored two-day workshop which was attended by speakers and delegates from IIT's located in Chennai, Kanpur, Guwahati and Mumbai, Dr Lachan Strahan, Deputy High Commissioner, Australia, said:

> The challenges confronted by all the nations are same....We must find ways of developing cleaner sources of energy. Solar energy must be a part of that solution; I know that there are fairly difficult challenges in converting solar energy's enormous potential into an energy source which can make contribution to our societies. What we need to do is to find ways to make solar energy more efficient and less costly...India has its own solar energy mission; it sets its ambitious targets for solar power generation. Australian Government has set its own renewable energy targets i.e. 20% by 2020...[12]

In the same workshop, Dr. C.K. Prahlada, Chief Controller, DRDO, A.K. Sood, Advisor, International Programme, D.S.T., Ministry of Science and Technology argued:

> ...Solar power should be cost effective and affordable for common man...The need of the hour is low cost, low weight solar batteries made of plastic or polymer. DRDO is encouraging institutes and students to carry on research in this area and in next ten years lot of opportunities exist for this in the solar energy sector.[13]

Increasing requirement for metallurgical coal to be met by imports: Indian companies are stepping up interest to secure coal resources in Indonesia and Australia to meet the power needs of the world's second-most populous country; echoing this, Australia & New Zealand Banking Group Ltd's Glenn Porritt, executive director and head of mergers and acquisitions in Asia said:

> We are seeing a lot of flow in terms of merger and acquisition interest or off-take interest from India into both Indonesia and Australia...We've been working on some transactions in Indonesia on thermal coal and I'm pretty surprised in terms of the number of Indian bidders....It's down to the demand, supply gap that India has and the incredible thirst that India has in terms of generating extra energy.[14]

India and China may be pressuring global supplies of coal, as the world's two fastest-growing major economies seek to power factories and homes and, in accordance with this development, India's Essar Group in March 2010 agreed to buy Trinity Coal Corp., following Tata Power Co. and Reliance Power Ltd. in buying overseas assets to shore up supplies to meet coal demand in India which could be 1.4 billion metric tons by 2020, exceeding domestic supply of 1.1 billion tons, according to Crisil Ltd., a unit of Standard & Poor's.[15] Coal India Ltd., the nation's monopoly producer, is looking at 10 proposals in Indonesia, Australia and the U.S. for strategic coal alliances, which may include taking equity stakes in mines, A.K. Sarkar, director of marketing, Coal India said: "Nothing will deter us from acquiring any strategic asset of any kind in order to continue to be the biggest supplier of coal," Sarkar said. "We've been a producer of coal but now we'll have to become an importer. We see this as an opportunity to increase our profits", adding Coal India may consider buying shipping units to help transport coal.[16]

Like Coal India, other Indian companies are also interested in acquisitions. For example, Essar is paying $600 million to acquire West Virginia-based Trinity to add 200 million tons of coal reserves while Reliance Power, controlled by billionaire Anil Ambani, bought three coal mines in Indonesia in 2008.[17] Currently, just under half of India's metallurgical coal requirements are met through imports and the Indian Government is aiming to limit the steel industry's reliance on imported metallurgical coal by allocating domestic coal mines to individual steel plants to ensure supply security, and a mechanism has been established to share excess coal between steel plants.[18]

Given the significant role Australian exports of coking coal play in India's large steel industry, the importance of coal as one of the mainstays of the bilateral trading relationship is unlikely to diminish; in fact, links between the Australian and Indian coal industries continue to increase - a coal and mining forum was held between the two countries in February 2006 and Indian companies have begun to invest in Australian coal mines—Gujarat NRE Coke's investment in NSW coal mines being a good example.[19]

Imports are expected to supply the majority of increased requirements for metallurgical coal because many Indian coal reserves remain underdeveloped, and more than 97 per cent of coal reserves are of lower grade coal, implying an increased reliance on imports for higher grade metallurgical coal.[20] Australia, as a major metallurgical coal exporter appears to be well-placed to meet India's requirements for metallurgical coal imports.

Australia is already the major supplier of metallurgical coal to India with an export value of $2.4 billion in 2006-07, accounting for around 95 per cent of India's metallurgical coal imports in 2006 and, because of its geographic proximity, appears to have a substantial freight advantage in supplying metallurgical coal to India over other main competitors — the United States and Canada.[21]

Opportunities for increased thermal coal exports: Opportunities may exist for Australia to meet the increasing demand for thermal coal in the Indian electricity sector as coal accounts for more than half of India's commercial energy consumption and almost 70 per cent of electricity generation and the 'Power for All' government program that is due for completion by 2012 aims to increase national electricity generation capacity by around 6 per cent a year, for a total capacity addition of 47 gigawatts.[22] This compares with actual capacity expansion of just over 3 per cent a year in the five years ended 2006 and the expansion of power generation capacity implies that there will be increased coal demand from the electricity sector that is unlikely to be met by domestic production alone.[23]

Import demand for LNG is expected to rise: Like other major world economies, India pursues fuel diversity in power generation and natural gas is playing an increasingly important role in meeting India's growing energy demand because of the fuel's environmental characteristics and greater efficiency and Indian industry is also eager to secure a reliable, cost effective fuel source. Since the commissioning of India's first LNG import terminal in 2004, LNG imports rose rapidly to 6.2 million tons in 2006, just under a quarter of India's natural gas consumption and LNG imports are likely to continue to play an important role in meeting India's energy demand.

To date, Australia has had a limited role in supplying LNG to India, with trade restricted to a few spot cargoes but India's growing gas requirements and desire for diversity in gas supply sources may lead to an increase in Australian exports of LNG to India.[24]

There are currently a number of LNG supply projects in the Asia Pacific region, including Australia, both existing and planned, that have the capacity to meet India's long term gas requirements but the current world LNG market is characterized by a tight supply-demand situation and so, competition from major LNG importing countries that are willing to pay higher prices may be a constraint to India securing long term LNG supplies.[25]

In 2009, India's Petronet LNG signed a 20-year agreement to take gas from the massive Gorgon project which is a joint venture partner between Exxon Mobil Corp and Petronet, India's largest LNG importer and, under the sales and purchase agreement, Exxon Mobil will supply about 1.5 million tons per annum of its share of LNG from the proposed Gorgon LNG project over 20 years.[26]

Australia approved and operationalized this massive energy project that is a joint venture by Chevron, Shell and ExxonMobil (which signed a contract worth 21 billion dollars with India's Petronet) to supply natural gas worth tens of billions of dollars to China and India, augmenting its resources boom but was careful to impose 28 conditions to protect wildlife affected by the Gorgon LNG plant off Western Australia; Roy Krzywosinski, Gorgon's Australian managing director indicated: "The Gorgon project is Australia's largest single resource project and is set to deliver significant economic benefits and create around 10,000 indirect and direct jobs during peak construction" and added the plant was "globally and nationally significant", with an economic life of at least 40 years, adding it had been sited to minimize environmental impact.[27]

According to an ExxonMobil Statement, the gas will be delivered to Petronet's new LNG terminal under construction at Kochi in southern India and its vice-president Australia LNG Luke Musgrave noted: "This historic agreement is the first long-term sale of LNG from Australia to India" and Trade Minister Simon Crean saw the deal as a major boost to Australia's profile as a green energy provider while Petronet managing director Prosad Dasgupta reiterated:

> I am very pleased to finalize this long-term agreement for the provision of LNG to our new terminal in Kochi, supporting more than $US2 billion ($2.4 billion) of related energy infrastructure investment in India...Energy consumers in Kerala State will now have access to a clean-burning base load fuel, which will enhance the economic development of the region and maintain the pristine ecology of Kerala.[28]

The Australian Bureau of Agriculture and Resource Economics expects "that LNG exports to India will increase to 8.1 million tons per annum" and that there has been strong Indian interest in Australia as a source for LNG" while Australian regional governments are keen to meet this demand, e.g. a submission from the Western Australian Government noted the potential for long-term LNG supply partnership with India given the state's vast reserves of LNG.[29] The 2008 Submission from the Department of Resources, Energy and Tourism provided a summary of the present state of the Indian LNG market: India has been importing LNG since 2004 and in 2007 imported 8.42 million tons of LNG and to date, this LNG trade has consisted of several spot cargoes with expectation that Indian LNG imports will increase to 12.6 million tons per annum (mtpa) by 2015 and 21.1 mtpa by 2020 - this will involve an expansion at the existing import terminals and /or new LNG terminal projects.[30]

In the private sector, Indian companies such as Petronet LNG signed a A$12.5 billion contract with ExxonMobil Corp for procuring LNG from its Gorgon project in Western Australia and, under the deal, Exxon's subsidiaries, Mobil Australia, Mobil Australia Resources Company and Mobil Exploration and Producing Australia will annually supply 1.5 million metric tons of LNG to Petronet's Kochi terminal in Kerala.[31] Australia appears to have considerable potential to expand its LNG production and companies such as Woodside, BHP Billiton, Chevron, Shell and ExxonMobil retain an interest in supplying India in the future and the outlook for Australian LNG exports to India may have improved significantly, with Shell signing a memorandum of understanding (MOU) with India's Gujarat State Petroleum Corporation to supply up to 0.5 million tons of LNG, which could be sourced from the proposed Gorgon project.[32]

Experimental coal bed methane: In 2004, a research partnership to boost India's energy program was undertaken by Australian scientists from the University of NSW and an agreement worth more than $AUD1 million was signed with the Oil and Natural Gas Corporation of India, taking the form of a 18-month collaborative project with the University's School of Petroleum Engineering to explore suitable technologies for the exploitation of coal bed methane gas from coal seams in India.[33]

Professor Val Pinczewski, Head of UNSW University's School of Petroleum Engineering (a department with more than 20 years expertise in coal bed methane technologies), focused on energy solutions in the form of an alternative form of gas production or coal bed methane which is basically methane gas/natural gas produced conventionally by the petroleum industry from underground gas reservoirs.[34] The only difference between conventional natural gas and coal bed methane is the way that the gas is actually trapped within the rock because, in conventional reservoirs, it is contained in the pore spaces between the sand grains and in coal it is actually absorbed onto the surface of the rock – in other words, the gas is part of the coal, and it's produced when the organic matter, which makes coal is actually formed.[35]

Some experts in India see coal bed methane as a possible partial answer to their energy problem, having about the sixth largest coal reserves in the world and, looking to tap into that to produce the gas so as part of a fact-finding mission, they visited Australia's Sydney Gas Company, hoping to learn and obtain Australian technologies that are used by the petroleum industry to produce conventional gas- basically drilling a hole, drilling a well into the coal seam.[36]

Coal, unlike conventional gas reservoirs, have seams that are very impermeable which means that it is very difficult for gas to move through the coal seam, so in order to fracture these seams, once the well is drilled, high pressure water is pumped into the well to fracture the coal seam and that creates large cracks in the seam which allows gas to actually move towards the well and be channeled to the surface.[37] These are relatively well-established technologies and the problem with applying these technologies is that coal seams are extremely variable in their properties and the trick in having a successful project as well as commercially successful operation is to be able to tailor this conventional technology to the particular characteristics of a seam.[38]

UNSW's researchers worked alongside personnel from the Oil and Natural Gas Corporation of India in the development of the technology and laboratory studies while interpretative work for field tests were carried out by the Indian team who also carried out field work, drilling the wells and testing the wells; after which the Australian team developed protocols for the Indians, collected data from drilling/testing wells and interpreted that data into mathematical models to optimize a development plan for the Indian energy industry.[39]

Wind power: Indian Pune-based Suzlon entered the Australian market and secured a contract to design, procure, construct and commission a wind farm with 45 units of the S88 – 2.1 MW wind turbine through the AGL (Australian Gas Light Company) and the deal consisted of 95 megawatts of wind turbine capacity installed at Hallett, 220 kilometers north of Adelaide, the largest wind farm in Australia upon completion.[40] In a company statement, Dan Kofoed Hansen, the CEO of SEA said: "This is an exciting day for Suzlon, and one that we've worked hard to reach in Australia" which was echoed by Tulsi Tanti, CEO and Chairman of Suzlon Energy Limited, the parent firm of Suzlon, based in Pune, a city in Western Indian State of Maharashtra, who said:

> Suzlon is proudly continuing its expansion globally with its entrance into the Australian market with such a well-respected customer...Suzlon Australia's team has professional experience and history in EPC contracting, whilst our India-based group has extensive experience in successfully providing total wind farm solutions. I believe the Suzlon group's combined background knowledge and expertise is set to deliver an outstanding wind power plant for AGL.[41]

Suzlon provided five years (starting from 2006) of maintenance and service on all wind turbines under the pact with AGL, while Suzlon Energy Limited of Pune supplied the S88 wind turbines for the AGL wind farm also installed 45 units of its S88 – 2.1 megawatt wind turbine for AGL on the Brown Hill Range, Hallett. AGL, headquartered in Sydney, is a major retailer of natural gas and electricity in Australia which purchased Southern Hydro that owned renewable energy assets consisting of hydro power stations and an existing wind farm, with total generating capacity of 736 megawatts.[42]

Another Australian firm, Mission New Energy Limited, is an integrated global renewable energy company with operations located in Australia and India amongst other locations and the company is listed on the Australian Securities Exchange with the head office located in Perth, Australia and its key areas of business comprised the production of biodiesel, Pharmaceutical grade refined Glycerine, the cultivation of Jatropha Curcas and electricity generated from wind turbines (including Wind turbines supplying electricity to the state utility in India)[43] Mission's wind power business provides electricity to the state utility of India.[44]

Rural energy. In the near future, remote villages and small towns in rural India as well as the Australian outback may be powered by self-sufficient sustainable energy-based mini-grids because Australia's national science agency, the Commonwealth Scientific and Industrial Research Organisation (CSIRO), is working with The Energy and Resources Institute (TERI) of India on projects aimed at meeting the energy needs of populations, which are not near the national power grid. *"In fact, both CSIRO and TERI are working on similar technology. but with different constraints. While we hope to free rural communities of their dependence on diesel generated power, India wants to electrify its rural villages,"* explained Dr Glenn Platt, research group leader at the CSIRO who elaborated on the new grids based primarily on solar energy, but with wind and natural gas as back-up, will substantially help reduce emissions with no need for costly infrastructure or fuels [The CSIRO is in an advanced stage of research because of its simulator which helps recreate the power requirements of a small town complete with peak consumption periods, cuts in supply as well as demand. In India, TERI is doing similar research in two locations].[45]

CSIRO's Energy for Buildings Manager Dr Stephen White, on the other hand, is trying to explore a sustainable way to use solar thermal power for cooling.

> "In Australia, we want to use the technology to provide air conditioning in rural households, but for India it will be more feasible to use it to create 15-KV community food stores to check wastage of produce due to the lack of good storage facilities."

Dr White explained and he elaborated that in India, TERI is already working on a prototype with assistance from Thermax, while another prototype is coming up in New Castle. "We hope to share our research findings and develop a feasible model," he said.[46]

Faced with one of the highest per capita emission levels in the world, Australia appears to be banking on solar energy as one of its options to take it towards a low carbon future and the country has announced an AUD 1.5 billion solar flagship program aimed at producing 1 gigawatt of capacity by 2015. The Australian Solar Institute (ASI), as part of the initiative, is working on producing cheaper solar photovoltaic cells and promoting the new solar thermal technology to replace coal but "cost is our main challenge. Solar energy costs three times more than traditional energy and we have to convince to spend for the longer term. The aim is to take mobile generation across the country like mobile phones," said Mark Twidell, the CEO of ASI; "our research is primarily aimed at improving technology to make solar power cheaper and efficient".[47]

Conclusion: Australia's potential role in India's energy security appears to be a complimentary one: Australia appears to be well-positioned to partner India in this area, through exports of fuels, energy investment opportunities in Australia and collaboration in areas of common interest such as new mining technologies.[48] Austrade's National Manager for Infrastructure and Major Projects, Jeff Turner said Australian companies were well-placed to assist India's development:

> The way to modernize the mining sector is to utilize the best available MTS (mining technology and services). This is the driving force behind the take up of Australian technology by the Indian mining industry...India is rapidly moving towards environmentally sustainable options in coal mining, and there is strong interest in all clean coal technology from Australia. Coal washeries are a major opportunity for Australia. In fact, some people in India have referred to the move to washing coal as the 'washery boom'...Not only is there a growing acceptance in India that it's environmentally unsustainable to burn coal with an ash content of around 30 to 40 per cent, but that it's also not economical to transport unwashed coal over

> large distances...Australian software, especially mine management systems, continues to do well in the market. Other key areas are equipment and services for underground mining. India is increasingly moving towards large, modern underground mines as surface coal and minerals are exhausted.[49]

Australian energy minister Martin Ferguson AM sought Indian investments into the island nation's energy sector and offered India long-term supply of energy sources and clean technologies by appointing a dedicated investment commissioner in Mumbai in 2010 to facilitate cross-border flow of investments and also showcase before Indian investors and businesses its latest blocks on offer for oil and natural gas exploration later 2010; "in resources and energy, we have a long-term relationship. With the growth in the Indian economy, it is going to expand dramatically over the next decade," said Ferguson as Australia is the biggest exporter of coal and the fifth largest exporter of LNG.

With higher investments, Australia hopes to be the second largest LNG exporter within five years.[50] The minister met with Cabinet ministers and businessmen during his visit to India and argued that Australia is strategically placed to meet the growing energy needs of the Indian economy, citing 2009's Australian $25 billion deal between Australia's Exxon Mobil Corporation's subsidiaries and Petronet LNG Limited for long-term supply of LNG as a milestone in cross-border trade in the energy sector (India is also a major buyer of Australia's coal and wants to expand the association further).[51]

In Feb 2010, Australian energy minister Martin Ferguson AM said that Australia has also been encouraging India's huge investments in its coal industry: "We have a favourable environment with respect to foreign investments. Our foreign investment policy is non-discriminatory", adding that the state does not interfere with market forces and offers partnerships and joint ventures with Indian firms in development of clean technology and sharing the research outcomes because India is investing heavily in research and has committed a 20% cut in carbon emissions by the end of the next decade with a focus on solar thermal, geo-thermal and biomass sources.[52] In Feb 2010, Australian energy minister Martin Ferguson AM said his government wants to take forward the activities of five working groups for co-operation set up in 2009 in the areas of mining, coal, power, petroleum and natural gas and new and renewable sources of energy.[53]

For future development, Australian Prime Minister, Kevin Rudd's government invested 50 million dollars over five years for the Australia-India strategic research fund, a joint initiative of the Australian and Indian governments, supporting fifty projects across the spectrum of scientific disciplines including astronomy, climate change and evolution, malaria vaccines, the impact of global warming on agriculture, water management, computing and biotechnology; Rudd added:

> The additional 50 million over five years for the Australia-India strategic research fund will commence from financial year 2009-10...I have already seen where such collaboration can lead to ground breaking research, investigating how—can be used to clean up oil contamination in water. In fact the fund which will be Australia's largest bilateral research fund is already supporting 50 projects across the spectrum of scientific disciplines.[54]

Australia contributed a million dollars for an innovative Australia-India solar cooling research project between CSIRO and the Energy and Resources Institute which aims to develop a zero emissions solar cooling system for use in remote rural communities in un-electrified areas; Australian PM Rudd added: "We will contribute to a further million dollars to extend the TERI and the CSIRO collaboration working to provide a emissions free solar cooling electricity and pure drinking water for rural areas".[55]

REFERENCES

Abare government economic research agency, "Australian Commodities" dated December 2007 quarter 07.4 in the Abare website [downloaded on 1 March 2010], available at www.abareeconomics.com, 2007.

APH Australian Government, "The economic relationship: Business engagement—energy, resources and agriculture", in APH website [downloaded on 1 March 2010], available at www.aph.gov.au

AUstrade media release, "Australia shares mining expertise with India, Indonesia" dated 21 November 2007 in the Austrade media website [downloaded on 1 March 2010], available at www.austrade.gov.au/Australia-shares-mining-expertise-with-India-Indonesia/default.aspx+Australia+India+energy&cd=226&hl=en&ct=clnk&gl=sg

Austrade media release, "Australia's world class resources sector draws major Indian delegation" dated Tuesday, 4 September 2007 in Austrade media release website [downloaded on 1 March 2010], available at http://www.austradegov.au/default.aspx? ArticleID=7239

Digihelp.com, "Suzlon to set up Australia's largest wind farm" dated 2 February 2006 [downloaded on 1 Jan 2010], available at http://www.digi-help.com/pub/suzlon-australia-wind-farm.asp

DNA India, "Solar energy can be used to combat climate change" dated 9 Feb 2010 in the DN India website [downloaded on 1 March 2010], available at http://www.dnaindia.com/scitech/report_solar-energy-can-be-used-to-combat-climate-change-experts_1345658.

Livemint.com and the Wall Street Journal, "Australia approves huge gas project to supply China, India" dated 26 August 2009 in the Livemint website [downloaded on 1 March 2010], available at http://www.livemint.com/2009/08/26115727/Australia-approves-huge-gas-pr.html.

Mission NewEnergy Limited, "CORPORATE PROFILE" in the Mission NewEnergy website [downloaded on 1 March 2010], available at http://www.missionnewenergy.com/AboutUs.php and http://www.missionnewenergy.com/.

Pearson, Madelene and Natalie Obiko Pearson, "India Is Seeking Coal Deals in Australia, ANZ Says" dated 10 March 2010 in the Bloomberg website [downloaded on 20 March 2010], available at http://www.bloomberg.com/apps/news?pid=20601072&sid= aigoS2sA8V5s

Prasad, Gireesh Chandra, "Australia seeks investments in energy sector" dated 6 Feb 2010 in the financial express website [downloaded on 1 March 2010], available at http://www.financialexpress.com/news/australia-seeks-investments-in-energy-sector/576161/.

Radio Australia, "India's Energy Program – Coal Bed Methane Gas" dated 24 April 2004 in the ABC Radio Australia website [downloaded on 1 Jan 2010], available at http://www.abc.net.au/ra/innovations/stories/s1094894.htm. Rajan, Nandagopal, "India, Australia join hands for solar research" dated 16 Dec 2009 in Indian Express [downloaded on 1 March 2010], available at http://www. indianexpress.com/news/India—Australia-join-hands-for-solar-research/554711

Thaindia News, "Australia to invest 50 million dollars for Australia-India strategic research fund: Rudd" dated 12 November 2009 in the Thaindian website [downloaded on 1 March 2010], available at http://www.thaindian.com/newsportal/india-news/australia-to-invest-50-million-dollars-for-australia-india-strategic-research-fund-rudd_100273623.html

The Age, "First Australia-India long-term LNG deal reached August 11, 2009" in the Age website [downloaded on 1 March 2010], available at http://www.theage. com.au/ business/world-business/first-australiaindia-longterm-lng-deal-reached-20090811-efui.html

NOTES

1. Abare government economic research agency, "Australian Commodities" dated December 2007 quarter 07.4 in the Abare website [downloaded on 1 March 2010], available at www.abareeconomics.com, 2007, p. 684
2. APH Australian Government, "The economic relationship: Business engagement—energy, resources and agriculture", in APH website [downloaded on 1 March 2010], available at www.aph.gov.au, p. 27.
3. *Ibid.*, p. 26.
4. *Ibid.*, p. 30.
5. Austrade media release, "Australia shares mining expertise with India, Indonesia" dated 21 November 2007 in the Austrade media website [downloaded on 1 March 2010], available at www.austrade.gov.au/Australia-shares-mining-expertise-with-India-Indonesia/default.aspx+Australia+India+energy&cd= 226& hl=en&ct=clnk&gl=sg
6. *Ibid.*
7. *Ibid.*
8. Austrade media release, "Australia's world class resources sector draws major Indian delegation" dated Tuesday, 4 September 2007 in Austrade media release website [downloaded on 1 March 2010], available at http://www.austrade.gov.au/default.aspx?Article ID=7239
9. *Ibid.*
10. *Ibid.*
11. *Ibid.*
12. DNA India, "Solar energy can be used to combat climate change" dated 9 Feb 2010 in the DN India website [downloaded on 1 March 2010], available at http://www.dnaindia.com/ scitech/report_solar-energy-can-be-used-to-combat-climate-change-experts_1345658.
13. *Ibid.*
14. Pearson, Madelene and Natalie Obiko Pearson, "India Is Seeking Coal Deals in Australia, ANZ Says" dated 10 March 2010 in the Bloomberg website [downloaded on 20 March 2010], available at http://www. bloomberg.com/apps/news?pid=20601072&sid= aigoS2sA8V5s

15. *Ibid.*
16. *Ibid.*
17. *Ibid.*
18. Abare government economic research agency, n.1, p. 688.
19. APH Australian Government, n.2, p. 26-27.
20. Abare government economic research agency, n.2, p. 688.
21. *Ibid.*
22. Abare government economic research agency,n.1, , p. 688.
23. *Ibid.*
24. *Ibid.*, p. 689.
25. *Ibid.*
26. The Age, "First Australia-India long-term LNG deal reached August 11, 2009" in the Age website [downloaded on 1 March 2010], available at http://www.theage.com.au/business/world-business/first-australiaindia-longterm-lng-deal-reached-20090811-efui.html
27. Livemint.com and the *Wall Street Journal*, "Australia approves huge gas project to supply China, India" dated 26 August 2009 in the Livemint website [downloaded on 1 March 2010], available at http://www.livemint .com/2009/08/26115727/Australia-approves-huge-gas-pr.html.
28. The Age, Website, n.26.
29. APH Australian Government, n.2, p. 28.
30. *Ibid.*
31. *Ibid.*
32. *Ibid.*, p. 29.
33. Radio Australia, "India's Energy Program – Coal Bed Methane Gas" dated 24 April 2004 in the ABC Radio Australia website [downloaded on 1 Jan 2010], available at http://www. abc.net.au/ra/innovations/stories/s1094894.htm.
34. *Ibid.*
35. *Ibid.*
36. *Ibid.*

37. *Ibid.*
38. *Ibid.*
39. *Ibid.*
40. Digihelp.com, "Suzlon to set up Australia's largest wind farm" dated 2 February 2006 [downloaded on 1 Jan 2010], available at http://www.digi-help.com/pub/suzlon-australia-wind-farm.asp
41. *Ibid.*
42. *Ibid.*
43. Mission NewEnergy Limited, "CORPORATE PROFILE" in the Mission NewEnergy website downloaded on 1March 2010], available at http://www.missionnewenergy.com/About Us.php and http://www missionnewenergy.com/.
44. *Ibid.*
45. Rajan, Nandagopal, "India, Australia join hands for solar research" dated 16 Dec 2009 in Indian Express [downloaded on 1 March 2010], available at http://www.indianexpress. com/news/India—Australia-join-hands-for-solar-research/554711
46. *Ibid.*
47. *Ibid.*
48. APH Australian Government, n.2, p. 30.
49. Austrade Media Release, n.5.
50. Prasad, Gireesh Chandra, "Australia seeks investments in energy sector" dated 6 Feb 2010 in the financial express website [downloaded on 1 March 2010], available at http://www.financialexpress.com/news/australia-seeks-investments-in-energy-sector/576161/.
51. *Ibid.*
52. *Ibid.*
53. *Ibid.*
54. Thaindia News, "Australia to invest 50 million dollars for Australia- India strategic research fund: Rudd" dated 12 November 2009 in the Thaindian website [downloaded on 1 March 2010], available at http://www. thaindian. com/newsportal/india-news/australia-to-invest-50-million-dollars-for-australia-india-strategic-research- fund-rudd_100273623.html.

53. *Ibid.*

3

India-Australia Energy Cooperation: Possibilities and Challenges

Pankaj Jha

Energy security can be defined as an adequate and reliable supply of energy at a reasonable price. Following this definition, the economics of energy security examines the economic consequences of volatile oil prices and the effectiveness of its mitigation measures mainly for oil importing countries. The recurrent impacts of high oil prices lead to deceleration in economic growth, a higher inflation and an increase in the unemployment. Apart from the energy security for oil importing countries, the energy security for oil exporting countries in specific and depletable resource based economies in general requires those economies to progress both the ultimate depletion of resources and the eventual loss of customers. The transition to renewable capital based economy is suggested as a solution for ensuring energy security.[1]

Energy security concerns are thus linked to the need to ensure a continuous availability of energy at prices that the country can afford. These concerns are currently exacerbated by a growing sense of competition and the feeling that one needs to tie up resources as quickly as possible to ensure that the country's needs are covered in the event of either economically or politically induced shortages. While diversifying, and especially planning for a longer term end to the hydrocarbon domination through a greater dependence on energy efficiency and renewable in the short term, it is important to eschew energy securing strategies that are competitive. Such strategies can only bid up prices of oil properties, and even result in conflict situations, besides cerating distrust, and greater global insecurity. Energy securing strategies should be avoided. Rather, transnational energy infrastructure projects should be seen as ways to strengthen bilateral economic and political ties. The need is for collaboration and partnership, and the building of trust.[2]

It is increasingly evident that for energy securing strategies to succeed, energy security concerns need to be integrated into foreign policy making, which in turn needs to be more imaginative and bold so as to ensure that what follows is a not greater conflicts and global insecurity. Building trust, for example, will need greater dialogues with oil producers and consumers. The former petroleum Minister,Mani Shanker Aiyar's proposal for a Pan Asian Gas Grid, stretching from Russia and Central Asia in the West through South Asia to Japan and Korea in the East to link producers with large consuming countries, is a bold and imaginative plan that would do much to help connect the region. Beyond this, countries should share new technologies in cleaner conventional fuels and in renewables; and support policies of engagement and not isolation of countries in West Asia, given that they are key energy providers in the short term and long term.[3]

The case of India and Australia qualifies more as a stage for bilateral energy cooperation rather than a buyer-seller relationship. This can be stated owing to few major factors. These are:

- India's energy security is predominantly relying on the secure supplies from the West Asia and Africa.
- Australia has not clearly devised the policy with regard to its energy exports and there is time and again domestic resistance to supply of uranium and other energy resources.

- India has not started seeing Australia as a major country from where energy supply could be secured, though there have a few MoUs and also energy agreements for long term supply.
- India and Australia have been vulnerable to the fluctuating oil prices and thus act as partners in securing the energy supplies as well as creating stability in oil market which has seen fluctuations in the couple of years.

These issues put India and Australia as the cooperating partners for energy and not limited to that the energy efficiency; sharing best practices and streamlining the FDI policy in energy sector as well as guidelines for energy usage and conservation need to be charted out in the two countries. This paper would look into varied aspects of energy cooperation which includes multilateral cooperative framework, energy policy, non-renewable and renewable energy sources, power generation, coal, natural gas as well as reducing carbon emissions and research in the field of energy efficiency between the two countries.

Energy Policy in India and Australia

India has been one of the largest consumers of energy. This issue gets multiplied by the fact that it is one of the largest importers of energy. Energy is an essential requirement for economic development and an important prerequisite for improving quality of life. Within commercial energy, oil & gas have been playing an increasingly important role in the development of economies throughout the world and India is no exception. In the last 50 years, the oil & gas sector has taken giant strides to meet the growing energy needs of the Indian economy. The country has built up a large petroleum industrial network encompassing every facet of the oil & gas business including exploration, production, refining, transportation and marketing. It is imperative to have a long-term policy for the hydrocarbon sector in order to facilitate meeting the long-term needs of the country. Issues such as energy security for strategic and defence purposes, making the hydrocarbon sector globally competitive and ensuring the development of free market in the hydrocarbon sector need to be addressed whilst formulating a hydrocarbon policy for India. The Government of India has come out with a policy document "India Hydrocarbon Vision 2025- which lays down the framework which would guide policies for the hydrocarbon sector for the next 25 years.[4]

The radical restructuring of the Indian economy since 1991 has led to opening up of the economy to the private sector. Recent initiatives in Oil & Gas exploration, Natural Gas, refining, marketing and infrastructure have resulted in enormous opportunities for private enterprise in the high growth areas. Out of 26 sedimentary basins in the country, production has so far been undertaken in only 7 basins and almost two-third of the total sedimentary area remains unexplored/poorly explored. Out of a hydrocarbon resource base of around 30 billion tonnes, in place, reserves account for 6.8 billion tonnes. The E&P policy entails carrying out extensive and intensive exploration to achieve a Reserve Replacement Ratio of more than one, while achieving a zero impact on the environment. One of the major milestones in Exploration is the opening up the vast areas in non-producing, frontier basins and deep-water offshore areas both by DGH as well as National Oil companies. Reconnoitry surveys in deep water areas led to offering 12 deep-water blocks in NELP-99 out of which 7 blocks have been awarded. ONGC has already discovered oil in deep water offshore east coast and there might be more discoveries as further areas are opened up in future. The NELP has provided internationally competitive terms keeping in view the relative prospectively perceptions of Indian basins along with expeditious and time bound finalisation of contracts.[5]

The demand for hydrocarbon in the country is growing at the rate of 6.5-7% per annum and India already is the eighth largest consumer of oil and is expected to be the fifth largest consumer in the next twenty years. With domestic crude production remaining almost static for the past five years, India has to depend largely on import. Without doubt exploration policies and techniques aimed at maximizing reserves accretion will be single most important factor for sustainable growth, calling for continued research and development in the frontiers of technology to evolve cost effective methods for adding petroleum resources. Another area of focus is the requirement of more natural gas in the country and India is likely to emerge as the largest growth center for use of natural gas. To reduce pollution, accommodate rising electric power generation and diversifying its energy portfolio, numerous projects are under way to increase India's usage of the green fuel. The natural gas policy framework envisages conventional gas availability through domestic production as well as pipeline and Liquefied Natural Gas (LNG) imports besides tapping unconventional sources such as Coal Bed Methane (CBM), Gas hydrates and underground coal gasification. The Central and State Governments have approved several sites for LNG imports and Petronet LNG lid; a joint venture company is the torchbearer in this arena. The Government is also considering to produce coal bed methane and several blocks would be soon on offer with the best terms available in the world. The CBM policy and the best fiscal terms for CBM were approved by the Government in 1997. A National Gas Hydrates Programme is in place and various R & D studies are in progress to develop vast resources of Gas hydrates in Western and Eastern offshore and Andaman areas. India is amongst the only 4 - 5 countries in the world where R &. D work on gas hydrates has started.[6] India has been trying for securing its energy supplies as well as looking for alternatives like wind energy, nuclear energy and solar energy. In fact, with regard to nuclear energy it has signed and ratified the Indo-US nuclear deal so as to shift its reliance on nuclear energy from thermal power generation for electricity in the long run.

In the case of Australia, energy supply is utilised for export and for meeting Australia's domestic consumption needs. Energy exports account for 66 per cent of domestic energy production and domestic consumption accounts for the remaining 34 per cent. Australia is the world's eighth largest energy producer, accounting for around 2.4 per cent of the world's energy production. Given Australia's large energy resources, Australia is well positioned to continue to supply a significant proportion of the world's energy needs, while maintaining domestic energy supply. The rate of growth in Australia's production of energy has been increasing. Over the 10 years from 1996-97 to 2006-07, energy production increased at an average rate of 4.3 per cent a year, compared with 3.4 per cent over the previous 10 years, being driven largely by a growing global demand for energy. The main fuels produced in Australia are coal, uranium and natural gas. In 2006-07, Australia's energy production was dominated by coal production, which accounted for 54 per cent of total Australian energy production in energy content terms, followed by uranium with a share of 26 per cent and natural gas with a share of 11 per cent. Crude oil and Liquefied Petroleum Gas (LPG) represented 7 per cent of total energy production, and renewables represented 2 per cent. The Australian energy industry is an important part of the economy. The coal, petroleum, gas and electricity industries contributed around $57 billion to industry gross value added in 2006-07, representing 6 per cent of the Australian total. The oil and gas extraction industries were the largest contributors to industry value added, followed by the coal mining industry and the electricity supply industry.[7]

Though the two countries have been looking towards each other for quite some time but tangible results with regard to developing understanding and creating common ground for negotiations in the field of energy security started sometime in 2005. Not only the bilateral negotiations but also multilateral initiatives need to be highlighted which form the basis for looking for energy cooperation between the two countries.

Multilateral Framework

India and Australia have been dialogue partners of ASEAN and also members of the East Asia Summit (EAS). Among other things non traditional threats have been discussed at length at all these organizations but particular emphasis has been made with regard to energy. The EAS, through its Energy Cooperation Task Force, has progressed activities to promote regional energy market integration to help strengthen energy security. Australia has led on this initiative by leading a study to develop recommendations for promoting regional integration of EAS energy markets. Other areas of interest include energy efficiency and biofuels and the potential contribution they can make to advancing energy security in the region.[8] The inaugural EAS Energy Ministers Meeting in Singapore in August 2007 endorsed the recommendations of the ECTF in three identified work streams addressing Energy Efficiency and Conservation (led by Japan); Biofuels (led by the Philippines); and Energy Market Integration (co-chaired by Singapore and Australia).[9] Though not much work has been done in this regard but it clearly envisions the role of major energy consumers and suppliers in developing an integrated energy sharing network and also sharing of energy efficiency practices in the larger geo-political region of East Asia.

Also, Asia Pacific Economic Cooperation (APEC) which was formed in 1989 has been envisioning the role of energy security in developing consensus among the member countries. Though, India is not a member of the organization but it might become a member when the moratorium on new membership ends. The APEC Energy Working Group (EWG) is actively working to advance regional energy security. The Asia-Pacific region is characterised by increasing demand for energy, rising incomes and growing levels of urbanisation, which results in a growing demand for energy. Australia sponsored the APEC EWG Energy Trade and Investment Roundtable in Cairns, Australia, in early November 2009. The Roundtable addressed identified barriers to energy trade and investment in the region and developed a draft Plan-of-Action which will be further refined before submission to APEC Energy Ministers for their endorsement when they next meet in Japan in 2010.

The EWG recently established two Task Forces to progress APEC Energy Minister's directives;

- Renewable Energy & Energy Efficiency Financing Task Force to work with the private sector and financial institutions to facilitate greater investments in clean and more efficient energy infrastructure and technologies. On completion of its work program EWG members decided to terminate this Task Force at EWG35

- Biofuels Task Force to help APEC Member Economies better understands the potential for biofuels to displace oil in transport.[10]

But the initiatives in the multilateral framework need to come to conclusion with regard to the pricing of resources, sharing ,grid and energy networks as well as energy dumps for safeguarding the region from price fluctuations and supply disruptions. There is also need for raising consensus about the price banding of the energy resources as well as long term strategy in this regard. Though multilateral initiatives have their own utility in terms of building consensus and cooperative security on energy but in the case of the two countries bilateral cooperation has been showing much promise.

Energy Cooperation- Looking for Complementarities

Bilateral energy and minerals cooperation with India is fundamental to Australia's strategic partnership. Australia is considered by India to be a large, stable and reliable supplier of energy and resources – products India needs to fuel its growth. In 2008-09, India was Australia's fourth largest merchandise export market, and seventh largest two-way trading partner. Resources and energy exports to India in 2008-09 were valued at around AUD 13.6 billion.[11] In fact, coal comprises of largest component of imports by India. Sensing this aspect of energy cooperation Joint Working group was formed. Australia-India Joint Working Group on Energy and Minerals (JWG) was established in 2000. Its purpose was to address trade and investment issues in the energy and minerals sector, to exchange information on policy developments and to identify possible commercial opportunities. While the first three meetings outlined the agenda and objectives of JWG, the fourth India-Australia JWG meeting was held in New Delhi on 8-9 June, 2005 to look at the areas of cooperation. GSI, IBM and

MECL have shown interest in entering into collaboration with their Australian counterpart agencies for state-of-the-art technology in exploration and exploitation of minerals.[12] There has been significant progress in the bilateral energy relationship following the Australia-India Joint Working Group (JWG) on Energy and Minerals held in New Delhi on 8-9 June 2005. Further discussions on a number of key initiatives agreed at the JWG, including a joint LNG trade study and a possible Australia-India Coal and Mining Forum, took place during the visit to India on 23-25 August the same year by John Hartwell and Tania Constable from the Resources Division, Department of Industry, Tourism and Resources (DITR). An Australian oil and gas exploration road show, coordinated by DITR, Geoscience Australia and the Australian High Commission in New Delhi, was organized in India on 19-20 September 2005 to promote acreage release and exploration opportunities. This event was prepared in cooperation with the Indian Ministry of Petroleum and Natural Gas. Indian officials attended a road show in Australia in November 2005 to promote opportunities associated with the forthcoming release of coal bed methane blocks. The Australian High Commission has been working with the Indian Directorate General of Hydrocarbons, Australian companies and state government representatives to ensure Australian business can gain the most benefit from this visit.[13]

The special purpose vehicle (SPV), International Coal Ventures Ltd (ICVL), formed by SAIL, Rashtriya Ispat Nigam Ltd., NMDC, NTPC and CIL for scouting coal mines abroad, is now considering picking up stake in some mining companies in Australia, Canada, Indonesia, Africa and Mozambique. Coal Ministry official said ICVL not only planned to pick up minority/majority stake in the overseas mining companies, but was also exploring the option of entering into joint ventures for developing the coal property. The SPV is even open to taking over greenfield coal projects from the identified mining firms. To meet a sizable coal requirement of its partner companies, ICVL is also in the process of picking up over 10 per cent stake in Australian mining firm Gloucester Resources.[14]

The 5th round of JWG consultations was held on 2-3 July 2007 in Canberra and discussed areas of mutual interest such as coal and clean coal technology, trade and investment, and sustainable mining and opportunities for projects under the Australia-India Strategic Research Fund. The fifth meeting of the Australia-India Joint Working Group on Energy and Minerals was held on 2nd and 3rd July, 2007. A Protocol was signed at the end of the meeting. The Working Group discussed issues related to power, coal, mining Forum, Oil and Gas, Renewable Energy, mining and mineral processing, Asia- Pacific Partnership on Clean Development and Climate, etc.[15] The next meeting was held in 16-17 March 2009, in India. To strengthen the resources relationship and to provide a framework for long-term collaboration with industry, Australia proposed an Australia-India Resources Strategy (under the auspices of the JWG) comprising:

- *Coal Action Plan* which aims to promote the further development, transfer and deployment of low emissions coal technologies. Identified activities include: information exchange on low emission coal technology issues; participation in international forums on the proposed Global Carbon Capture and Storage (CCS) Initiative; and collaboration on existing projects under the Asia-Pacific Partnership on Clean Development and Climate (APP) Coal Mining Task Force.
- *Power Action Plan* aims to promote the further development, transfer and deployment of clean energy technologies, including CCS in the power sector and participation in international forums on the proposed Global Carbon Capture and Storage (CCS) Initiative. Identified activities include: continued collaboration on existing projects under the Asia-Pacific Partnership on Clean Development and Climate (APP) Power Generation and Transmission Task Force; and exploration of opportunities to promote scientific cooperation, possibly through the Australia-India Strategic Research Fund, on issues of mutual interest such as geothermal energy production.

- *Mining Action Plan* aims to promote the further development, transfer and deployment of clean technology in the mining and minerals sector. Identified activities include: collaboration on existing projects under the Asia-Pacific Partnership on Clean Development and Climate (APP) Aluminium Task Force; and exploration of opportunities to promote scientific cooperation, possibly through the Australia-India Strategic Research Fund, on issues of mutual interest.
- *Renewable and Clean Energy Action Plan* aims to promote the further development, transfer and deployment of renewable energy technologies in power production and the uptake of clean energy technologies. Identified activities include: promotion of information exchanges on renewable and clean energy issues; identification and pursuit of opportunities to facilitate two-way trade and investment flows in relation to renewable and clean energy technologies and environmental services; continued collaboration on existing projects under the Asia-Pacific Partnership on Clean Development and Climate (APP) Renewable Energy and Distributed Generation Task Force; and exploration of opportunities to promote scientific cooperation, possibly through the Australia-India Strategic Research Fund, on issues of mutual interest including solar technology.
- *Petroleum Action Plan* aims to promote the further development, transfer and deployment of clean energy technologies in the petroleum sector. Identified activities include continued collaboration on existing projects under the Asia-Pacific Partnership on Clean Development and Climate (APP) Cleaner Fossil Energy Task Force; and exploration of opportunities to promote scientific cooperation, possibly through the Australia-India Strategic Research Fund, on issues of mutual interest, including carbon capture and storage.[16]

Apart from these there is increasing stress on research and development also. The Australia-India Strategic Research Fund

(AISRF) is a component of the previous government's Australian Scholarships package, with funding of $20 million provided over five years commencing FY 2006/07. The AISRF aims to facilitate and support Science and Technology research cooperation between Australia and India. The fund assists Australian researchers to increase their participation in leading edge scientific research with Indian scientists, to raise the profile of Australian research, and to support the development of strategic alliances between Australian researchers and Indian researchers. It is administered by the Dept of Innovation, Industry, and Science & Research.[17]The trickle down effect for these research initiatives is sure to reach energy sector also.

Australia also initiated the Global Carbon Capture & Storage (CCS) Initiative which will provide a mechanism to coordinate and leverage national and regional CCS initiatives to deliver the goal of launching 20 large-scale CCS demonstration projects globally by 2010. The proposal includes the establishment of the Global Institute to coordinate the network of the existing national centres around the world. The Global Institute will accelerate the delivery of a diverse portfolio of fully-integrated, commercial-scale CCS projects by 2020. Australia is taking a leadership role in driving this Initiative and is preparing to fund the Global Institute (up to $100 million per annum), which will be headquartered in Australia. The Indian Government has been formally invited to join the Global Institute.[18] Australian energy minister Martin Ferguson AM had sought Indian investments into the island nation's energy sector and has offered India long-term supply of energy sources and clean technologies. Australia appointed a dedicated investment commissioner in Mumbai in 2010 to facilitate cross-border flow of investments. The energy minister showcased before Indian investors and businesses its latest blocks on offer for oil and natural gas exploration later this year.[19] So in terms of possibilities, there is no dearth of securing the energy supply as well as search for possible areas of cooperation. This includes coal bed methane, LNG, gasification of coal, rural electrification programmes, transmission efficiency in electricity, solar energy, renewable power generation, green technologies and joint research in promoting energy efficiency. The partnership has not only been limited to the energy sector only but it has percolated down to climate conservation and clean energy also.

Asia-Pacific Partnership on Clean Development and Climate (APP)

As part of the APP, Australia cooperates closely with India on collaborative efforts between industry, government and researchers in the development, deployment and transfer of cleaner, more efficient technologies. The Australian Government has announced $100 million to support the initiative and has provided in-principle funding for over 60 projects, 27 of which involve India, either bi-laterally or multi-laterally. Total Australian investment involving India is well over $43 million. Whilst the Indian Government has not made any similar formal funding package announcements on the APP initiative, India provides in-kind support and/or financial contributions on a project by project basis, such as access to sites/ infrastructure – e.g. Power plants upon which to test technology and provision of land. Coal India was a joint host with RET of an Asia Pacific Partnership Workshop on Mine Rehabilitation, Closure and Completion held in Kolkata in April 2008.[20]

The then Australian Prime Minister Kevin Rudd (now Foreign Minister), during his visit to India in November 2009, undertook the initiative to increase partnership with India in science and research. He pledged more than $70 million in areas like straddling energy, agriculture and environment. Energy cooperation has also been highlighted in the Joint Statement by the Prime Ministers of the two countries. The solar cooling research project, a joint research project between Commonwealth Scientific and Industrial Research Organization (CSIRO) and TERI, has been earmarked for developing a zero emission solar cooling system. It would be aimed at remote rural communities in un-electrified areas. The two countries can also enter trilateral partnership agreement with Indonesia for exploration in and around the islands of Java and Sumatra. So it is important that the two countries should work on joint research, joint exploration and sustainable energy supplies. This should include entering into long term supply contracts for building confidence as well as prolonged interdependence.

Energy security and climate change are serious challenges facing the international community. The Prime Ministers reiterated that Australia and India believe that a comprehensive outcome at the Copenhagen Conference, in accordance with the principles and provisions of the UNFCCC and the Bali Action Plan, is critical to meeting the challenge of climate change. Rudd noted India's plans to meet its future energy requirements by exploring and developing all sources of energy, including nuclear, renewable and non-conventional resources.[21] Both sides recognized the benefits of enhancing bilateral commercial exchanges of renewable and non-renewable energy resources. The two Prime Ministers agreed that energy security concerns are best met by reconciling the long-term interests of both energy producing and energy consuming countries through a truly open and competitive energy market. Both sides also expressed their willingness to join efforts which promote a cooperative response to any global energy crisis, noting the important role of open and transparent energy trade and investment markets. The Prime Ministers agreed that meaningful progress in the areas of energy security and climate change should be made through national, bilateral and multilateral efforts in a manner that does not limit the possibilities of accelerated economic and social development. The leaders agreed to work to address these global challenges.[22] So, there is a steady evolving confluence of ideas between the two countries and the leaders are trying to streamline the efforts both in renewable and non-renewable sectors. These initiatives have been boosted because of the efforts of the private sector in terms of investment in each other countries and looking for feasibility in investment in mining and other energy sectors.

Cooperation in Non-Renewable Energy

In July 2005, Tata Steel announced agreements to buy a 5% interest in the Carborough Downs Coal Project located in

Queensland. Majority owned and operated by a subsidiary of AMCI Holdings Australia, the Carborough Downs coal project is estimated to have a life of 14 years and approximately 58 million tonnes of raw coal is expected to be mined during this period. The clean coal envisaged to be produced will be low-ash coking coal and PCI coal, highly suitable for steel making. Tata Steel also signed an offtake agreement for a proportion of the production over life of the project.[23]

India and Australia have stepped up their cooperation in the resources and energy sector, by signing five action plans to deliver concrete outcomes. Strong commercial links continue to drive the energy relationship. India's first long-term LNG supply contract was signed in August 2009.[24] India's Petronet LNG has entered a US $ 20 billion agreement with Exxon-Mobil for Gorgon project in Western Australia. Also Indian companies like ONGC have signed an MoU with Australia's Arrow Energy for cooperation in Coal bed Methane (CM) sector. The cooperation would be in joint participation in blocks in India and abroad, research in the area of production of Coal bed methane (CM) as well as transfer of technology in CM Sector.[25] Not only bilateral cooperation but there is possibility of cooperation in Timor Sea and Timor Leste.

During the year 2009, Reliance farmed out 25% participating interest in Block K in East Timor [26] to Oil India Limited and Indian Oil Corporation Limited.[27]

Reliance now has 14 blocks in its international E&P portfolio including 3 in Peru, 3 in Yemen (1 producing and 2 exploratory), 2 each in Oman, Kurdistan and Colombia, 1 each in East Timor and Australia, with total acreage of 99,000 sq km.[28] On May 22, 2006, just a few days before the security situation in the tiny country deteriorated rapidly, East Timor had named the successful bidders for six offshore exploration areas within its part of the Timor Sea. Five of the areas went to Italy's Eni, and the sixth went to India's Reliance Industries.[29] The Joint Venture participating interests in JPDA 06-103 offshore in Timor Sea are: Oilex (JPDA 06-103) Ltd (Operator) 10%; Videocon JPDA 06-103 Limited 25%(1); GSPC (JPDA) Ltd 25%(1); Bharat

PetroResources JPDA Limited 25%(1); Japan Energy E&P JPDA Pty Ltd 15%.[30] Apart from that there are possibilities in the sector of wind energy, low cost electricity generation, solar power and Liquefied Natural Gas. The two countries, for which the supply of uranium has been the bone of contention, should look for other areas which can amplify the cooperation between the two countries. This also includes looking for joint exploration in and around the Asia-Pacific region more particularly in offshore exploration, in order to share escalating oil rig costs and sharing of best practices. Even though, Australia is very conservative with regard to oil and gas exploration rights in Timor Gap owing to treaty, there are possibilities with regard to exploration in the region especially when Reliance had bid for the exploration rights in the region in the past. Also, Tata has been looking for western coal fields for providing regular coal supply for its power projects in India. Though the energy cooperation between the two countries is still in its infancy, there is huge potential in terms of low emission power generation, low cost energy for rural households, solar energy, tidal energy and wind energy. In this context, it would not be prudent to talk only about nuclear energy but look for complementariness in the energy sector both in terms of renewable and non- renewable energy.

Cooperation in Renewable Energy

With regard to the renewable energy, Suzlon in one of its initiatives has invested in Australia. Suzlon will install 45 units of its S88 – 2.1 megawatt wind turbine for AGL at the Hallett Wind Farm to be located approximately 220 kilometers north of Adelaide, in South Australia. With the increasing demand and the advantage of being an end-to-end solution provider in its field of activity, Suzlon plans to increase its presence within India, and around the world. It already has a presence in over 40 locations around the world – including Australia, China, Europe, India, New Zealand, South Korea and the USA.[31] India's Tata Power has big plans to generate electricity from geothermal energy in India and abroad and is eying projects to produce 1,500 mega watts, or a big chunk of Indonesia's geothermal target of 9,500 mw, by 2025.[32] Origin Energy Ltd, the Australian electricity and gas retailer, and India's Tata Power Co. may bid to develop a geothermal power project in Indonesia; the Sydney-based company said.[33] India is already expanding its renewable energy sources involving wind and solar energy. The country has also significant hydropower potential, a lot of which has already been harnessed. With geothermal energy, India will further strengthen its clean energy portfolio, and open the road for further investments in this sector. Marine and tidal energy have not yet been mentioned in any detailed context, but this energy source is sure to find its way into the country's renewable energy mix in the future as well.[34]

These areas seek India- Australia cooperation. There are still few irritants in the energy cooperation between the two countries and the prominent one is the issue of Uranium supply to India for peaceful nuclear power generation purposes.

The Uranium Tangle

Australia's uranium export policy acknowledges the strategic significance which distinguishes uranium from other energy commodities. Australian policy has consistently recognised that special arrangements need to be put in place to distinguish between the civil and military applications of nuclear energy. Australia's uranium export policy embodies fundamental tenets first outlined in 1977, adjusted to reflect a number of international and domestic developments in the intervening period. It provides assurances that exported uranium and its derivatives cannot benefit the development of nuclear weapons or be used in other military programs. This is done by precisely accounting for amounts of Australian-Obligated Nuclear Material (AONM) as it moves through the nuclear fuel cycle. At the same time, the policy recognises the needs of customer countries and the nuclear industry for predictability about the way Australia exercises the non-proliferation conditions governing its uranium supply.[35]

In summary, Australia's policy is that:

- Australian uranium may only be exported for peaceful non-explosive purposes under Australia's network of bilateral safeguards Agreements, which provide for:

- coverage of uranium exports by IAEA safeguards from the time they leave Australian ownership,
- continuation of coverage by IAEA safeguards for the full life of the material or until it is legitimately removed from safeguards,
- fallback safeguards in the event that IAEA safeguards no longer apply for any reason,
- prior Australian consent for any transfer of AONM to a third party, for any enrichment beyond 20 per cent of uranium-235 and for reprocessing of AONM, and
- physical security requirements;
- Australia retains the right to be selective as to the countries with which it is prepared to conclude safeguards arrangements;
- non-nuclear weapon state customer countries must at a minimum be a party to the NPT and have concluded a full scope safeguards Agreement with the IAEA;
- nuclear weapon state customer countries must provide an assurance that AONM will not be diverted to non-peaceful or explosive uses and accept coverage of AONM by IAEA safeguards; and
- Commercial contracts for the export of Australian uranium should include a clause noting that the contract is subject to the relevant bilateral safeguards arrangement.
- The Australian Government announced in 2005 a further tightening of Australia's export policy by making an additional protocol with the IAEA (providing for strengthened safeguards) a pre-condition for the supply of Australian obligated uranium to non-nuclear weapon states.[36]

But there is a change in the policy with the coming of the Kevin Rudd led Labour government. The main components of the Labour Party policy are:

- overturning its 25-year ban on new uranium mines
- leaving the decision to develop new uranium mines to the state governments
- pursuing more effective international export control regimes and tighter controls on nuclear technology transfer, and
- opposing all uranium-related activities other than uranium mining and exportation.[37]

Even though Bob Hawke government had given signals for the supply of uranium to India, Kevin Rudd's labour government changed stance due to domestic compulsions and his party stance on uranium supplies. It is a strange policy option where it supplies uranium to China which is the biggest proliferator of nuclear weapons. Canberra argues that since Australia has taken the same stance with other countries like Pakistan, India must understand and respect its policy predicament. The ruling Labor Party maintains a ban on uranium sales to countries that have not signed the Nuclear Non-Proliferation Treaty, despite U.S. President Barack Obama supporting Indian membership of the 45-nation Nuclear Supplier Group.[38] The Indian Foreign Minister S.M. Krishna during his visit to Australia in January 2011 had asked the Australian government to review its uranium export policy as it is expected to come for review in later part of the year 2011[39] during Labour Party meeting in Australia. This shows how vital Australia's uranium is for India's nuclear energy. But, the uranium issue should not dominate the energy ties because India already has secured supplies from Kazakhstan and Russia. The energy cooperation between the two countries is also facing few emerging challenges which include climate change and the rising prices of energy in global market.

Future Perspectives

During Minister for Resources and Energy Ferguson's 2008

visit to India, five Strategic Action Plans were signed between the Department of Resources, Energy and Tourism and the respective Indian Ministries of: Coal; Mining; New and Renewable Energy; Petroleum and Natural Gas; and Power. The Action Plans seek to promote and enhance awareness of opportunities in two way trade and investment, increase bilateral cooperation and collaboration; and identify and address barriers to important trade and investment opportunities.[40]

At the sixth JWG meeting, Australia and India developed individual three-year work programs for each of the five Strategic Action Plans. The work programs identified a range of activities to be carried out between 2009 and 2011 including:

- capacity building (including secondments to renewable energy agencies)
- two-way technical exchanges on power generation, new and renewable energy, and geoscience data storage and mapping
- secondments of Indian officials to Australian policy agencies, safety and regulatory authorities, and technical and research organisations
- two-way education and training at educational institutions and within industry.[41]

Three technical and policy exchange workshops have already taken place which covered issues relating to mining and mineral exploration, geothermal, new and renewable energy, and power. Further, workshops are planned for later, which would cover two-way education and training and secondment of Indian officials to Australia. Both countries also committed to disseminate information on upcoming bilateral conferences related to power generation, and new and renewable energy technologies and policy development. The Department had compiled two calendars for power and new and renewable energy related events which were planned after 2009 and for future to ensure both countries are aware of relevant conferences being held in India, Australia and around the world. It is hoped that these events will provide further opportunities for ongoing collaboration between Australia and India on the mutually important issues related to power generation, and new and renewable energy, as well as continuing to strengthen the broader strategic partnership Australia and India benefit from.[42] India and Australia need to iron out their differences with regard to energy price banding and must enter into long term agreement. While China is trying to invest in the mining and energy sector in Australia, Indian companies must also take initiatives in this regard. Also the joint exploration and production projects should be taken up by the companies of the two countries on real time cost and profit sharing basis.

Conclusion

India- Australia energy cooperation preceded the thinking about the strategic partnership and formed a part of larger economic cooperation. Australia always has figured an important source for India's energy requirements and prior to any policy articulation companies have been scouting for energy resources in the sparsely populated country. Though, Australia has been keen on exporting its energy but the domestic compulsions as well as nuclear inhibitions have undermined the huge strategic potential of energy exports. India embarked on the Australian energy through various companies like Tata, Coal India Limited as well as Suzlon Power and had made great inroads into the energy supply market of Australia. The latest in the series, namely the long term agreement with Petronet, shows that this energy supply line is more secure than those of West Asia owing to the hyperactive piracy in the Gulf of Aden. But, for the energy cooperation to take a rather concrete shape, it is important for both the countries to highlight their constraints as well as areas of engagement. Few areas which could be fruitful in terms of cooperation would be R&D in gas hydrates in the Indian Ocean, Coal gasification projects, developing energy efficiency and also renewable energy. One area where both countries can work productively is the cutting of transmission losses because of the fact that electricity generation and transmission costs are quite high in India and also the end users i.e.. consumers have to pay a much higher price for electricity in

India. Also in the areas of wind energy and tapping of tidal and wave energy the countries can cooperate on an equal footing, though there is lack of policy articulation in India. There is also vast potential with regard to technology sharing and efficient technologies but for that the technical research institutions must come together. Also with regard to solar energy there are few areas where the two countries can share the best practices especially when India is seeking solar energy for electrification of rural households. Uranium supply, though a contentious issue, the two countries can look for understanding each other's position. Australia should also take into account that how other countries like Russia and Kazakhstan have formulated their Uranium supply agreements with India and how they are addressing the concerns with regard to nuclear proliferation. There is a serious need for greater understanding and long term agreement for energy supply, so that the two countries can configure their energy cooperation for the future.

NOTES

1. Oungho Chang, "The Economics of Energy Security," in Virendra Gupta and Chong Guan Kwa eds. *Energy Security: Asia-Pacific Perspectives,* Manas Publications, New Delhi, 2010, p.35.
2. Ligia Noronha, *India's Energy Situation in Energy Perspectives on Singapore and the Region,* Institute of Southeast Asian Studies, Singapore, 2007, p.141.
3. *Ibid,* p. 141.
4. Avinash Chandra, *An Overview of India's Hydrocarbon Policy,* World Energy Council Indian Member Committee, at http://www.indiaworldenergy.org/download/avinash.pdf (Accessed 24.4.2010)
5. *Ibid.*
6. *Ibid.*
7. *Energy in Australia 2009,* Department of Resources Energy and Tourism, at http://www. abare. gov.au (Accessed 22.4.2010).
8. "Australian Energy Engagement with China," at http://www.iea.org/papers/Roundtable_SLT/ Australia2_Mar09.pdf (Accessed 20.4.2010)

9. *Ibid.*
10. "Australian Energy Engagement with China," n.8.
11. "Bilateral Minerals and Energy Cooperation with India," at http://www.ret.gov.au/resources/enhancing/bmec/Pages/India.aspx (Accessed 24.4.2010)
12. *International Cooperation: Annual Report 2006-07,* Ministry of Mines, p.64 at http:// mines. nic. in/anrep06-07/english/chapter8.pdf(Accessed 14.4.2010)
13. *Australia-India Focus,* July - September 2005, Issue No.3 at http://www.dfat.gov.au/ aic/ newsletters australia india focus 2005 jul sep.pdf (Accessed 25.4.2010).
14. "ICVL eyes stake in coal mining companies abroad ," at http://www.hindu.com/2008/12/20/stories/2008122052621400.htm (Accessed 23.4.2010)
15. "Australian Energy Engagement with China," n.8. Also refer to http://www.ficci-b2b.com/site/ MINES.pdf(Accessed 23.4.2010)
16. "Australian Energy Engagement with India," n.8.
17. *Ibid.*
18. *Ibid.*
19. "Australia Seeking Investment in energy sector," at http://www.financialexpress.com/news/ australiaseeksinvestment sinenergysector/576161/(Accessed 24.4.2010)
20. "Australian Energy Engagement with India," n.8.
21. "Joint statement with the Prime Minister of India," Hyderabad House, New Delhi, November 12, 2009, at http://www.pm.gov.au/node/6323 (Accessed 25.4.2010).
22. *Ibid.*
23. *Australia-India Focus,* n.13.
24. "Joint Statement, India-Australia Foreign Ministers Framework Dialogue," 13 October, 2009, New Delhi.
25. "Projects Info," at http://www.constructionupdate.com/products/projectsinfo/2009/Feb-02-08/ 007.html (Accessed 04.5.2010).
26. For details about the commercial agreement in Timor Sea, see "Timor Sea Treaty," at http://www. mof. gov.tl/en/rc/DPR/CurrentLaws/en/TIMORSEATREATY.pdf (Accessed 10.5.2010).

27. *Quarterly Review, Sriram Insight,* at http://www.shriraminsight.com/ Market_reports/ Reliance. pdf?q=reliance-industries (Accessed 2.5.2010).

28. "Growth through Energy Security for India," at http://www.ril.com/ html/business/ exploration_ production.html(Accessed 10.5.2010).

29. Geoff Hiscock, "East Timor eager to tap resources," at http:// edition.cnn.com/2006/WORLD/ asiapcf/05/31/timor.australia.gas/ index.html (Accessed 24.4.2010).

30 "Australia: Oilex to sidetrack Timor Sea Lolotoe well after mechanical problems, at http:// www. energy-pedia.com/ article.aspx?articleid=138443 (Accessed 23 4.2010).

31. "Suzlon Enters Australian Market to Build Australia's Largest Wind Farm for AGL," at http://www. suzlon.com/images/ Media_Center_Press_release/ 81_AGL_Press_Release_ Rv_Final.pdf. Also see http://www.statemaster.com/encyclopedia/ Suzlon-Energy (Accessed 21.4.2010).

32. "Tata Power with Big Plans on Geothermal Energy," March 29, 2010 at http://thinkgeoenergy. com/ archives/4256(Accessed 26.4.2010).

33. Origin, "Tata may develop geothermal power project in Indonesia," at http://www.business-standard.com/india/news/origin-tata-may-develop-geothermal-power-project-in-indonesia/387710/ (Accessed 28.4.2010).

34. "India implementing geothermal energy R&D and demonstration program," at http://www. renewbl.com/2010/05/05/india-implementing-geothermal-energy-rd-and-demonstration-program.html (Accessed 29.4.2010)

35. "Nuclear Non-Proliferation, Trade and Security," at http:// www.dfat.gov.au/security/ aus_uran_ exp_policy. html (Accessed 26.4.2010).

36. "Submission on Uranium and Nuclear Power to Senate Committee on Fuel and Energy," August 2009 at http://www.aph.gov.au/Senate/ committee/fuelenergy_ctte/submissions/ sub0129.pdf (Accessed 28.4.2010).Also see Nuclear Non-Proliferation, Trade and Security at http://www.dfat.gov.au/security/aus_uran_exp_policy.html (Accessed 26.4.2010).

37. *New Development's in Australia's Uranium Policy,* at http:// www.mallesons. com/ publications/2007/May/8911400w.htm (Accessed 29.4.2010).

38. *"No sales of uranium to India, says Australia,"* January 20,2011, at http://nuclearnewsaustralia. wordpress.com/2011/01/ (Accessed 19.7.2011).

39. "Lift ban on uranium sale to India, Krishna urges Rudd," at http://www.thehindu.com/news/ national/article1104826.ece/ (Accessed 19.7.2011).

40. "Bilateral Minerals and Energy Cooperation with India," at http://www.ret.gov.au/resources/ enhancing/bmec/Pages/India.aspx (Accessed 27.4.2010).

41. *Ibid.*

42. *Ibid.*

4

To Be or Not to Be: Indo-Australian Nuclear Relations

S. Uttam Kumar Jamadagni

Introduction

The controversy surrounding the nuclear liability bill not only brings to fore citizen's rights and redressal processes[1] in India but also the significance of India's relations with nuclear supplier nations. Of special interest is the case of Australia, which is though in a position of great uranium wealth reluctant to supply it to India. But what is of note is that there has now been a change in leadership with Kevin Rudd making way for Australia's first woman Prime Minister Julia Gillard. As Deputy Prime Minister, she visited India in August-September 2009 to strengthen relations strained due to the reported series of racist attacks against Indian students.[2] It is to be seen whether the rigid stance of no-supply is reviewed to a more beneficial decision. Some of the policies which directly affect Indians like immigration (to now focus on 'skilled immigration') have been reinvented.[3] Thus both enthusiasm and skepticism cloud the expectation on the prospect of future India-Australia ties.

Relations between India and Australia have been quite interesting. Australia and India enjoy similar forms of democratic government, and many other commonalities like English as a link language, cricket as a tradition. As a rising power in Asia, India has come under renewed focus. As an energy dependent economy India must rely on other nations in the region and beyond for supply of fuel to produce energy. Among some of the issues that are bones of contention between India and Australia is the nuclear factor.

To understand the significance of the nuclear fuel supply in bilateral relations, a panoramic view of Indo-Australian relations in general is warranted. There have been many points of discontent in the relations between the two countries. The Cold War and the following years laid severe stress on the relations. Australia has been one of the fiercest critics of India's nuclear policy especially weaponisation. The first nuclear explosion was "unsettling" to the Australian officials.[4] This policy also has not been consistent for the "evangelical fervor" that was shown in denouncing India's nuclear explosion. The second Pokharan explosion was a new low in the relations. There was severe criticism of Indian and Pakistani experiments but the similar explosions of the British and the French even closer to Australian territory were accepted and clearly show double standards. In fact her reaction to India's Pokharan II explosion was among the harshest. Australia withdrew her High Commissioner Rob Laurie in protest and termed it "terrible".[5] The condemnation of Pokharan II explosions also included suspension of defence links by recalling the defence attaché and suspending foreign aid programs.[6] There was normalization of relations only two years after the tests.

The recent attacks on Indian students have been yet another talking point where the then visiting Australian Premier Kevin Rudd had to assure that such attacks would be dealt with "the full force of Australia's law enforcement and criminal justice systems."[7] A change in the government has also meant hardening of stance on some issues nuclear supply being one of them. The paper would aim to examine the import of nuclear issue in the past, present and future Indo-Australian relations.

The Seed of Power

The salience of the nuclear supply problem between these two countries must be examined in the backdrop of the status of nuclear energy and its associated processes in Australia's own political and economic map. Nuclear energy is principally produced from uranium and Australia is the second leading producer of uranium in the world.

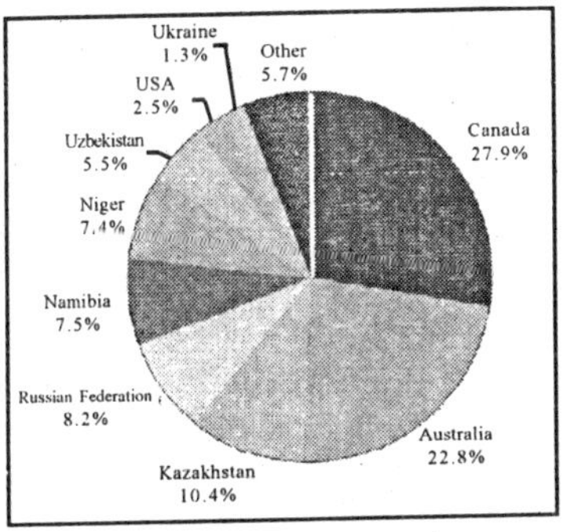

Figure 1 Uranium Producers of the World

Source: http://www.worldenergy.org/documents/fig_uranium_6_3.gif

The choice of nuclear energy as opposed to coal or other resource based generation of electrical power is because it is comparatively cleaner than the rest. When the world is concerned with drastic cuts in carbon emissions, nuclear energy seen as "greenhouse gases-free" is the most preferred method of power production.

India on the other hand, is an energy deficient country. A large population and thriving economy raise the demand for more energy. India's energy demands are estimated to grow dramatically with economic growth. Presently, power generation in India is predominantly coal-based but this is a primary carbon emitter. It is expected that the capacity of coal stations would treble in the next decade which would add 955 million tonnes of carbon emissions annually.[8] India is also looking at supply of Australian coal. Instead, if nuclear power plants are built then carbon emissions are estimated to be cut substantially. Currently, however, only 3% of India's energy needs are met by nuclear sources.[9] The gap between supply and demand is hoped to be bridged by increasing the capacity of nuclear power plants and other means. Following the uranium fuel cycle India also needs "yellowcake" supply to sustain its nuclear power stations. India has to import from other countries to meet this need. Australia being one of the leading uranium producers in the world has supplied these yellowcakes to China but the reluctance to sell the same to India a country with an 'impeccable'[10] track record by Australian standards is termed unreasonable.

Uranium Policy - Down Under

The problem with Australia supplying nuclear fuel crops from the policy stance adopted by Australia in relation with non NPT signatories. Australia's uranium export policy is based on the tenet that the nuclear goods exported cannot be used to develop weapons. The recipient countries must agree to full scope, full life safeguards and assurance of non divergence to non-peaceful purposes.[11] Australia is a unique country in that, though it has one of the largest uranium reserves in the world it neither has a single nuclear power plant nor a weapons program. There has been stiff opposition to suggestions of nuclear power usage for power generation. However, it has supported even the Manhattan Project by supplying uranium.[12]

The uranium mining is totally export oriented. There has been an export policy that supplies uranium to countries that have full scope safeguards under the South Pacific Nuclear Free Zone agreement of 1985 that states that nuclear goods would not be sold to countries that refuse to open all of their facilities to international inspections.[13] This has excluded India from the recipient list.

Turn a Blind Eye

In keeping with the Labour government's leaning towards China there has been discrimination in nuclear policy too. China as one of the fastest growing economies is energy deficient. China has 9 nuclear power plants and plans to build 30 more in the next 15 years. Australia has concluded an agreement with China in 2006 to not only provide uranium fuel but also allow Chinese companies to prospect for "new uranium deposits and open mines in Australian territory".[14] Australia would export 20,000 metric tones of uranium annually to China from 2010. This might be technically correct as China is an NPT signatory. But her assistance to Pakistan and Korea in developing their weapons program should not be forgotten. In contrast, India in spite of being a non-NPT state has neither transferred nuclear technology to a third country nor helped another state to acquire weapons. The behaviour of India as a responsible nuclear power state has been well appreciated as "impeccable".

Policy Progress

There has been difference in approach by the various parties in government. Menzies' liberal party sought to follow a policy to acquire tactical nuclear weapons in the least.[15] The Howard government though bitterly opposed supply of uranium to India finally watered the policy substantially to offer uranium sales to India. While officially it was reiterating the no sale policy, privately it had proceeded with negotiations on facilitating the export of uranium to India. This is seen as towing the American line of nuclear cooperation. The position changed in 2007 but the incumbent Labour government reversed the decision to sell uranium to India. Even the Labour Party which was against exporting nuclear goods to non NPT signatories did not prevent the passage of waiver in the NSG meet that allowed nuclear goods to be exported to India. It is puzzling why a country which could derive economic benefits from a decision that it has allowed others to do so while preventing itself from enjoying such gains. The reiteration of Labour party opposition to sale of uranium to India as a non-nuclear proliferation signatory was later pegged to the condition of the conclusion of the 123 Agreement between the US and India.

Australia with Japan then set up the International Commission on Nuclear Non-Proliferation Disarmament (ICNND) which in its final report recommended that countries outside the purview of current safeguards must be "given access to nuclear materials and technology"[16] upon exhibiting a strong commitment to disarmament and non proliferation. It has now been accepted that not supplying uranium to India "is a lost cause"[17] and hence Australia cannot be "consumed by NPT theology" but work through the difficult issues raised by the status of nuclear technology in today's world. However, the pressures from the uranium industry to continue exporting have also driven nuclear policy of Australia. The uranium mined in the three places of Beverly, Olympic dam and Ranger is exclusively meant for the export market.

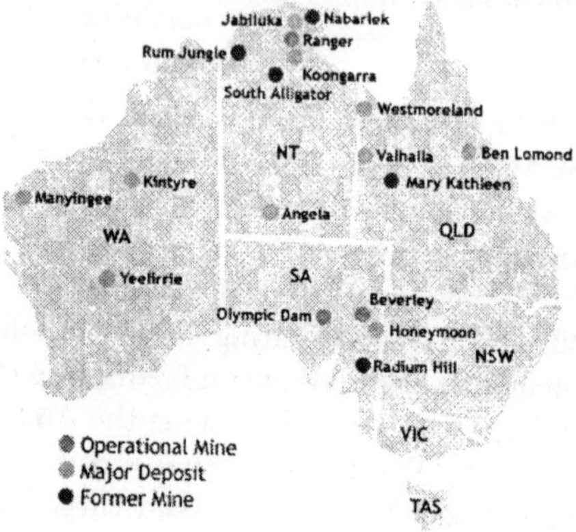

Figure 2 Map of Australia's uranium mines

Source: http://www.australianuranium.com.au/images/Bakers%20-%20Australian%20Uranium%20Projects.jpg

The 45 countries including USA, Australia, Japan, Russia, China, France and Germany which make up the NSG, denied India access to nuclear technology after the 1974 nuclear explosion. Nuclear Suppliers' group lifted a 34-year-old nuclear trade embargo on India in 2008 after the American President Bush indicated that there is a need to "adjust international regimes to enable full civil nuclear energy cooperation and trade with India".[18] The Indo US nuclear agreement has meant waiver of norms under the nuclear suppliers' group's rules. [19] Now there is growing support in Australia in favour of providing uranium to India. The arguments are based on 'climate change' logic, business sense and non-proliferation ideals too.

Eco-friendly Energy Source

The environment argument has taken the debate to another level. Nuclear energy is seen to be cleaner, greenhouse gases-free than the polluting fossil fuels like coal. Coal has contributed substantially to pollution and lack of electricity has led to several pollution-related deaths in India. The Asian Brown cloud phenomenon resulting due to pollution has been seen a catalyst in the global warming process. The Carbon emissions could then be drastically reduced especially by countries that are energy deficient and whose energy needs are growing substantially. If they adopt fossil fuel methods there is fear that the carbon emissions that are seen to primarily contribute to climate change would increase manifold. Hence, adoption of nuclear way of power generation is recommended. Countries like India and China would need nuclear fuel in substantial quantities that can be supplied by surplus countries like Australia. Professor Tim Flannery, an Australian climate change expert, even termed Australia's refusal to sell uranium to India as "immoral".

Uranium and Indigenous People

Uranium export could also help indigenous people of Australia. Most prospective uranium rich lands are located in reserved territory. If bans on mining are lifted and royalties paid for uranium mined in such areas, the native communities like the Martu people of Western Australia can improve their plight. The support for increasing uranium exploitation and export has been growing over the years within Australia.

Conclusion

The Australian nuclear export policy rested on the belief that

NPT signatories and non signatories who accept full scope safeguards are alone eligible for nuclear goods transfer. But the emergence of nuclear powers like India and Pakistan outside the ambit of NPT warrants a relook at the mere technicality of treaty signature. The stance of Australia has changed considerably from the ban on sale of uranium resources to India. Owing to the international pressure and the futility of adhering to inadequate international regimes, Australia is forced to alter its stand on the nuclear issue. The track record of non proliferation of India has to be considered instead of harping on a mere technicality. The American shift to conclude a civil nuclear agreement has stipulated international inspections and safeguards for civil installations. Many other countries like Russia, U.K., France and Canada have either inked civil nuclear agreements with India or are in the process of forging such relations.[20]

Australian export policy guidelines have been applied discriminatorily to aid countries like China who are known proliferators. The stance of no sale has been gradually watered down to now agreeing for a sale that has been temporarily put off for reasons of party politics. The former party in power, the Conservative party, falling in line with US diktats had decided to supply uranium fuel to India. The Labour government while overturning the Howard agreement to sell yellowcakes to India, left the door ajar by pointing to additional protocols that would be adhered to in the wake of the 123 agreement between India and USA. While officially there seems to be no change in the nuclear policy of Australia there is an expectation that the incumbent government with a change in leadership would be left with few options but to join the ranks of countries like America to begin transfer of nuclear fuel to India. This would be in the political, economic and environmental interests of not only India but Australia too. It is evident that the supply of nuclear fuel would remain a significant point in Indo-Australian relations in the long term, whether or not the issue is resolved in the near future.

NOTES

1. "A deeply flawed bill, Editorial, *The Hindu,* March 16, 2010.
2. http://www.topnews.in/people/julia-gillard
3. "Australia's new PM Julia Gillard suggests she would favour skilled immigration", *DNA India,* June 27, 2010 http://www.dnaindia.com/world/report_australia-s-new-pm-julia-gillard-suggests-she-would-favour-skilled-immigration_1401943
4. Jim Walsh, "Surprise Down Under: The Secret History of Australia's Nuclear Ambitions", *The Nonproliferation Review,* Fall 1997, p.13.
5. http://cns.miis.edu/archive/country_india/reaction.htm#australia
6. Book Review by Duane Bratt of Richard Broinowski, "Fact or Fission? The Truth About Australia's Nuclear Ambitions", *Journal of Military and Strategic Studies,* Summer 2004, Vol. 6, Issue 4 http://www. jmss.org/ jmss/index.php/jmss/article/view/212/229
7. Matthew Franklin, "Rudd soothes India's concerns over attacks on students", *The Australian,* November 13, 2009 http://www.theaustralian.com.au/politics/rudd-soothes-indias-concerns-over-attacks-on-students/story-e6frgczf-1225797290372
8. Gavin Atkins, *"Why Australia should export uranium",* http://us.asiancorrespondent.com/ gavin-atkins-shadowlands/why-australia-should-export-uranium.htm
9. For a detailed report see http://pmindia.nic.in/India%E2%80%99s%20Nuclear%20Energy%20Programme%20and%20the123%20agreement.pdf
10. "Uranium politics, *Frontline,* Vol. 23, Issue 8, April 22 – May 5, 2006, http://www. hinduonnet. com /fline/ fl2308/ stories/20060505001006100.htm
11. http://www.dfat.gov.au/security/aus_uran_exp_policy.html
12. Jeffrey S. Lantis, "Elections and Enduring Realities: Australia's Nuclear Debate", *Arms Control Today,* April 2008, http://www.armscontrol.org/act/2008_04/Lantis
13. *Far Eastern Economic Review,* http://www.feer.com/review-federation/2008/february/ Challenges-Lie-Ahead-for-Rudd
14. Purnendra Jain, "Australia's discriminatory uranium policy", *Asia Times Online,* April 1, 2006.
15. Walsh, p.5.

16. "Uranium exports to India on cards", *Indian Express,* December 16, 2009, at http://www. indianexpress.com/news/ australia-may-lift-its-ban-on-uranium-sale-to-india/554806/

17. *Ibid.*

18. "Radical shift a risk until world agrees on new nuclear rules", *The Age,* August 15, 2007, at http://www. theage.com. au/news/editorial/radical-shift-a-risk-until-world-agrees-on-new-nuclear-rules/2007/08/ 14/1186857509735. html#

19. "India crosses a nuclear hurdle with NSG waiver", *Business Line,* September 7, 2008, http://www. thehindubusinessline.com/2008/09/07/stories/2008090751320100.htm

20. See, "India, France ink nuclear deal, first after NSG waiver", *Indian Express,* October 1, 2008, at http://www.indianexpress.com/news/india-france-ink-nuclear-deal-first-after-nsg-waiver/368048/; 'India-Russia civil nuclear agreement practically sealed', *The Hindu,* December 7, 2009, at http://www. thehindu.com/ 2009/ 12/07/stories/2009120757180100. htm; UK, India sign civil nuclear accord, *Energy Business Review,* February 15, 2010 http://nuclear.energy-business-review.com/news/uk_india_sign_civil_nuclear_deal_100215/and "India, Canada sign civil nuclear deal", *The Times of India,* June 28, 2010, at http://timesofindia.indiatimes.com/india/India-Canada-sign-civil-nuclear-deal/articleshow/6100127.cms

5

India-Australia Defence Cooperation

Vijay Sakhuja

India and Australia are two important players in the Asia Pacific Region and share many of their strategic interests. Further, there is a broad convergence of their security concerns that pivot on *maintaining a rules-based global security order,* fostering multilateralism, diplomacy through the United Nations, upholding institutions that enhance international security, and an enduring stability in the wider Asia-Pacific region. Both partners also see several benefits in cooperative measures that support international efforts to counter terrorism, fight piracy, stop drug smuggling/ gun running/human smuggling, counter proliferation of weapons of mass destruction, and addressing emerging common challenges like climate change and pandemics. Being maritime nations their interests stretch from the Indian to the Pacific Oceans that have emerged in geo-economic and geo-strategic significance. Also, their geo-strategic location in the Indian Ocean confers a unique opportunity of maintaining stewardship of the oceanic domain through cooperative and convergent strategies that would stabilize the global commons even as they contend with maritime security.

Defence Cooperation

India's engagement with Australia is premised on dialogue

and cooperative security. Being important maritime states, naval cooperation has been high on the agenda and has witnessed greater focus. Both countries support initiatives that challenge disorder at sea. Besides, the natural and human induced disasters evoke convergent concerns since they are linked with economic interdependence and trade.

Indian and Australian naval forces have developed good working relations that cover a wide spectrum of issues including (a) maritime cooperation and military exchanges; (b) high level and staff level talks; (c) training exchanges; (d) ship visits; (e) participation in multilateral naval initiatives such as the Indian Ocean Naval Symposium (IONS), MILAN, the Council for Security Cooperation in the Asia Pacific (CSCAP); (f) Memorandum of Understanding on Defence Co-operation signed in March 2006 and (g) bilateral maritime security operations working group established in 2007.

Australian White Paper on Defence

At this juncture it will be useful to examine very briefly the Australian White Paper on defence titled 'Defending Australia in the Asia Pacific Century: Force 2030' released in May 2009. The White Paper can provide a sound framework for enhancing India-Australia defence cooperation. The Paper notes:

> India is an important partner for Australia given our shared democratic values, our maritime interests, and our commitment to combating regional and global terrorism and maintaining a rules-based global security order. As India extends its reach and influence into areas of shared strategic interest, we will need to strengthen our defence relationship and our understanding of Indian strategic thinking. In the near term, we are looking for opportunities to expand high-level defence dialogue, building upon annual talks between the Chief of the Defence Force and his Indian counterpart. We should also increase education and training exchanges and practical cooperation in areas

> such as defence information sharing, counter-terrorism and peacekeeping.

Further, the White Paper observes:

> Australia and India will have a strong mutual interest in enhancing maritime security cooperation in the Indian Ocean, where we both have key strategic interests to manage. Maritime trade through the eastern Indian Ocean is particularly important for both countries, and we will explore opportunities to work together with India to ensure that those waters are kept secure and open over the decades ahead. The Government has specifically directed Defence to examine opportunities for increased bilateral maritime cooperation.

This is a welcome development; however, the above must be tampered with the following perspective on India. The White Paper notes that India, "will also seek defence capabilities commensurate with its strategic weight and widening interests, including through the modernisation of its armed forces and the maintenance of a credible nuclear arsenal." Australia is concerned about India's military modernization and nuclear capabilities. Such expressions are not new to India. India's expanding economy provides it the critical ballast for enhanced external engagement and a stronger voice and stake in international affairs.

India must contend with the extra regional military (particularly naval) presence in the Indian Ocean deployed in support of 1991 Operation Desert Shield/Desert Storm in Iraq, Operation Enduring Freedom (OEF) in 2001 in the Persian Gulf-Arabian Sea and Operation Iraqi Freedom (OIF) in 2003.

On an average 16-18 warships are deployed in the Gulf of Aden for anti-piracy operations. In January 2009, a multinational task force CTF 151 was established whose mandate is counter-piracy in the Gulf of Aden, Arabian Sea, and Red Sea. The NATO naval flotilla began operations in October 2008 and the EU task force was deployed in December 2008 to provide security to vessels carrying humanitarian assistance to Somali under the UN World Food Programme. Russia has deployed its warships since October 2008. Warships from Australia, China, Japan, Malaysia, Singapore, and South Korea have also deployed their ships in the Gulf of Aden.

China Factor in India-Australia Relations

In September 2007, the navies of Australia, India, Japan, Singapore and the US had engaged in one of the biggest naval manoeuvres in the Bay of Bengal. These initiatives did not appear to have gone well with Beijing. In May 2007, Beijing issued a demarche' seeking an explanation from New Delhi, Washington, Tokyo and Canberra on the purpose of holding a meeting on May 24-25 in Manila, Philippines. Sun Shihai, Deputy Director of the Institute of Asia-Pacific Studies under the Chinese Academy of Social Sciences (CASs) has noted, "The so-called democratic alliance is not good for Asia... Any attempts to take China as a rival or contain China will not work".

Although India and Australia had in the past engaged in bilateral exercises, war games of such a magnitude were the first.[1] Australian Defence Minister Brendan Nelson had stated that "... Australia's position is that we are prepared to have quadrilateral discussions on trade, economic, cultural and other issues. We do not wish to have formal quadrilateral strategic dialogue in defence and security matters...We do not want to do anything which is not necessary and which may otherwise cause concern in some countries, particularly in China." [2]

The Australian White Paper on defence makes note of the ongoing Chinese military modernization, its evolving power projection capabilities, and opaqueness in defence plans. The Chinese commentators have reacted sharply to Australia's 'China threat' thesis. Likewise, the paper, though not as explicit as on China, is concerned about India's military modernization and nuclear capabilities. A recent study by Australian Strategic Policy Institute (ASPI), an Australian think tank has noted that:

> The government [Australia] acknowledges the need to rebuild the relationship, but that won't be easy. India's policies can be distorted by domestic social developments and politics and by threat perceptions, as well as by its land border disputes with China. Inevitably, there'll be policy differences—and some of them, such as on nuclear issues, will be substantial.[3]

At the 2009 Shangri-la Dialogue, Australia's Prime Minister Kevin Rudd said that "Australia by definition is a maritime power, with maritime interest, and we are therefore deeply focused on the importance of the Indian and Pacific Oceans in our own long-term security" and security cooperation with India was a priority matter.[4] The ASPI paper however, notes "*The relationship with India must be one of equal partners. This might be hard: India seems reluctant to treat Australia on an equal basis. This will create problems should India extend its reach and influence into areas of common strategic interest.*"[5]

Be that as it may, the prospects of the India-Australia defence cooperation could still be based on cooperation and convergence on issues of mutual interest and the imperatives to explore measures for security and safety specifically in the context of maritime based threats and challenges. The Indian and Pacific Oceans provides the theatres of operations for India and Australia, given that this sea space is witness to the growing density of shipping between the two regions.

Australia would like to join the Indo-US Malabar exercises and as a gesture of reciprocity has invited India to join the ADF multilateral exercises Kakadu and Pitch Black. According to Foreign Minister Stephen Smith "I said it would be a good thing if we joined that [Malabar naval exercises], just as we host a couple of multilateral exercises in Australia - Kakadu and Pitch Black. He [Indian Foreign Minister] said he would get back to us on that,"[6] India supports multilateralism so long as it is within the framework of the UN and is also bound by internationally accepted legal framework. This issue is discussed in greater details later in the paper.

The Benign and Humanitarian Roles

The mission and roles of the Indian Navy in Humanitarian Assistance and Disaster Relief (HADR) operations are premised on cooperative security. India's offer of assistance during the 2004 Indian Ocean Tsunami has been a signature policy. Indian Navy deployed thirty two naval ships, seven aircraft and twenty helicopters in support of five rescue and relief missions. Although this speaks volumes of the efficiency and the operational readiness of the Indian Navy, what is noteworthy is that the Indian Navy was deployed in Sri Lanka, Indonesia and Maldives, while its own shores had been battered by the massive Tsunami waves. Likewise the Australian Defence Force (ADF) personnel and equipment, medical and health support assets, engineers with their water purification systems were mobilized as part of the Tsunami disaster relief operations.

HADR contingencies would be more frequently in occurrence in the future and the offer of assistance as demonstrated during the 2004 Indian Ocean Tsunami would emerge as the new template of multinational maritime operations in the humanitarian spectrum. There is a critical need for India and Australia to devise a comprehensive strategic and tactical response in humanitarian missions of the two armed forces and more specifically the navies who have enormous platform and capabilities to cope with and respond to adverse impacts of climate change.

In the context of HADR, maritime forces of India and Australia would have to adapt to new strategies that are focused on capacity building and response mechanisms. Reconfiguration of force structure would imply the need for expeditionary platforms whose focus would be on humanitarian missions.

Climate Change

The Indian Ocean basin is quite replete with the symptomatic effects of climate change. As a result of this change, the shoreline of some countries has had adverse impact resulting in erosion of coastal areas. Further, there are fears that sea water level rise would lead to small islands being submerged resulting in major human displacement.

At another level, the issue of 'climate refugees' gains salience for India and Australia. People of Maldives may soon be climate refugees due to changes in the sea level that could inundate large parts of the archipelago. The President of Maldives has observed "we can do nothing to stop climate change on our own and so we have to buy land elsewhere. It's an insurance policy for the worst possible outcome. After all, the Israelis [began by buying] land in Palestine... We do not want to leave the Maldives, but we also do not want to be climate refugees living in tents for decades," Maldives is now looking towards India and Sri Lanka to offer them space on their territory since Maldives enjoys common culture, cuisines and climates.[7] Maldives is also looking towards Australia since it is a large country and can offer space to Maldives. The Maldives government is considering a 'sovereign wealth fund' from its burgeoning tourist industry.

Climate Change and Navies

While the navies engage in operational missions related to climate change, the necessity for some introspection and housekeeping is critical. As noted earlier, the shipping industry is a significant contributor of green house gases (GHG). Naval vessels, though very small in number when compared to global shipping fleet need to address the problem of climate change through proactive measures. The shipbuilding industries have begun to take measures to reduce emissions and address possible technological requirements associated with global climate change. The issues relate to identification of GHG emitting substance inventory on board ships, Ozone Depletion Substances (ODS) used on board ship's refrigeration and firefighting systems and their phase out plans and also identifying Halon alternatives, and fuel-efficient machinery for propulsion.

Australian Marine Defence Mission

Australian defence industry is exploring opportunities for joint venture partnerships with Indian defence industry in the maritime, aerospace and military domain particularly in communications sector, command and control systems, multi-sensor data fusion; signal processing, phased array radar, navigation and positioning aids, logistics support systems and self-monitoring propulsion systems, UAVs and Sonars. Australia has a proven capacity in the construction, integration, modification and support of naval vessels and their sub-systems. According to Peter Linford, Senior Trade Commissioner, South Asia, "Australia has capability spread across the entire maritime security spectrum with expertise in submarine systems development, integration and high-pressure hull fabrication, ship construction, modular fabrication, systems integration, platform integration, sub-system design and maintenance services, patrol boat design and construction and high speed naval vessel design and construction."[8]

Regional Submarine Rescue Organisation

In 2007, industry specialists noted that over the next ten years, Asian navies were projected to acquire 83 submarines at a cost of US$55 billion i.e. a little more than half of the total spending and this would result in doubling the regional submarine force. Similar tends continue in 2009, and according to Jane's Defence Systems Forecast, over the next ten years, 80 to 100 submarines could be added to the Asian naval inventory. The above estimates for submarine acquisition are indeed very promising clearly indicating that there is a 'submarine frenzy' in the region.

Australia plans to buy twelve submarines, India's inventory includes sixteen vessels and six more will be inducted, Malaysia has acquired two, Indonesia and Singapore operate two and four boats respectively and Vietnam has placed orders for two vessels from Russia. It is quite natural that these will be deployed to monitor each other's activities through shadowing or snooping and can come dangerously close to each other. It will be useful to start discussing the merits of establishing regional mechanisms that promote safety and security of submarines. It is therefore important to designate submarine training areas to prevent accidents and establishing 'Hot Lines' for submarine operations.

Impediments of Defence Cooperation

Limits of Maritime Multilateralism

It has been acknowledged that a secure maritime environment can never be achieved by the efforts of a single country; it requires mutual understanding and cooperation of all the countries in the region. For that, it is necessary to share the common values on the benefits of maritime multilateralism to be enjoyed by the whole maritime community. India's security perspectives are based on the benign, constabulary and humanitarian premises of cooperation. Further, India would like to cooperate with other nations under the United Nations conventions thus developing a worldwide network to uphold global order. While India-US maritime cooperation is on an upward trajectory, the Indian government has not been supportive of some of the US maritime initiatives such as the PSI and the '1000 Ship Navy' initiative and in that context India has ruled out joining the above initiatives and would prefer a UN approach to address these issues. Further, it will be important to note that India would be more driven by its penchant for strategic autonomy that it has gained with its economic growth and the new robustness of its capabilities.

Military Cooperation with Pakistan

A possible India- Pakistan conflict appears to worry Australia. The White Paper observes that "the miscalculation between India and Pakistan leading to conflict" remains a major concern. India is aware of Pakistan-Australia defence cooperation that involves strengthening Pakistan's security and stability by doubling military training to the Pakistan Army and expanding strategic dialogue. Also, Pakistan is providing logistics support and transit facilities to carry out its role in Afghanistan.

So long as the military cooperation between Australia and Pakistan is limited to training, bilateral exercises, port calls, etc and keeping in mind that India and Australia have 'common interests and shared objectives' in promoting peace and stability in the region, India would not be very much concerned. However, in case their cooperation involves sale of military hardware, it could impact on bilateral relations. This is particularly important keeping in mind that in 1988 Australia transferred 50 Mirage aircraft to Pakistan in return for a mere $A36million. This transfer had provoked an outcry in India, since these were to be deployed against India. However, India acknowledges Australian humanitarian and medical support to the victims in the earthquake in Pakistan. Also India is supportive of Australian participation in Pakistan sponsored Aman 2009 exercises.

Lack of Trust

Despite these convergences and upsurge in bilateral maritime cooperation, India-Australia defence relations have had their share of bitterness. In the aftermath of the 1998 Indian nuclear tests, in a rather harsh and brash move, Australia suspended defence cooperation with India and the government unceremoniously ordered Indian Defence Attaché and other Indian military personnel undergoing training to leave Australia at very short notice. New Delhi was disappointed by this move and the general perception was that Australia was acting in concert with the US. Interestingly, the US was quick to mend fences with India, but it took sometime for Australia; but defence relations were re-established and witnessed significant improvement since 2000.

India's sensitivities also emerge from incidents at sea that appear to make the Indian Navy quite wary of the Australian intentions. In 1997, Australian Orion aircraft presumably based at Butterworth, Malaysia, buzzed Indian naval ship INS Delhi in the Bay of Bengal. This was not an isolated incident, but there have been instances when Australian patrol aircraft had dropped sonobuoys (an underwater listening device) against Indian naval vessels operating in Southeast Asia waters. In the past, Australia had deployed its *Oberon-class submarines off India to conduct 'perilous intelligence-gathering operations' to monitor naval activity,* [9] *which is of concern to India.*

Concluding Remarks

In summation, the twenty-first century has well begun with the rediscovery of the global maritime based economic interdependence in which India and Australia are important partners. Both should think of their defence related interactions more like commercial transactions, where both gain better security as a result of their engagements. There is immense potential and capacity to harness the existing engagements and explore newer vistas for bilateral cooperation. Such an engagement has the potential to enhance the stability and growth of the Asia-Pacific region as also other regional and trans-regional frameworks.

India-Australia engagement is determined by the norm of synergy of relations based on convergence of interest. Further, the defence cooperation is shaped by common geo-strategic perspectives and security challenges, emergent geo-economic trends and synergy in contending asymmetric and transnational threats. In this age of globalization and asymmetric conflicts, the preference of cooperative and convergent approaches to global and regional security is critical for both partners since the objectives of their economic development and security are intertwined.

Further, the Indian Navy is in a position to share its operational efficiency gained through diverse sources of collaboration and cooperation pivoting on naval exercises, acquisitions from diverse sources and integration with domestic systems, and joint development of naval hardware that have witnessed phenomenal successes. Further, the Indian navy has gained qualitatively in operational competence through its partnerships with several maritime forces and would immensely gain from its interactions and engagements with the Royal Australian Navy.

NOTES

1. Sandeep Dikshit, " Biggest joint naval exercise in Bay of Bengal in September", *The Hindu*, July 13, 2007.
2. "No quadrilateral security alliance including India: Australia", available at http://news.outlookindia.com/item.aspx?487705 accessed on March 15, 2010.
3. Sam Bateman and Anthony Bergin "Our western front: Australia and the Indian Ocean", *Australian Strategic Policy Institute Paper*, 2010, p.34-35.

4. Keynote Address by Kevin Rudd, Prime Minister, Australia at the 8th IISS Asian Security Summit, *The Shangri-La Dialogue,* Singapore, May 29, 2009.
5. Sam Bateman and Anthony Berginn n. 3, pp.34-35.
6. Amanda Hodge, "Stephen Smith aims for India war game", *The Australian,* October 15, 2009
7. "Paradise Almost Lost: Maldives Seek to Buy a New Homeland", *The Guardian,* November 10, 2009.
8. Huma Siddiqui, "Australia explores marine defence prospects in India", *The Financial Express,* May 09, 2009
9. Geoffrey Barker, "The Mystery Boats", *Australian Financial Review,* November 23, 2003.

6

India-Australian Partnership in the Asia-Pacific Region

A. Subramanyam Raju

India and Australia are democracies with shared colonial heritage, members of the Commonwealth of Nations and littoral countries in the Indian Ocean. Both of them are members of ASEAN Regional Forum and the East Asia Summit. They have agricultural economies with a developing industrial base. Their shared concerns relate to trade, financial and human links between the two countries, disarmament, globalization, environment, state sponsored terrorism, weapons of mass destruction. Australia supports India's membership of the UNSC and the latter welcomes the former as an observer in the SAARC.

There were misperceptions and differences between the two countries during the Cold War period. While Australia misunderstood India's nonalignment policy and treated India as ally of the former USSR, India could not understand Australia's preoccupation with its fear of communism and considered it as a client state of the US. India felt that Australia had "no opinion of (its) own on the great international issues or freedom to express it".[1] The former High Commissioner Peter Heydon told in Canberra that the main reason keeping both countries apart was the Indian view that "We have no real national personality of our own, we are copies of the UK domestically and of the US in foreign affairs".[2] Both the countries defended their national and security needs differently and took different paths during the cold war period. Australians never recognized the importance of the Asian region. They are a European people who look to Europe and are alien to Asia. One of the Australian newspapers noted: "Australians are a European people who look to Europe for our origins and our culture. Our religious faith, our national philosophy, and our whole way of life, are alien to Asia".[3] Indifferent personal relations between Robert G. Menzies and Jawaharlal Nehru also played a significant role in the development of unsound relations between the two countries.

However, after the end of the cold war, both the countries began understanding and realizing the importance of each other. Australia is looking for cordial relations with India which is a growing and promising economic giant and an emerging important player in the international politics maintaining close relations with the US. Besides, India has the largest navy and coastguard and it could be considered as an important element in Australia's maritime security. India is equally looking for cordial relations with Australia because latter's cooperation is required to increase its presence in the Asia-Pacific region; to protect the sea-lanes of the Indian Ocean region; its concern for growing China's presence in the region and to enhance its trade in the region. Both the countries have recognized the cooperation between them to tackle maritime threats i.e. terrorism, piracy, drugs trafficking and arms smuggling.

An attempt is made in this paper to focus on issues: maritime cooperation, nuclear issue and climate change. Further, the paper would focus on possible areas of convergence of interests and how they can play constructive roles to ensure peace and stability in the Asia-Pacific region.

Maritime Cooperation

India, in terms of geographical size, economy and geopolitical location, occupies a pivotal position in the Indian Ocean region. It has 7,500 kilometers of coastline and 48,000 sq. km. of exclusive economic zone in the Indian Ocean region. It had been given the status of pioneer nation in 1987 to explore and exploit the resources in the sea bed and allocated 150,000 sq.km of sea bed by the UN Sea bed authority for mining in the central Indian Ocean. Its trade through the Indian Ocean is increasing rapidly. Thus, it became necessary for India to strengthen its navy to defend its economic and strategic interests. Indian navy expounded a maritime doctrine in 2004 to enhance its capability. It is clearly evident that the Indian navy initiated several maritime security and capacity building measures such as countering piracy and played a constructive role in times of crises like tsunami not only in India but also in Maldives, Sri Lanka and Indonesia. However, the Indian navy and other security forces failed to prevent the terrorists' attacks in Mumbai (26/11/08 attacks). Since the non state actors' activities through sea are expected to increase, strengthening Indian security forces particularly navy is vital. The sea lanes of communications (SLOCs) are important for India's trade, because it largely depends on sea for its trade. It is expected that its oil imports would reach 82.2 per cent by 2010 and 91.6 per cent by 2020. Most of its oil imports originate in the Middle East and pass through the sea lanes via Pakistan. It is to be noted that there were several occasions when India was not supplied oil from the region due to political instability. Regarding India's need to develop its naval force in the Indian Ocean region, K.M.Panikkar stated: "...India's security lies in the Indian Ocean, that without a well considered and effective naval policy, India's position in the world will be weak, dependent on others and her freedom at the mercy of any country capable of controlling the Indian Ocean. India's future, therefore, is closely bound up with the strength she is able to develop gradually as a naval power".[4]

During the Cold War period, Australia was greatly concerned about Indian naval expansion, perhaps next to Pakistan. It questioned the motives behind the Indian naval expansion.[5] Australian concern revolved not around any fear that India's growing power projection capability might threaten 'Australian security interest or trade routes', but rather the possibility that might provoke naval build ups by its neighbours.[6] Australia did not oppose the US presence in the Indian Ocean region as it considered the US presence was necessary to protect shipping lanes, as oil from Middle East passed through the region. Australia abstained from voting on the proposal to make IOZP in 1971 at the UN, because it was neither practical nor realistic approach.[7] It supported the presence of the US naval forces in the region. There was a strong security link between Australia and the US through ANZUS (Australia, New Zealand and the US) treaty. However, after the cold war, India and the US realized the importance of cooperation between them in the region. India and the US navies are closely engaged in building maritime synergies through various means: goodwill visits, joint naval exercises, exchange of personnel, information, technology, etc. and such relationship gained greater thrust after the US campaign against Al Qaeda. Emerging India-US strategic security operations reflect on India-Australian relations too. For instance INS Godavari (60 ships) participated along with other visiting navies at the Sydney International Naval Review in 1998 and the Royal Australian Navy (RAN) participated in the International Fleet Review hosted by India at Mumbai in February 2000. Similarly Australia also perceived the importance of India's role in the region.

India is an important maritime player in the region. Of the 90 per cent of India's trade carried out through sea, over 40 per cent of its trade is through Malacca Straits. Ninety five per cent of its trade by volume and seventy per cent by value moves by sea. India has positioned itself as a major supplier of efficient and cost effective manpower to the shipping world with a market share of around seven per cent. It would be difficult for any country to tackle the maritime security threats without any collective cooperation with other countries. Hence India and Australia realized that both need to work towards tackling threats emerging from the sea.

Nuclear Issue

India detonated its first nuclear device in 1974. The peaceful explosion was part of India's research and development programme. Rejecting the arguments of the Westerners regarding the 1974 explosion, Indira Gandhi stated in an interview to the Danish Television on 28 June 1974: "The thinking of the world has been conditioned by the fact that most nuclear countries have thought of nuclear energy only in terms of military uses. Therefore, they find it very strange that there is a country which has the capacity and which wants to use it merely for peaceful and development purposes".[8] After twenty four years it again carried out a series of tests in May 1998. The difference between 1974 and 1998 tests was that the Indian government in 1974 maintained that the test was a peaceful explosion, and in 1998, there was no reference of peaceful tests. After the 1998 tests, India claimed a nuclear weapon state status. India, though not a party to the NPT, did not violate the rules. India's nuclear policy is guided by the disarmament approach to security. It has a strong desire to acquire nuclear capability, as this would compel the world to give it respect and prestige. It believes that real security is possible only through global disarmament and not by disarming the non-nuclear states. India rejected the NPT and CTBT[9] on the ground that they are discriminatory. These treaties failed to provide equal treatment between the NWS and NNWS. India considers all states to be equal. It does not believe in dividing the states into 'nuclear haves' and 'nuclear have-nots'.

Despite recognizing importance of India, the nuclear tests became a setback temporarily to the emerging India-Australian relations. Australia suspended bilateral defence relations with India, withdrew its Defence Adviser from its High Commission in New Delhi, suspended non-humanitarian aid and postponed indefinitely all ministerial and senior official visits. It maintained that its reaction to the tests was based on its stand against the proliferation of nuclear weapons. The then Prime Minister John Howard referred to the tests as "an ill-judged step".[10] Australia did go out of its way to alienate India, a country where its economic stakes are very high and with which it has been trying to improve relations.

Australian reaction to the tests might have been different had there been in Australia a long term and deeper knowledge of the history of nuclear technology developments in South Asia. It should have enhanced its engagement with India than imposing sanctions. It was strange that Australia was criticizing India on nuclear non-proliferation, when Canberra had allowed Britain to undertake atmosphere nuclear tests spreading radioactive debris. Canberra did not criticize France, as it did against India, when the former conducted tests in the Pacific in 1995-1996. It had been adopting anti-Indian posture at various world fora. However, later Australia supported India at the International Atomic Energy Agency; Nuclear Suppliers Group-lifting a thirty four year old ban on nuclear trade with international community. The sale of uranium to India is a case in point. The Kevin Rudd Government, posing as a non-proliferation hawk, did not think before scrapping the landmark deal negotiated by the former conservative Prime Minister John Howard to sell uranium to India for its nuclear energy program. Australia was technically "right" on that. India is a non-signatory of the NPT and is not entitled to receive enriched uranium from other nations. Notwithstanding Australia's refusal to sell uranium to India, the two countries today vowed to push their ties to a "strategic partnership" and decided to enhance their cooperation in economic, defence, energy and various other fields.

The South Pacific nuclear free zone - not to engage in nuclear trade with any state that does not allow full scope, which is comprehensive international safeguards over all of their nuclear facilities. Australia would be violating itself, its South Pacific nuclear free zone treaty commitments, by selling uranium to India. However, Australia must realize that India was a responsible state with advanced nuclear technology. India is a nuclear weapon power in its own right and needs to be treated as one.

Nuclear generation is attracting countries to increase the diversity of their energy supplies, improve energy security and provide a low-carbon alternative to fossil fuels. For instance, China, the US and India, which are the world's three largest coal-consuming nations, are projected to expand their nuclear capacity significantly over the next twenty five years.

India is presently able to produce about three per cent (4000 Mw) nuclear energy. In 2002, the installed electricity capacity was about 139 giga watts. During 2002-2003 electricity production was about 639 terrawatt hours (twh), where sixty seven per cent from coal-based stations, twenty per cent from oil and gas, ten per cent from hydro and three per cent from nuclear. India's requirements of energy by 2052 indicate that the total installed capacity will have to be about 1,350 gigawatts and the total generation about 8,000 twh. Of this, the coal and hydrocarbon (oil and gas) contributions would have gone down to forty seven and sixteen per cent and hydro to eight per cent. The nuclear component is required to go up to twenty six per cent.[11]

Realizing its energy needs, India has recently signed an agreement with the US on peaceful nuclear energy cooperation. Through this agreement India is expected to produce about 20,000 Mw by 2020 and double this by 2030. The Nuclear Supplier Group (NSG), which treated India in the past three decades as a pariah, has agreed to trade nuclear commerce with the latter. India's main focus on nuclear energy is not only to meet the demands but also to reduce its green house emission.

On two grounds, Australia may reconsider the decision taken by the previous government regarding supply of uranium to India: a) climate change dimensions and b) Australia can check and verify whether uranium supplied by it is used for peaceful purposes. Or it, like the US, can have a safeguard agreement to open up the plants for international inspections. It must understand that ban on uranium sales to India is the biggest obstacle in India-Australia energy ties.

Climate Change

The discourse on climate change reveals that the entire humanity would face numerous problems (rise of sea level, migration, of people who live in low lying areas, environmental hazards, cyclones, droughts, impact on health, on crop yield, water scarcity and so on) in the near future due to green house gases (GHGs: CO_2, methane, nitrous oxide, hydro fluorocarbons, perfluorocarbons, and sulfur hexafluoride) emissions. Climate change poses different challenges for many countries including India and Australia. Climate change has a major influence on sea level change. It is estimated that the rate of global sea level rise was between 0.1 and 0.2 meters (about 3.9 to 7.9. inches) during the twentieth century and this rate of sea level rise was ten times that of previous 3,000 years. Since the end of the ice age, transfers of mass from ice sheets to the oceans have raised sea level by 120 meters. Global ocean heat content, according to the IPCC, has increased since late 1950s. Due to the impact of climate change, it is expected that the sea level will grow up. As a result people, who live in coastal areas/low-lying areas, will have to suffer. It is estimated that by 2050, about 250 million people may leave their places due to intensifying monsoon flooding, desertification and reduced food production. Most of the coastal states (including India and Australia), which are dependent on coastal fishery and agriculture, are likely to be affected. If a one-meter sea level rise were to take place today, it would displace seven million persons in India. Furthermore, intrusion of sea-water in the ground water and changes in temperature can reduce agricultural and fishing incomes. Australia's coastline will have erosion and inundation from about 8-88 cm increase in global sea level. Climate change will have impact on Australia's environment, economy and health.

Though for both India and Australia, coal continues to be important to economic development, as responsible players in the region, it has become compulsory to mitigate their GHGs emission through initiatives such as: improve energy efficiency, transport, power generation and reduce the energy-intensity of industrial production, afforestation and wasteland development and population reduction, which will improve environmental quality and limit human health hazards from air pollution.

Possible Areas of Convergence of Interests

Cordial relationship between Australia and India has been

developed since end of the cold war. India is now starting to look east, to the rest of Asia, to fuel its economic growth. And Asia is beginning to take India seriously as a potential regional economic power. In looking east, India is also looking to Australia and towards the Pacific region. Though it still continues to have differences with India over nuclear issue, Australia emphasized that "bilateral relationship is much deeper and broader than one set of issues alone." Australia realized that there were better economic opportunities in India than in East and Southeast Asia.

The first official India-Australia Strategic Dialogue was held in New Delhi on 30 August 2001. India has the largest navy and coastguard of any littoral state between the two most important commercial straits in the world-Hormuz and Malacca. Australia's maritime trade towards the west passes through the Strait of Lombok and then through Malacca. Thus, India has become important to Australia in its maritime security. Partnership between India and Australia is important for the peace and stability of the Asia- Pacific region. India has civilization and historic links with the Asia-Pacific. People of Indian origin are present in almost all the countries of the region and play a significant part in the business and professional activities there. Australia has a maritime border with these countries. Cooperation is important since the Asia-Pacific region faces some formidable challenges such as the increasing nexus of trafficking in drugs and illegal arms, human trafficking, armed piracy and above all terrorism. From preventing failed states becoming havens for terrorism to cooperation in protecting the sea lanes of the Indian Ocean, there is scope for a broader and deeper agenda between Australia and India. Thus, in the Indian Ocean and the Asia-Pacific region as a whole, the two countries are obvious partners in any future arrangement for a stable balance of power. The growth of the world economy in the next decade will be decided by Asia. The regional architecture of the Asia-Pacific is undergoing considerable transformation towards the establishment of the Asia-Pacific Community (APC) by 2020 to suit the region's changing geo-political landscape in the twentyfirst century. The APC is envisaged as a regional institution spanning the "entire Asia-Pacific region, including the US, Japan, China, India, Indonesia and other states of the region". Both countries along with the US have concerns for Chinese expansion in the Malacca Straits. The perspective clearly indicates an upward shift in the trajectory of India-Australia relations notwithstanding irritants to a closer engagement between the two democracies in recent times. India's growing clout in the global arena makes it difficult for Australia to ignore its presence altogether. The fact that India is a "very significant power" and a neighbour in the region suggests that closer ties are sought after as Australia recognizes the criticality of the relationship. Both countries need to play a constructive role and collaboration between them is essential for the peace and stability in Asia-Pacific region.

REFERENCES

1. Walter Crocker, *Australian Ambassador,* Melbourne: Melbourne University Press, 1991, p. 200.
2. Letter, 5 July 1958, *Australian Archives: A 838/2:169/10/1,* p. 4.
3. Cited in *Sydney Morning Herald,* 22 January 1950, p. 2.
4. Cited in K.M.Panikkar, *India and the Indian Ocean,* Bombay: George Allen Unwin, 1945, p. 92.
5. A.W. Grezebrook, "The Indian Naval Build Up: Has Defense Central Got It All Wrong", *Pacific Defence Reporter,* February 1990, pp.14-15.
6. For details see Tim Huxley, "India's Naval Expansion and Australia" *Contemporary South Asia,* vol.1, no.3, 1992, pp. 407-423.
7. *UN Yearbook 1981,* vol. 25, New York: UN Publications, p. 34.
8. Brahma Chellaney, *Nuclear Proliferation: The US-Indian Conflict* (Hyderabad: Orient Longman, 1993), p. 39.
9. For India's perspective on NPT and CTBT, see A. Subramanyam Raju, *Indian Women Scientists' Perceptions of the Nuclear Issue,* New Delhi: WISCOMP, 2005), pp.16-18.
10. See *The Times,* 13 May 1998.
11. M.R.Srinivasan, "New Opportunities for Nuclear Energy", *The Hindu,* 2 August 2005, p.10.

7

India - Australia Relations: Towards Building a Genuine Strategic Partnership

G.V.C. Naidu

Introduction

India-Australia relations are poised to take off if the recently concluded comprehensive 'strategic partnership' agreement at the time of Prime Minister Kevin Rudd's visit to India in late 2009 is any indication. It acquires considerable political salience because Australia was the eighth country to be accorded that status by New Delhi. It is hoped that, unlike in the past, the renewed interest in each other, underscored by a growing awareness of the need to forge close links, would ensue in building a genuine strategic partnership that is not only longer lasting but does not become a victim to political misunderstandings that marked the history of bilateral relations since the early 1950s. The basic requirements to construct a comprehensive and mutually beneficial relationship are in place now: a more propitious political environment, vibrant economic relations, and vital common strategic stakes. Obviously, there is more to India-Australia relations than either shared colonial legacy or the famous three "c's"—Commonwealth, cricket, and common language. Given that both are influential littoral states of the Indian Ocean and are key powers in the Asia-Pacific, their interests intersect. Both these regions are at a crossroads undergoing unprecedented transformation, which will have enormous implications for India and Australia.

The paper, apart from providing a brief backdrop, deals with two specific areas that are of concern to India and Australia, that is, the Indian Ocean and the Asia-Pacific. So far, there have been few tangible bilateral actions specifically aimed at evolving certain common strategies to deal with these two issues. It argues that unless the scope of bilateral relations is constantly widened by incorporating areas of mutual interest, there is a danger of these relations suffering the same fate that they did for a long time.

Backdrop

On the eve of India's Independence, the political bonhomie was very conspicuous. Indian Prime Minister Jawaharlal Nehru saw Australia as part of Asia and wanted it to play an active role in regional affairs. In his opening remarks at the historic Asian Relations Conference in April 1947, he observed: "We welcome also observers from Australia and New Zealand because we have many problems in common, especially in the Pacific and in the Southeast region of Asia, and we have to co-operate together to find solutions." On the eve of India's Independence, the then Australian Foreign Minister Herbart Evatt of the Labour Government remarked: "Our geographical proximity and our common interest in the affairs of the Indian Ocean and South-East Asia naturally throw our lots closely together." It is well known that it at Nehru's instance, Australia and New Zealand were invited to the Bandung Conference in Indonesia in 1955 as observers. He said, "Australia and New Zealand are almost in our region. They certainly do not belong to Europe, much less to America. They are next to us and I should like Australia and New Zealand to come nearer to Asia."[1]

The creation of Commonwealth provided an opportunity for the top leadership of India and Australia to meet occasionally in the initial years of its formation in the early fifties. They, however, started drifting politically once the cold war gained momentum with Australia joining the American camp and India, after dabbling with the non-alignment, gradually drifting towards the former Soviet Union. The only time when their armed forces met were during multilateral naval exercises that used to be held in the 1950s and 1960s under the auspices of the Commonwealth near Trincomalee port in Sri Lanka called the Joint Exercises Trincomalee (JET). Growing hostilities between India and Pakistan led to their end in the mid-1960s.

Although India and Australia did not have major bilateral political problems or issues of dispute, their differences were heightened by certain developments. For instance, India was highly critical of American military presence in the Indian Ocean whereas Australia in general perceived it as necessary to provide a counterbalance to the Soviets as well as contribute to stability. The developments that followed the communist victories in Indochina in the mid-1970s, especially the rift between Vietnam and China and Vietnamese military deposing the Pol Pot regime had tremendous impact on India's East Asian policy. India, aside from humanitarian dimension, saw an opportunity to develop political solidarity and strategic partnership by supporting the Vietnamese action in Cambodia, which led some to believe that India and Soviet Union along with Vietnam were trying to check the American and Chinese influence in the region. Some Australian commentators saw Indian naval expansion as an attempt to project power into Southeast Asia, where it had considerable interests at stake.

By the mid-1980s, the political gulf between the two countries had widened so much that some Australian analysts went to the extent of voicing concerns about the Indian Navy posing threat to the Cocos (Keeling) Islands, because they lie some 2,700 km. away from Perth.[2] It was probably the clearest pointer to the kind of communication gap that had set in. It, of course, partly due to Indian Navy's failure to explain its modernisation and its security compulsions to embark on acquiring such capabilities— chiefly the second aircraft carrier from the UK, and a Charlie-I class nuclear-powered submarine on lease, TU-142 MR long-range maritime reconnaissance aircraft and modern Kilo-class conventional submarines from Russia, and a variety of sea-going ships being built indigenously— that were seen as attempts to acquire power projection capabilities. Strong reactions from Australia and a few Southeast Asian nations were also in part due to expansion of the Andaman base facilities in the Bay of Bengal close to the crucial Malacca and other straits. Whereas the truth is that many of them were due to decisions taken in the 1970s but, given Indian notorious red tape and slow pace of implementing decisions, came into fruition only from the mid-1980s onwards.[3]

The dispatch of Indian troops under garb of a peacekeeping force to Sri Lanka in 1987 at the height of conflict between minority Tamils and majority Sinhalese, the swift naval operation that subdued an attempted coup in the Maldives 1988, and growing assertiveness in the neighbourhood in tandem with its rising military capabilities were dubbed as India's Monroe Doctrine. The creation of a Marine Command Force and considerable increase in strategic sea and airlift capabilities only reinforced the disquiet about its intentions in Southeast Asia and the Indian Ocean. There had also been a few incidents of the Australian navy snooping on Indian ships on high seas in the Indian Ocean, which raised suspicions in New Delhi about Australian intensions. The root cause of much of this antagonistic perception was the cold war and the two countries belonging to the opposite camps. Thus, only after the end of the cold war India-Australia relations started looking up and the Indian Navy played a major role in this endeavour.

Post-Cold War

As part of an initiative to build confidence and allay concerns, the Indian Navy undertook a series of measures such as inviting senior officers from Australia to the Andaman military facility as a measure of assurance, which was followed by a series of bilateral exercises. Perhaps this was also the first occasion that the navies of the two countries met after a long time. Objective assessments of the Indian Navy, in particular concerning the Andaman facility, also helped ease the previous misunderstanding.[4] No question that an unprecedented turnaround in India-US relations too had great impact on Australia's India policy. Australia soon became a major focus of the Look East Policy that New Delhi launched in the early 1990s and expectations were quite high from Canberra. Defence relations were established starting with the exchange of senior officers for training. Australia too on its part began a series of pro-active measures to promote India rightly forecasting its potential. Starting with the launch of the Australia-India Council in 1992, which played (in fact it continues to) a key role in several programmes, the Department of Foreign Affairs and Trade's comprehensive report entitled *India's Economy: at the Midnight Hour* (a similar report in 2001) and the India Today Festival in 1994, the Look West Strategy in 1995, and the Australia-India New Horizons Campaign in 1996. At a time when the two were beginning to warm up towards each other, India's 1998 nuclear tests put paid to whatever initiatives that had been taken and relations were dealt a severe setback. While Canberra had reasons to be annoyed with Indian actions, the manner in which it went about condemning New Delhi at the ASEAN Regional Forum (ARF) meeting and other international fora (while letting China off lightly for its 1995 tests) left Indians terribly upset.[5] India did not violate any international agreements that it was party to nor posed a threat to Australia's security even remotely. In any case it is no secret that till late 1970s, Australia harboured ambitions of acquiring nuclear weapons. More importantly, Australia's own security continues to be strongly underpinned by a huge American nuclear umbrella.

Australia soon realised that its hardline policy was out of sync with emerging realities: India was becoming a significant factor in the Asia-Pacific and Indian Ocean security and that was the reason why Americans had begun secret parleys with Indian interlocutors soon after the nuclear tests. As a result, in 2000 Australia and India renewed their defence relations and efforts began to re-engage with each other. However, the 9/11 events probably acted as a major catalyst to forge deeper security relations. For one, even as the full gamut of terrorist organisations and their global networks and the threats they posed to global security started to unfold, it turned out much of it had been concentrated in the Indian Ocean rim region— from eastern Africa to the Middle East and from South Asia to Southeast Asia. And for another, it became apparent that there was no way terrorism could be tackled without strong and enduring international cooperation. India's location as a frontline state fighting terrorism for several decades acquired considerable importance in counter-terrorism efforts.

A flurry of activities spurred by the conservative governments in the US, Japan and Australia resulted in the creation of new security consultative mechanisms such as the three-way talks among these, which included heads of state, foreign and defence ministers meetings. The security cooperation agreement that Japan concluded with Australia in March 2007 was an important development not merely for the two countries but for India as well, for Japan strongly pitched for New Delhi's inclusion in security discussions during a summit meeting of George Bush, John Howard and Shinzo Abe in September 2007.[6] Abe, in fact, during a visit to India in August 2006 had already spoken of creating an "arc of freedom and prosperity" in the Asia-Pacific.[7] India agreeing to participate in the quadrilateral signalled a major shift in its policy. Importantly, this forum along with the March 2006 India-Australia MoU on defence cooperation provided the much needed shot in the arm to propel India and Australia relations.

The most visible aspect of the new bonhomie was the first-ever large scale multilateral exercises in September 2007: the 13th Indo-US Malabar exercises in the Bay of Bengal in which for the first time Australia joined the US, Japan, and Singapore in such manoeuvres hosted by India.[8] Unfortunately, although these were not aimed at any particular country but to promote greater inter-operability among friendly countries, Australia chose to withdraw from the quadrilateral after Kevin Rudd's Labour Party came to power. The initial misgivings that Rudd was developing relations with China at the cost of India were soon dispelled and efforts began to reinvigorate India-Australia relations even though Canberra's wavering on natural uranium supplies to Indian civilian reactors remained a sticky issue. Notwithstanding a series of attacks on Indian students in Victoria which appeared to vitiate the environment, the two countries managed to sign a 'strategic partnership' agreement during Prime Minister Rudd's sojourn tc India in November 2009 (thus Australia becoming one of the nine nation who have signed such agreements with India), which is expected to bring the relationship back on track.

The *Joint Statement on Security Cooperation* is comprehensive encompassing a number of areas of mutual interest, such as maritime security, counter-terrorism, working together in East Asian regional multilateral fora, disaster management, universal disarmament and non-proliferation and seeking a peaceful world free of nuclear weapons. Importantly, the *Statement* also mentions the creation of "comprehensive framework for the enhancement of security cooperation between the two countries." Furthermore, it elaborates various mechanisms of cooperation including high-level visits and consultations between National Security Advisors.[9]

While this provides the framework to consolidate the process of bilateral security cooperation, the tricky part would be to develop the 'action plan' with specific measures to advance security cooperation that the *Statement* mentions.

Major Areas of Convergence

Indian Ocean

Thanks to the critical sea lines of communications that carry vast amounts of trade, the Indian Ocean is the 'new maritime silk route' connecting the east with the west. It is regaining its prominence, both because of serious problems it is beset with and huge opportunities it offers. Since non-traditional security issues have emerged as the biggest challenges not merely for the rim countries but virtually for the entire world, it is important to find new approaches to address these problems. Given that the nature, intensity and complexity of the threats, it has become imperative to evolve multilateral cooperative arrangements.

Perhaps no other ocean is so geostrategically located as the Indian Ocean flanked by some of the most important regions, which cannot only seriously endanger international peace and security but can also significantly contribute to global prosperity. With over one-third of the world's population residing in its littoral, its economic and human resource potential is immense. If the energy rich Persian Gulf, with its nearly two-thirds of global oil and about 30 per cent of gas reserves, constitutes the lifeline to drive the economic vibrancy in East Asia and Europe, the rim is also home to countries that are politically volatile and hotbeds of global terrorism. Safer shipping is hampered by the persistent threat of piracy from the Gulf of Aden to the straits in Southeast Asia and the threat of maritime terrorism is present and real. More importantly, the Indian Ocean region also has seen rampant illicit and clandestine exchange of WMD technologies and systems.

The ocean's economic criticality can be gauged by the fact that more than 60 oil tankers pass through this ocean daily, which is expected to dramatically increase up to 200 in the next decade or so. More than 80 per cent of hydrocarbon requirements of East Asia, which includes global economic power houses like China, Japan, South Korea, and India, are met with imports from the Middle East that traverse through the Indian Ocean. Interestingly, while over 40 per cent of the global trade (with some 100,000 ships a year at present) transits the Indian Ocean, only 20 per cent is conducted among the littoral countries of the region, which means 80 per cent of trade is carried out by extra-regional countries, which signifies how critical this ocean is to countries outside the region. That Australia's prosperity and security to a considerable extent are dependent on the Indian Ocean is obvious because its growing links with East Asia, whose economic and security stakes are, as noted, invariably linked to the Indian Ocean security. If the current century were to be Asian century as indications suggest, the Indian Ocean is going to be a key cog in that. Hence, it is but natural that Australia attaches so much importance to this region. India's unique contribution to the Indian Ocean security is also acknowledged by the US for the first time as the 2010 Quadrennial Defense Report states: "India's military capabilities are rapidly improving through increased defense acquisitions, and they now include long-range maritime surveillance, maritime interdiction and patrolling, air interdiction, and strategic airlift. India has already established its worldwide military influence through counterpiracy, peacekeeping, humanitarian assistance, and disaster relief efforts. As its military capabilities grow, India will contribute to Asia as a net provider of security in the Indian Ocean and beyond."[10]

As one of the leading littoral nations, for Australia the security of the Indian Ocean region naturally is paramount in view of its growing linkages with Southeast Asia and India. For instance, the India-Australia bilateral trade has grown from US $4.55 billion in 2004-05 to 12.56 bn in 2008-09, an average annual increase of nearly 30 percent. India was Australia's fourth largest merchandise export market and seventh largest merchandise trading partner in the financial year 2008-2009.[11] The criticality of the Indian Ocean is even more telling given its geographic location. Even as the Indian economy gallops (the third largest in PPP terms), the rate of its external trade is more than 25 percent a year. And, more than 95 percent of it sea borne. Equally significant, the November 2008 horrific attacks on Mumbai by a handful of terrorists were sea borne.

Surely, the Indian Navy is the largest in the Indian Ocean littoral and it is undergoing a fundamental shift in its expansion and the role it seeks to play, however it has its limitations. There is a strong case to revisit the inactive Indian Ocean Rim Association for Regional Cooperation (IOR-ARC) forum, which can serve as a good platform to deal with its security problems in a cooperative framework and also reinvigorate it to promote economic cooperation. India now likely to be more inclined to extend full support unlike in the past. Similarly, the Indian Ocean Naval Symposium (IONS), which has been instrumental in bringing the navies of the region together on a common platform has enormous potential not simply as an endeavour to build confidence but also undertake a series of other security-related initiatives. Yet, there appears to be no major joint efforts to collaborate in ensuring the Indian Ocean security.

Asia-Pacific Security

Asia-Pacific is witnessing unprecedented changes and never before the interests of both India and Australia were so vitally linked to developments here. Until recently, both had been marginal players with limited stakes, but that has undergone a transformation. Seven out of top ten Australian trading partners in 2009 were East Asian nations, while for India it was three (but likely to grow consequent to signing of a spate of CECA/CEPAs and FTA/RTAs.) India's trade has seen the fastest growth with East Asia compared to any other region since the launch of economic reforms in the early 1990s. Both Australia and India are active participants in several regional multilateral frameworks—economic and security—and have a vital interest in the evolving regional economic and security architecture.

The region, however, presents a complex picture: it is economically the world's most vibrant region, but is also beset with a myriad security concerns too, both traditional and non-traditional, that can seriously undermine peace and stability. If the present trends continue, it is estimated that the combined GDP of China and India would reach 50 percent of global GDP between 2030 and 2040. China is already the largest manufacturing nation and India is consolidating its position in ICT and other service sectors, whereas Japan's hold over advanced technologies is unlikely to diminish any time soon. Already East Asia's GDP is more than the US and the EU put together. Apart from the three mega economic powerhouses, East Asia is also home to a large number of economic tigers, from Australia to Vietnam, which are significantly contributing to regional economic dynamism.

Even as East Asia hogs the global limelight, it is also undergoing enormous changes within. The intra-regional trade is growing rapidly: at around 58 percent, it is far more than North America and slightly less than the EU (at 62 percent). Similarly, with over 40 percent of global population, the East Asian market too is expanding phenomenally fuelled by the rise of new economic powers such as China and India and rising incomes. This trend also indicates declining importance of traditional markets such as the U.S. and EU for Asian exports. As opportunities grow, East Asia is attracting huge investments. Interestingly, much of this is market-driven. Indeed, frenetic attempts are underway across the entire region to further promote regional cooperation and integration through bilateral and multilateral comprehensive cooperation agreements. A variety of ideas to promote a sense of identity and enhance cooperation are being floated: Yukio Hatoyama's East Asian Community and Kevin Rudd's Asia-Pacific Community that deserve greater attention.

On the other hand, the region also has to grapple with a number of challenges as well. The implications of the rise of new powers and the kind of relations that govern them, a large number of highly emotive border/maritime boundary disputes involving virtually every country of the region, lingering historical legacies and suspicions, uncertainties about China's long-term goals and ambitions, and innumerable unconventional security threats need to be factored into any security assessment of the region. Perhaps the most fundamental problem is the lack of a classic balance of power and cooperative security frameworks failing to take roots.

Against the above backdrop, India and Australia together can play a unique role, for, unlike most other nations in the region, they do not have a baggage of the past to worry about, nor do they have a record of interference or intervention in domestic affairs of other countries. What is more, they have no pending border/ boundary problems (India-China border is a different case). Developments in this region directly impinge on their interests, yet there is no bilateral framework between India and Australia to consult and arrive at some common understanding on the question of regional security in the Asia-Pacific.

Conclusion

India-Australia relations have great potential but some amount of political reticence seems to be holding them back and that is because of certain irritants— chiefly the uranium supply. It is a bind that Australia is in need to be overcome to send a strong political signal. Simultaneously, it is equally prudent to focus on those on which their interests converge instead of allowing differences coming in the way. For obvious reasons this was not possible during the cold war and in the post-cold war as till recently mutual stakes were limited and hence both sides failed to pay serious attentions to bilateral relations. That is beginning to change with the Indian economy growing rapidly, which requires natural resources to fuel that growth, and Australia looking for markets for its products. Importantly, both are looking for strategic partners. This comes out starkly when seen against the background of qualitative shifts in bilateral trade and steadily improving security cooperation. It is to be noted that so far India and Australia have been leading powers of the Indian Ocean region but their interests neither clashed nor converged. However, that is likely to change the major resurgence of the Indian Ocean along with the emergence of a multitude of security challenges, which offer opportunities for these two to forge close links. Both have to build solid defence links encompassing a range of activities starting with evolving common strategies on disaster management, counter-proliferation, counter-terrorism, counter-piracy, sea lane security, etc. Similarly, the Asia-Pacific region that is witnessing tectonic shifts both in its security and economic outlook provides innumerable possibilities for consultations and building common strategies. Progress on this front has so far been limited because they failed to look beyond a few regional multilateral frameworks, in particular the ARF and the East Asia Summit, in which they are members. Unfortunately, both these (many others as well) have failed to live up to their expectations and hence the need for India and Australia to evolve a different kind of consultative mechanism in the region.

Evidently bilateral interactions are limited and mechanisms to guide them are inadequate. The Joint Statement on Security Cooperation issued in November 2009 is exhaustive, but the challenge is to create appropriate institutional mechanisms for regular consultations along with regular high-level visits.

NOTES

1. Quoted in Prime Minister Kevin Rudd's speech, "From Fitful Engagement to Strategic Partnership," at the Indian Council of World Affairs (ICWA), November 12, 2009, http://www.icwa.in/aupmspeechfull.html
2. See for instance, A.W. Grezrbrook, "The Indian Naval Buildup: Has Defence Central Got it all Wrong?" *Pacific Defence Reporter*, February 1990, quoted in P.V. Rao, ed. *India and Australia: New Horizons* (Hyderabad: Society for Indian Ocean Studies, Osmania University, 2003), p. 132.
3. Some of these issues are dealt with in detail in G.V.C. Naidu, *Indian Navy and Southeast Asia,* (New Delhi: Institute for Defence Studies and Analyses and Knowledge World, 2000).
4. D.N. Christie, *India's Naval Strategy and the Role of Andaman and Nicobar Islands,* Working Paper No 291 (Canberra: Strategic and Defence Studies Centre, Australian National University, 1995), p. 18.
5. See G.V.C. Naidu, "The Manila ASEAN Meetings and India", *Strategic Analysis,* November 1998, pp. 1163-1177.
6. *"Japan wants India to join talks with US Australia"*,September 7, 2007, http://news.yahoo.com/s/afp/20070907/wl_sthasia_afp/apecsummitaustraliausjapanindia_070907065944
7. The quadrilateral idea expectedly drew sharp reactions from China. The Indian prime minister reportedly clarified to the Chinese premier Hu Jintao that this was not a military alliance and was not attempt to gang up against China. "No Question of ganging up against China," *Times of India,* June 27, 2007, http://timesofindia.indiatimes.com/ India/No question of ganging up against China/articleshow/2155268.cms
8. These were militarily the most significant exercises that India ever participated in.
9. *India-Australia Joint Declaration on Security Cooperation,* November 12, 2009, http://www.india.embassy.gov.au/ndli/pa5009jsb.html
10. http://www.defense.gov/qdr/images/QDR as of 12Feb10 1000.pdf
11. http://www.dfat.gov.au/geo/india/india brief.html

8

India-Australia Relations: Strategic Cooperation and Beyond

Gopalji Malviya

Australia had figured prominently in India's foreign policy calculations during formative years. India's first Prime Minister Jawaharlal Nehru, the architect of India's foreign policy saw Australia "almost in our region". Nehru realised the geographical proximity of Australia and its potential role in Asia and accordingly Australia was invited as observer to the first Asian Relations Conference held at New Delhi in April 1947. Nehru looked for Pacific neighbours for lasting cooperation and finding solutions for problem concerning Asia. Nehru's insights on Australia's common destiny with India and our wider regional concerns were shared by Australia too. Australian Foreign Minister said on the occasion of India's Independence: "Our geographical proximity and our common interest in the affairs of the Indian Ocean and South East Asia naturally throw our lots closely together," thereby confirming and recognising India and Australia potential relationship in the context of the region.

But unfortunately India was seen very differently by the Australian in the 1950-60s. Their ideological mindset and perceptions on global and regional issues were conditioned by the cold war dynamics. Hence, they followed different routes towards their foreign relations. "Asian Consciousness" could not bring the two countries on the common platform. It was only India's New *Horizon programme* in October 1996 that triggered swing in Indo-Australian bilateral relations in terms of fresh look. The growth of India's economic and IT sectors were interwoven in its Look East Policy that attracted Australia's attention and perhaps opened new windows of convergence. There was strong feelings and reactions of academia, civil society and even in the ruling establishments that Australia should review its tough stands particularly after India's nuclear test after 1998. Pressure was mounted to look towards India with more positive approach towards traditional and non-traditional security issues.

Australia has long pursued its security interest by maintaining security partnerships with regional friends and neighbours. Building security partnerships and engaging regional states in defence and security dialogues helps to reassure states and offers a means by which potential problems can be resolved. Over the past few years, Australia has formalised and strengthened some key security relationship. For example, India and Australia have concluded a memorandum of understanding on Defence Cooperation in 2006.

Australia has long recognised the potential of India as a strategic partner, based on shared democratic tradition and common values and strategic interests. The current relationship between the two nations is reflected in strong economic ties– India is Australia's fourth largest export market- and burgeoning engagement in the areas of education, science and technology collaboration, and cultural exchange. From a defence and security perspective, our bilateral relationship mirrors the broader patterns of the relationship. We share high level strategic interests that shape and guide our interaction and continue to develop co-operative defence activities and personnel exchanges.

India and Australia share variety of strategic interests in bilateral, global and regional context with the prime interest in combating international terrorism, non-proliferation of weapons of mass destruction, securing maritime lane of communication and energy and resource security. We also share an interest in a range of transnational security challenges such as disaster, environmental degradation and international crime.

Taking forward the decision to upgrade its relations to the level of strategic partnership, India and Australia agreed to create a comprehensive framework for enhancement of Security Corporation. India and Australia have upgraded their relationship to that of 'Strategic partnership' and signalled their intention to increase cooperation on security issues. As for the defence dialogue and cooperation within the framework of the Memorandum of Understanding (MoU) on Defence Corporation signed in March 2006, the mechanism to carry it forward includes Defence Policy, talks between Senior-level officers, staff and service to service exchanges including exercises. Indian defence market and Industry is highly competitive and restricted. However, there is a wide scope for India- Australia greater military cooperation particularly in the changing strategic landscape in the region. It is desirable, particularly in the congenial and warm political relations that exist today. This may also provide strategic transformation in bilateral relations in future.

Economic growth and military might are two major components that are propelling India, which is emerging as a global power, to play a more prominent role at International theatre. India's large military-industrial complex, innovations and technical advancements have been consistent with its military requirements. India's *Navarathna (9 Public Sector Undertaking),* over 40 Ordnance factories, large network of Defence Research and Development Organisation (DRDO) and continued advancement in space technology and different missile programmes makes this country as one of the top few countries in the world. India's leadership in IT industries, its services and products are already established.

India and Australia demonstrated their commitment in a joint declaration on security cooperation that is likely to strengthen understanding and cooperation in wide ranging of security related areas that includes counter-terrorism, defence, disarmament, non-proliferation and maritime security issues. In November 2009, Indian Prime Minister Dr. Manmohan Singh and Australian Prime Minister Mr. Kevin Rudd expressed that this strategic partnership between the two countries is based on shared desire to promote regional and global security as well as their commitment to democracy, freedom, human rights and rule of law. The joint statement also affirmed their respect for each other's contribution for promoting peace, stability and development in Asia and beyond. This opened a new chapter of profound relationship. It is not very clear whether entering into a strategic partnership would facilitate change in Australian attitude and reluctance to sell uranium to India. However, the term connotes at least intent to develop deeper and broader ties between the two countries. Now with the new government under Julia Gillard is likely to move for a closer understanding that could bring a subtle change in Australia towards sale of Uranium to India.

Growing bilateral defence relationship between India and Australia could be traced to the year 2000 when ties were re-established. Exchange of military personnel, training, service links, establishment of strong strategic dialogue and maritime engagement constitute the prime agenda of this strategic discourse. Exchange of officers at Defence Services Staff College (DSSC), Wellington and National Defence College (NDC), New Delhi have provided qualitative training and enduring personal links apart from understanding the defence architecture of their respective countries. Indian military officers also participated in Australian course such as emergency management, peace operations and defence management. In recent years India and Australia have been engaged in series of reciprocal visits to defence institutions. This practice is certainly encouraging as it provides an opening for interaction among military officers of the two countries and also helps to develop deeper understanding of each other's strategic perceptions.

India's military requirements are large and ever growing; however, there are critical areas of military technology that India has to scout, may it be for acquisition, procurement or collaborative production. For almost five decades India has been over dependent on former Soviet- Russia for most of its military hardware. After the disintegration of the Soviet Union, the Russian Federation could not keep up quality of supplies within the agreed time frame. Inordinate delays, cost escalation, obsolescence and prolonged negotiations have hampered India's military readiness. Hence, there is a need for India to look around for alternative sources of military supplies. The strategic environment in and around India continues to be threatened and particularly with new types of traditional and non-traditional military challenges in India's land, sea and air space. Hence, close military co-operation with Australia could be one option that India may prefer.

While there is sufficient scope for a comprehensive engagement on various dimensions of security, maritime security cooperation would constitute an area of greater importance based on geo-political realities in Indian Ocean regions. Maritime concerns are potential areas for futuristic relationships. Australia may seek to increase interaction and create opportunity for bilateral maritime engagement. The converging strategic interest meets in the Eastern Indian Ocean Region. Australia as a maritime country seeks opportunities of greater interaction with Indian Navy. Indian Navy also realises the politico-strategic advantage of partnership with Australian Navy. Naval co-operations and greater interactions may lead towards system integration of ships building and submarine building technology, submarine escape and search and rescue operations, logistic and material management and networking. The Australian mine sweeping system has already secured a major order with Indian Navy which is the latest client for its innovative system that protects the ship from under water mines.

The intense desire of extreme competitive and restricted Indian defence market has now identified a new player: Australia is also searching for new opportunities in the business of defence cooperation. First ever Australian marine defence mission has visited India in early 2009. The delegation comprised nine leading defence industries displayed their expertise and capabilities in maritime security and offered the same to the Indian armed services. The Australian military experts were seeking to build strong partnership and looking for joint venture with the Indian defence establishment. The delegation was here to understand the Indian system of defence procurement and acquisition and offered high-tech value added competitive solution and entire spectrum of maritime security in submarine system development, integration and high pressure hull fabrication, ship construction, modular construction, system integration, platform integration, sub-system design, maintenance services, patrol boat design and construction of high speed naval vessel design. The presentations were made before key government department including the Ministry of Defence, Coast Guard and Border Security Force (BSF). The Australian military experts offered latest technology, including specialised safety, combat and security equipment, personnel protective apparel, chemical splash protection suits, satellite communication and software for the management of search and rescue missions and aerial maritime surveillance.

Participation of the Australian experts at the Aero India February 2009 was facilitated by the Australian Department of Defence and Regional Development, New South Wales, Australia Trade Commission, International Trade and Investment Promotion Agency and the Australian High Commissioner in India. This interaction was considered significant in defence, aviation and aerospace sectors. Australia has expertise in a wide spectrum of aerospace technology with proficiency in air systems integration, aircraft component avionics, pilot education training and aero maintenance training, general aircraft manufacture and maintenance and support. Australia is also looking for Indian cooperation in civil aviation sector with most modern systems and equipment. Australia is a major aviation and aerospace centre in Asia and Pacific region capable of dealing in civil and aerospace markets in India.

In the contemporary world it is difficult to separately characterise and classify global, regional and local threats. It is thus important to build strategic partnerships and coalitions of like-minded countries for lasting peace and security in the region. Cooperative approach of capacity building in defence preparations and military readiness would constitute a step forward. Economic and trade relations, that had accelerated over past two years, however, are not reflected in strategic and defence interactions, yet they provide for essential and basic ingredients for strong security relationships. This gap exists and could be addressed by both the countries.

Following areas could be vital for futuristic shared vision by both countries:

- Maintaining and securing sea-lane communication
- Smuggling and Proliferation of small arms in the region
- Drug trafficking and Narco-terrorism
- Illegal Migration and Human Trafficking
- Maintaining and Restoring Extra Regional Power
- Maritime Terrorism
- Cooperation in search and rescue operations in ocean disaster
- Sea Piracy and other Oceanic Crimes
- Protection of Ocean Environment and issues related to climate change.
- Sharing of Intelligence and Vital Information
- Energy Cooperation
- Ocean Partnership, Ocean Management, Ocean Governance.

The other areas that are important and may draw India-Australia joint venture and cooperation are:

- Rise of China, emerging tension and nuclear threat in Korean sub region.
- Changing contours of Sino-Japan relation and development of new security structure.
- Development in Indonesia, its stability and ethnic upsurge in Fiji.
- Nuclear proliferation related issues and commitment to global, complete and universal disarmament, to seek a peaceful world free of Nuclear Weapons.
- Areas of military modernisation, collaboration and transfer of military technology.
- Exploring the possibility to initiate a formal and periodic dialogue between Royal Australian Navy and Indian Navy and also to establish a naval hot line between the two countries.

India, USA, Japan and Australia which are all multicultural, vibrant democracies have lots in common but yet to form a viable institutionalised mechanism for better understanding of common threat, regional security, economic partnership and addressing maritime issues. These countries together could address non-military threats and could be catalyst for Asian Strategic Balance, particularly in the context of North Korea's nuclear programmes and tension growing due to politico-military development in the subregion. This group of four could also address Terrorism, Weapons of Mass Destruction and Small Arms Proliferation in Asian countries.

9

Australian Maritime Security Perceptions, Challenges and Responses

R.S. Vasan

Introduction

Both a continent and an Island, Australia with a coastline five times the length of the Indian Coast and an EEZ four times that of India by size is dependent on the seas surrounding her for trade and development. A study of the Australian maritime challenges reveals some very interesting factors in comparison to the ones faced around the Indian Peninsula. Australia claims to be both an Indian Ocean Power and an Asia Pacific entity. Traditionally the waters from East coast of Africa to the west coast of Australia constitute what is generally referred to as the Indian Ocean boundary .Being close to some of the South Eastern countries, Australia has certain perceptions about maritime terrorism and piracy issues in the region. Equally affected by the happenings post 9/11, and by a sense of affiliation with the west, it has chosen to be part of the multi national forces fighting the war against terrorism in distant locations in Iraq and Afghanistan. This desire to be part of the western coalition has brought Australian forces to this part of Asia.

In addition to maintaining law and order at sea, Australia has also challenges of illegal immigration, drug laundering and the use of the seas for other illegal activities including poaching. The study of contours of maritime security as perceived by Australia and also its impact on the neighbours make interesting study of how maritime nations shape polices and responses given their geographic location. It is obvious that one can not change one's neighbours and therefore would need to learn to live with them and manage them. The force level structures of the Australian Maritime Forces have evolved over hundred of years to cope with the emerging challenges and perceptions of security. With both bilateral and multilateral cooperation in the maritime arena becoming the order of the day, Australia like many other navies of the world is cooperating with other navies in different parts of the world to promote safety and security at sea.

Australia has a powerful navy and has challenges of safeguarding its EEZ and the maritime assets with its Navy. A study of the composition of its naval forces and the structure highlights the importance attached to this wing of Australian Defence Forces. Australia was extremely critical of India's nuclear effort that resulted in the Pokhran blast in May 1998. In fact, it went to the extent of expelling at short notice, Indian military officers who were undergoing various courses in Australia. However, in recent times, with the growing economic importance and clout of India, also possibly due to the strategic engagement of USA, Australia has engaged India, an Indian Ocean Region power, in a positive manner. The shape of maritime relations between the two countries and identification of areas of possible convergence/ dissent are important in the IOR calculus.

Geography

Both a continent and an Island referred to as a country down under, Australia a midle level power has many unique characteristics. It is blessed with a wealth of natural resources and has very good potential for trade and commerce in many commodities. It likes to consider itself as an Asia Pacific power.

Being an Island country, the country is entirely dependent on the seas for its economic, cultural, social and other forms of linkages with the rest of the world. Identified as a western country that follows US in its policies has many features of interest in terms of its maritime security perceptions. It is obvious that the perceptions of maritime security are shaped by geography and the nature of neighbourhood.

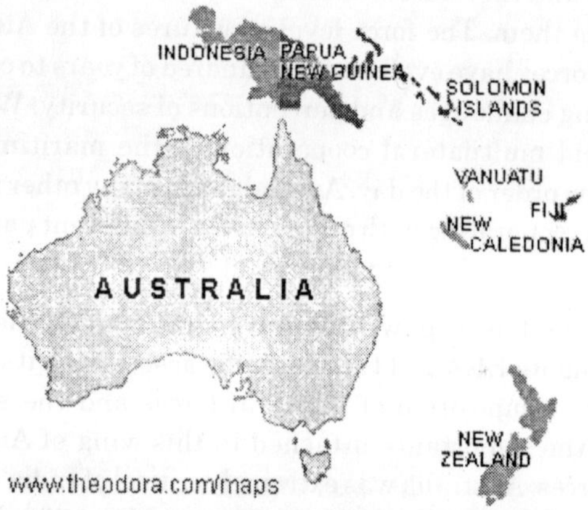

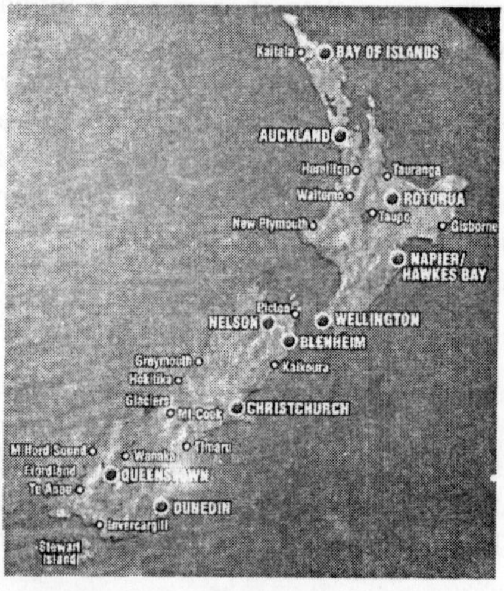

Australia's history, proximity to and continuing relationships with the South West Pacific result in commitment to support the security and stability of the nations of the region. It would be an important area of academic study to look at the way some of the relations have shaped with her neighbours despite some stark differences in cultural, economic, religious and political spheres. The need to engage the neighbours despite both perceived and actual differences at many levels was apparent to successive Governments in Australia and has shaped the relations in the neighbourhood. A very brief account of how the relations with some of the key countries in the neighbourhood would give an insight into thinking of Australian policy makers. Aspects of how these neighbours figure in the calculations of Australia is covered by a few examples in the succeeding paragraphs.

Indonesia: By reason of its geography and demography, Indonesia that houses the largest Muslims in the world is a defining element within Australia's strategic environment. The terrorist attacks on western targets and the phenomenon of jihadi terrorism have brought to fore the inescapability of engaging the Governments and the public in the muslim neighbourhood to bring about a secure environment. The resentment against the west post 9/11 has accentuated the climate of mutual distrust and animosity. The importance attached to relations with Indonesia is brought out by what the then PM of Australia Keating had to say in 1994 about Indonesia:

> No country is more important to Australia than Indonesia. If we fail to get this relationship right, and nurture and develop it, the whole web of our foreign relations is incomplete [and] ... the emergence of the New Order government of President Suharto, and the stability and prosperity which [it] has brought to [Indonesia] was the single most beneficial strategic development to have affected Australia and its region in the past thirty years...

It is clear that not much has changed since then and successive Governments in Australia have a compelling need to continue to engage Indonesia on many fronts in a positive and constructive manner.

FPDA: Fiver Power Defence Agreement is an agreement that was signed in 1971 between Australia, Singapore, Malaysia, UK and New Zealand provides cooperative mechanisms for protection of Singapore and Malaysia in the event of external aggression or threat to the safety and security of these countries. This came about as a result of UK to withdraw its forces from East of Suez in 1967. Since the commencement of joint exercises in 1981, the nature of joint exercises now involves both the naval and air units.

Papua New Guinea: Papua New Guinea another northern neighbour who gained independence from Australia in 1975, again has special security interest for Australia and the relationship with Papua New Guinea has been considered on equal terms to that envisaged vis-à-vis Indonesia. Australia remains the largest donor nation for this poor country.

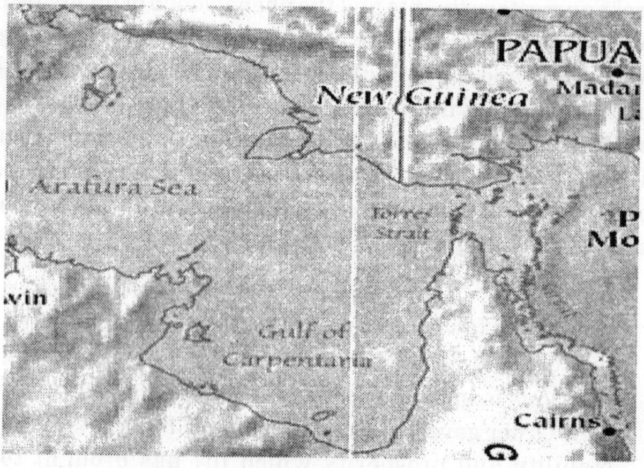

The issue of concern is the illegal immigration through the Torres Straits (see diagram above) between the two countries.

New Zealand: to the east of Australia enjoys good relations except in cricket perhaps and due to similarities of governance and culture, the relations have been good by and large. Even today, the two nations remember their association in World War I where both the Australian and NewZealand Armies fought together. The ANZAC (Australia and New Zealand Army Corps) day is commemorated on 25th April each year. ANZUS is a trilateral military treaty between Australia, New Zealand and US. However, New Zealand broke away from this alliance in 1984 over visit of nuclear armed ships to her ports. The military alliance is operative between Australia and US in the Pacific theatre. Australia, New Zealand has provided joint forces in East Timor and also forces for Operation Enduring Freedom in Iraq.

Fundamentals of Australia's Strategic Environment: Given its geographic location and its assessment of its own role certain assumptions can easily be made. In the strategic vision of Australia there is an assessment that it has key interests in the security and stability of the Asia-Pacific, including South East and North East Asia, the South West Pacific and North America. That kind of self assessment demands active engagement in different hemispheres of the globe and poses many challenges in its strategic engagements with countries as diverse as China, Indonesia and America. It is also very clear that physical security is dependent and driven by the initiatives in the seas around Australia. Some of the vital policy decisions regarding the maritime environment are triggered by security and stability issues in maritime South East Asia and the South West Pacific.

According to Prime Minister Rudd the three Pillar Policy include Engagements with UN, Engagements with Asia and Engagement with the US alliance. It is therefore very clear that Australia would reach out to Asian countries, US alliance and also engage itself with the UN (meaning participate actively and contribute positively in UN sponsored initiatives around the globe).

Regional Economic/Strategic Developments: In the perception of Australia, the economic development of East Asia is the key driver of change in the Asia-Pacific strategic system. Of the evolving new international power relationships, the most important according to Australian planners will involve the US, China and Japan. India does not figure in a big way yet in the over all scheme of strategic foresight. Australia plans to ensure avoidance of destabilising strategic competition between USA, China and Japan in areas of concern that would directly affect Australia. At another plane, prevention of the emergence within the Asia-Pacific region of a dominant power, or group of powers whose strategic interests are hostile to those of Australia is a crucial factor to be achieved.

Maintenance of a benign environment in South East Asia, particularly maritime South East Asia, which respects the territorial integrity of all states, has been considered to be an important geostrategic factor of stability to be achieved and promoted. Australia also plans to keep a watch on plans of extra regional military forces which may be planning to position forces in the neighbouring countries thus bringing the mutual strategic interests in to conflict. Thus Chinese overtures in the neighbourhood would continue to be watched.

Australia also has a stated policy about prevention of the proliferation of weapons of mass destruction (WMD). Despite the clearance for the Nuclear Suppliers Group being cleared to supply nuclear fuel to India, the current Government has reiterated that it would do business only with those who have signed the NPT. The clearance of Australia would also be important for India which is trying to improve its nuclear power generation capacity and potential to meet its ever increasing power demands.

Sino-Australian Relations–Energy Security

China continues to occupy the position as the largest trading partner of Australia. The reasons can be traced to the happenings in the early 19th century when many Chinese settled in Australia and have a strong base now in this country. By and large the equations have been on even keel particularly in the economic engagements despite reservations on human rights violation and Dalai Lama.

Despite some of the reservations about China, its human rights record and the its concerns on its military expansion, on August 19, 2009, Chinese petroleum company Petro China signed an AU$50 billion deal with Exxon Mobil to purchase liquefied natural gas from the Gorgon field in Western Australia, considered the largest contract ever signed between China and Australia. It is amply clear that as long as Australia is an energy provider and China the thirsty consumer, equations such as this one which add to the economic engagement would continue to be signed. China by this deal is assured a steady supply of LPG fuel for 20 years, and is a part of China's stated objective to achieve to identify and utilize relatively clean energy sources.

Australia-Japan Joint Security Pact, March 2007

The two maritime nations who share the Pacific Ocean have many common challenges and consider it beneficial to collaborate on security issues. Despite being on the opposite side during the world war, the relations have remained cordial and have many security connotations in various spheres. The Australia-Japan security pact that was signed in March 2007 encompasses many areas of collaboration. This pact includes the following:

a) Law enforcement on combating transnational crime, including trafficking in illegal,

b) narcotics and precursors,

c) people smuggling and trafficking,

d) counterfeiting currency and arms smuggling,

e) Border security Counter-terrorism,

f) Disarmament and counter-proliferation of weapons of mass destruction and their means of delivery,

g) Peace operations,

h) Exchange of strategic assessments and related information,

i) Maritime and aviation security,

j) Humanitarian relief operations, including disaster relief Contingency planning, including for pandemics.

ADF Tasks: The Australian Defence Force Tasks include measures listed below

(a) Defeat of Attacks on Australia (DAA)

(b) Defence of Regional Interests (DRI)

(c) Defence of Global Interests (DGI)

(d) Protection of National Interests (PNI)

(e) Shaping of the Strategic Environment (SSE).

The diagram below is illustrative of the way in which the Australian Defence Forces are tasked in diplomatic, constabulary and military roles in a calibrated manner. As indicated in the diagram, the diplomatic roles are conceived in a manner that would move from the benign to the coercive depending on the degree of involvement. The constabulary roles predominantly could be identified as the roles normally carried out by the Coast Guards. It may be noted that Australia does not have a separate Coast Guard as understood in the traditional way. The military roles envisaged include those operations from the sea and those conducted at sea. The component of Combat from the sea includes Maritime mobility, land strikes, amphibious operations, and support to land operations. Those envisaged as operations required at sea include intelligence collection and surveillance, Cover, Anti Shipping, maritime strikes, Containment by distraction, Barrier operations, layered operations, advance force operations and Naval Control of Shipping.

In order to meet the challenges as illustrated above a Joint Offshore Protection Command was set up in 2006. This was previously called as Joint Border Protection Command in 2005. The Multi Agency Command includes the Customs and the ADF from Canberra. The MAC is responsible for prevention of Illegal exploitation of natural resources. Illegal activity in protected areas, Prevention of Unauthorised maritime arrivals, Prevention of

Prohibited imports/exports, Maritime Counter Terrorism, Anti Piracy, Bio-security and measure to prevent Marine pollution.

ADF has a good mix of warships, submarines, patrol aircraft and Helicopters to meet the maritime obligations of surveillance and security. By a combination of action the ADF seeks to maintain dominance at sea in selected areas.

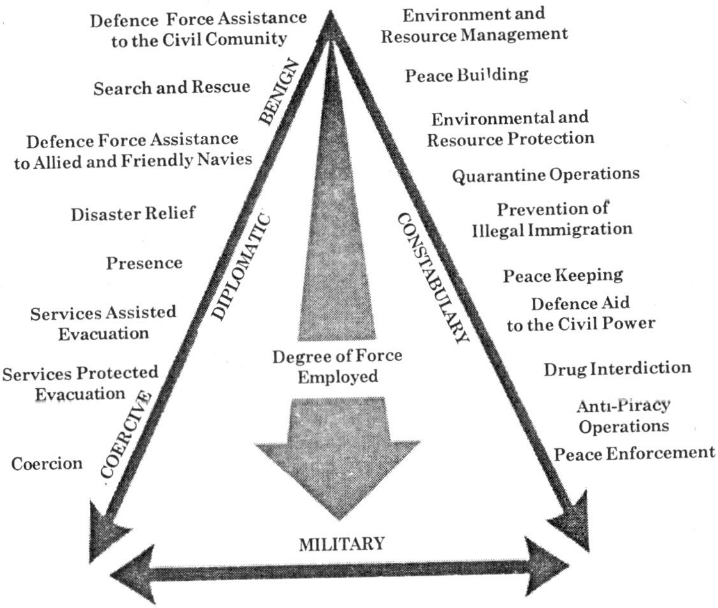

COMBAT OPERATIONS AT SEA

- Intelligence Collection and Surveillance
- Cover
- Against Shipping
- Maritime Strike
- Containment by Distraction
- Barrier Operations
- Layered Defence
- Advance Force Operations
- NCS

COMBAT OPERATIONS FROM THE SEA

- Maritime Mobility
- Land Strike
- Amphibious Operations
- Support to Operations on Land

The Scope of the Maritime Challenge

The importance given to the maritime power potential by policy makers can be easily understood when one examines the maritime challenges defined by the following parameters:-

a) Coast length of over 39,000 km

b) EEZ of 4mn Sq nm

c) Value of Australia's international sea freight: $200 billion (EX-IM)

d) Maritime trade tonnage: 600 million tonnes

e) Voyages to Australia by Foreign Vessels: 9000+

f) Registered Vessels: 2,500 Australian registered fishing vessels and 6,000 registered recreational vessels over 24 metres in length as at June 2003, as well as many thousands of smaller vessel

The value attached to the possession of a strong maritime force by Australia and the vindication of its stand was even more evident soon after the East Timor operations as highlighted by Maj General PJ Cosgrove AC, MC at a ANZAC lecture on 04 April 2000.

> Another military blinding glimpse of the obvious is the utility of sea power in the East Timor operation. The persuasive, intimidatory or deterrent nature of major warships was not to me as the combined joint force commander an incidental, nice to have 'add on' but an important indicator of national and international resolve and most reassuring to all of us who relied on sea lifelines.'

Environmental Protection: With increased maritime traffic, trade and activity at sea for off shore exploration there are greater challenges today than ever before in protecting the environment. Australia has also the responsibility of protecting the natural reef called the Great Barrier which has over 2000 kilometers of coral barrier. The grounding of coal carrier Shen Neng 1 (which was carrying 65,000 tons of coal and 950 tons of oil) on 03 April 2010 brought out the dangers to the fragile environment. Australia has realized that there is greater need for increased surveillance and stringent enforcement of laws in the surrounding seas under its control.

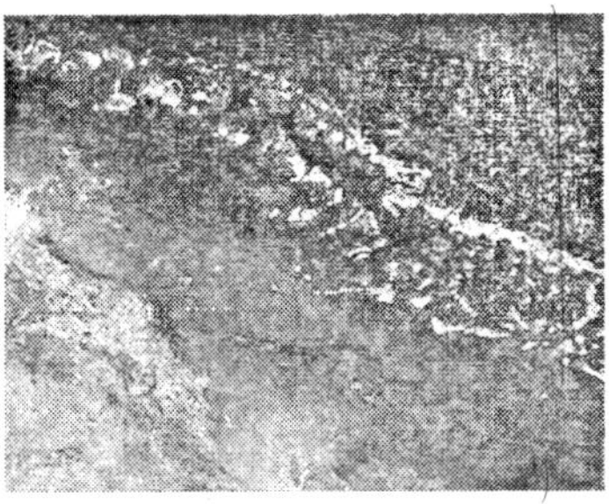

Coast Watch: The concept of engaging maritime security forces in the context of Australian maritime defence is unique in that, it uses private civilian agencies under the name of Coast Watch to undertake the tasks normally undertaken by the Coast Guard in other countries. The agency deploys aircraft and other craft to augment the tasks of the ADF.

Border Security: Historically, Australia encouraged many immigrants from many other countries around the world based on the political system that allowed refugees and asylum seekers. A very large number of Sri Lankan Tamils fled to Australia and have settled down.However, in many cases, the Sri Lankan Tamils also indulged in money laundering and other illegal activities.

Australia was compelled to announce that it will not accept claims of asylum by Tamils.

The Australian Government justified its change in policy after citing a report by the UNHCR stating that conditions in countries like Afghanistan and Sri Lanka were improving, making it safe for refugees to return. However, the Human Rights Watch in a letter to the Government said that this change in policy violated Australia's obligations under the 1951 Refugee Convention and the 1967 Protocol not to discriminate in the treatment of refugees.

Claims in Antarctica: Australia has claims over large tracts of Antarctica which is only recognized by UK, New Zealand and Norway. Japan does not recognise these claims in Antarctica. The race for claims by nations in both Arctica and Antarctica is hotting up with huge expectations of energy resources, mineral wealth and living sources.

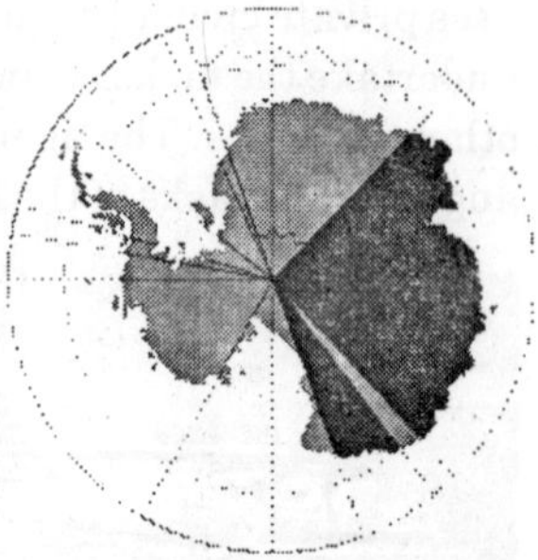

Sharing of maritime resources. There have also been issues of sharing the resources in disputed areas. While East Timor would have got just 18 percent of the gas/oil resources in the area till signing of the treaty on the day of independence of East Timor, post signing of the treaty on 20th May 2002, the resources are shared equally. Also the Timor Sea Treaty would run till 2057 for fifty years without entertaining any mutual claims. This new treaty replaced the earlier one known as the Timor Gap treaty signed in 1989 between Indonesia and Australia.

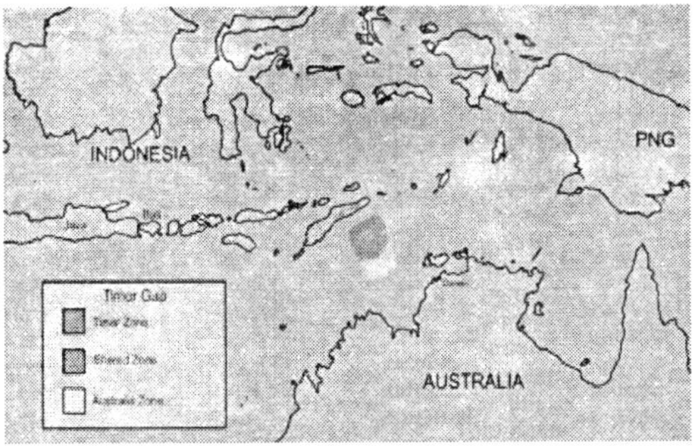

Milan. This paper is not complete without a mention of the initiative by India which was put in to effect in 1995. With all the reservations about India's naval expansion plans, Australia initially was not enthused by this initiative. With passage of time and with the change of perceptions about India, Australia also joined the initiative. What started as a meeting of the Navies from the region today has participation of over 13 navies including Australia. The biennial form of a regional meet at Port Blair in the Andaman and Nicobar group of Islands under the aegis of the Tri Services Commander (formerly Fortress Commander till the creation of the tri services command) has brought the maritime community together and has synergized their thought and action in many areas of cooperation.

Both India and Australia have come a long way since the acrimonious relations particularly after the Pokhran nuclear explosion in 1998. The officers who were undergoing defence courses in Australia were unceremoniously sent back. However, perceptions about India changed when it became evident that India was a responsible growing democracy and was not a hegemonic state as was believed earlier. The thawing of relations paved way for enhanced levels of interaction and engagement. Some of the statements made by both Australian and New Zealand naval officers reflect the sentiments and also indicate the way in which they want India to take centre stage in ensuring maritime safety in the Indian Ocean Region.

"Indian Ocean is your (India's) ocean. You need to man it. We are always looking for opportunity for joint exercises with Indian Navy, which is big in size,"

Commodore Ross Smith,
Maritime Component Commander, New Zealand

"Milan-2010 is a joint exercise. We are looking at a joint task force against piracy in the region in which all these nations can contribute."

CO of HMAS Glenelgs

Conclusion

Australia a country referred to as a continent down under is increasing its clout in the maritime arena both by trade and by its military growth. The country which is a vibrant democracy is also endowed with rich natural and mineral resources. The vastness of the continent imposes a heavy burden on the security services charged with the defence of the country. The nature of neighbourhood brings in additional responsibilities on Australia to maintain balance while simultaneously protecting its interests both in the Pacific and in the Asian context. Despite differences in approach, Australia would continue to ally itself with the US and the UK on most issues. The threat of jihadi terrorism from across the borders needs to be factored in the over all scheme of security preparedness. The maritime security is handled a little differently without a Coast Guard and also by commercial use of maritime power.

Australia has by and large cast aside its doubts about India. However, with the change of Government in Australia there is insistence on supplying the nuclear fuel, which is critical to India's energy needs, only to signatories of NPT. Regular enthusiastic participation in Milan at Port Blair has allayed fears of India's expansionist plans and has paved way for better understanding of each other's role and responsibilities in the Indian Ocean Region. India's leverage stems not just from the large number of students who contribute to the economy in the education sector but also due to the economic growth and its strategic importance in global affairs today.

Illegal entry would continue to challenge the authorities as many migrate to seek greener pastures in a prosperous country. Australian maritime forces would continue to keep their options open by participation in bilateral and multilateral exercises in different ocean areas. Exercises such as the Quadrilateral exercise in Bay of Bengal conducted in 2007 drew adverse reaction from China as it felt that this exercise was aimed at China. Notwithstanding such apprehensions, there is a greater need for these navies to work out contingencies for disaster mitigation and relief which is presently referred to as Humanitarian Assistance and Disaster Relief (HADR) operations.

There is commonality of purpose and intent between the two countries that needs to be nurtured. Areas of cooperation include Maritime Counter Terrorism (MCT), SAR and Marine Pollution Prevention (MPP). Enhanced regional initiatives in IOR to prevent foul play at sea that would promote the concept of safe seas. It is evident that the over all climate is conducive for constructive engagement to promote mutually beneficial initiatives.

10

US-Japan-Australia-India Quadrilateral Initiative: Opportunities and Challenges

S.Y. Surendra Kumar

One of the important debates in the 21st century is over the principal characteristic of international relations, whether it is a multipolar or nonpolar world. Many regard it to be multipolar world, where there are several distinct poles or concentrations of power like the United States (US), European Union (EU), Russia, China, India, Japan and so on. However, many like Richard Haass regard that international relations is turning out to be 'nonpolarity', i.e., "world dominated not by one or two or even several states but rather by dozens of actors possessing and exercising various kinds of power".[1] Some of the power centres are not necessarily Nation-States; it may be regional and global organisation, Non-Governmental Organisations (NGOs). In this context, one of the notable trends in multilateralism has been the emergence of various strategic groupings like G-20, G-4, Shanghai Cooperating Organisation (SCO), India-Brazil-South Africa (IBSA), Brazil-Russia-India-China (BRIC), and so on. Subsequently, there are many trilateral strategic dialogues like India-China-Russia, US-Japan-Australia, China-Japan-South Korea and so on attempting to achieve their strategic interest in the region and also to resolve the transnational issues. These trilateral initiatives in the process have given scope for quadrilateral initiatives like the US-Japan-Australia-India, which is yet to be formally institutionalised.

Quadrilateral Initiative

Generally, since 2000 the US, Japan, and Australia have pursued a formalized trilateral strategic grouping through frequent meetings of leaders and joint military exercises. For example, on the sidelines of Asia Pacific Economic Cooperation (APEC) summit in September 2007, leaders of the three countries reaffirmed the three-way strategic dialogue. Subsequently in October 2007 they carried out a joint naval exercise in the Pacific, west of Japan's Southern Kyushu Island that involved two destroyers and two P-3C anti-submarine patrol planes from Japan Maritime Self Defense Force (MSDF) and one P-3C patrol plane each from US Navy and Australian air force.[2] Against these developments, the then Japanese Prime Minister Shinzo Abe wanted to turn the trilateral security arrangements into quadrilateral with the inclusion of India.[3] This idea was also backed by the US Vice President Dick Cheney during his visit to Japan and Australia. In addition, the other base for backing this grouping was the formation of "Regional Core Group", by US-Japan-Australia-India to address the spearheaded relief work in the wake of the disaster caused by the Indian Ocean tsunami in December 2004. Thus, it was since argued that the four countries had successfully handled the Post-Tsunami crisis, they could very well concentrate on achieving shared strategic interest. As a result, in 2007 the idea of quadrilateral initiative emerged and in April 2007 the unpublicized first meeting took place at the rank of Assistant Secretary of four countries on the sidelines of ASEAN Regional Forum (ARF) in Manila.[4] Subsequently, the *Malabar 07* multilateral military exercise, which has traditionally been US-India bilateral exercise since 1994, was expanded to include Japan in April 2007 and was held off the coast of Okinawa. In September 2007, the second round of exercises also included Australia and Singapore. This five-nation exercise was held in Bay of Bengal, India featuring over 20,000 personnel, 28 ships, 150 aircraft, and 3 aircraft carriers.[5] All these developments indicated the possibility of a formal establishment of quadrilateral initiative; however, the initiative was yet to take off due to lukewarm and ambiguous response from India, Japan and Australia. Before understanding the reasons for quadrilateral initiative not taking off, it is important to examine the need for quadrilateral forum in the existing world order.

The Need for Quadrilateral Initiative

Asia-Pacific region is strategically very important to the US, Japan, Australia, India and also to China, as this region contains half of the world's population, six of world's ten largest countries, a substantial share of the world's savings pool, two of the most urgent cases of nuclear proliferation (North Korea and Pakistan) and the world's three most populous Muslim states (Indonesia, Pakistan and India); and it increasingly dominates America's and China's politics of trade.[6] Thus, the Asia-Pacific is of vital strategic interest to big and emerging powers. Apart from this, there are other reasons for forming the quadrilateral groupings such as:

Shared Values

The US-Japan-Australia-India are democratic countries sharing common values, like freedom, respect for human rights and rule of law, to they are committed. Thus, the quadrilateral forum can focus on promoting peace, democracy, counterterrorism, economic freedom, development and provision of humanitarian and disaster assistance in the Asia-Pacific region. Moreover, this alliance would go a long way in addressing the main irritants in the bilateral relations of the four countries.

Shared Security Objectives

This quadrilateral alliance would facilitate in addressing the shared security objectives in the region like rivalry between China and Japan, tension between India and China; North Korea's nuclear program; tension in Taiwan Straits; increasing competition for energy resources; instability and unrest in Myanmar and Thailand; and security challenges resulting from climate change. The region also threatened by sea piracy, terrorism, drug and material trafficking, illegal movement of persons and weapons of mass destruction, particularly in the maritime waters around Southeast Asia. Moreover, Indian Ocean has the busiest trade routes through which oil and gas is supplied across the globe, and the Malacca Straits, alone accounts for more than 25 per cent of world's maritime trade and terrorist groups like the Abu Sayyaf, the Jemaah Islamiya and Laskare-e-Jihad have reportedly planned terrorist attacks to disrupt the global supply chain system.[7] Although, Japan has advocated 'Naval Ocean Peacekeeping Force, India and other Southeast Asian countries have conducted frequent joint naval exercises. Subsequently, many countries have welcomed the formation of Regional Cooperation Agreement on Combating Piracy and Armed Robbery against Ships in Asia (ReCCAP). However, the quadrilateral initiatives can put in place collective and effective maritime cooperative security to protect the Indian and Pacific Oceans.

Rise of China

The international security environment is witnessing a power shift from the West to Asia, led by the rapid rise of China and India. More than India's rise, it is the rise of China which is a major source of concern for US, Japan Australia and also for India. Although, this concern has not been expressed formally by these countries however, their trilateral strategic dialogue and the quadrilateral efforts obviously indicate the increasing threat from China. For instance, China has successfully intensified its engagements in the Asia-Pacific region through trade and economic integration, particularly with Free Trade Agreement (FTA). China's strong diplomatic initiatives manifested in EAS, ASEAN+3 and the SCO is an attempt to develop an alternative security group to America's security partnerships in the region. Moreover, to address its energy security needs it has established a substantial naval presence along vital maritime chokepoints[8], popularly known as China's 'String of Pearls", a plan to acquire several strategically placed ports, naval bases and listening posts in friendly countries like Pakistan (Gwadar), Sri Lanka (Hambantota), Myanmar

(Sittwe) and Bangladesh (Chittagong) to protect the billions of dollars worth trade that pass through strategic sea lanes such as the Straits of Hormuz or the Malacca Straits to Middle East, Africa and Latin America.[9] The 'String of Pearls' also allows China to access several preferential resources and a market access at highly subsidized terms.[10]

This strategy does not have any parallel strategies either by the US, Japan or any power. Thus the rise of China remains a major concern for quadrilateral grouping. This concern was raised by the US Deputy Secretary of State Robert Zoellick in 2005 affirming that "US was in fact hedging against China by enhancing its diplomatic and military ties with Japan and especially with India". Furthermore, even the Australia's Defence White Paper, released in May 2009, indicated China's increasing military power and its assertiveness in Asia-Pacific region as a primary factor in Australia's future defence plans.[11] Hence, China's increasing economic, diplomatic and military power compelled countries like the US, India, Japan and Australia to rethink on the existing security arrangements and take initial steps that may lead to the formation of regional groups of nations with common interest and values.

Regional forums not Effective

Although, it argued that there are regional initiatives such as ARF, EAS and APEC forums, through which the four countries can achieve their strategic goals, however, these forums are too large and unwieldy to bear enduring results by themselves. Moreover, the APEC has focused mainly on trade liberalisation, while the ARF has dealt with confidence-building measures and preventive diplomacy, the ASEAN+3 and EAS processes overlap in membership and their explicit roles have yet to be clearly defined. This was also articulated by Australian Prime Minister Kevin Rudd while advocating the formation of "Asia-Pacific Community" (APC). He argued that "none of the existing regional mechanisms as currently configured were capable of engaging in the full spectrum of dialogue, cooperation and action on economic and political matters and future challenges to security".[12] However, there were mixed reactions from the countries towards APC. Thus, a smaller initiative like the quadrilateral involving important powers would go a long way in achieving the strategic interests of countries in Asia-Pacific region.

The Challenges

Although, there is a need for quadrilateral alliance to address the Asia-Pacific security concerns, but it is still not formally institutionalised for multiple reasons.

Lack of Unanimity

During the initial period, the US, Australia and Japan were very keen on the formation of quadrilateral alliance; however, due to India's reluctant in joining this group and change of regime in thc US (2008) and particularly in Australia and Japan (2007), the new governments were more inclined to view such democratic coalitions as too provocative and unproductive in an Asia-Pacific security context.

US: From pro-active to soft peddling

Bush administration was pro-active in forming trilateral and even quadrilateral security arrangements to achieve the US strategic interest in the Asia-Pacific region. The main objectives for grouping included: preventing dominance of Asia by any single power or a coalition of powers like China or its allies; continue to maintain system of alliance to facilitate the projection of American power; securing sea lanes of communication to facilitate American commercial access and the free flow of trade in the region.; and to promote American values such as democracy, and extend humanitarian and disaster assistances.[13] In addition, President Bush in September 2007 proposed the creation of "Asia-Pacific Democracy Partnership" to promote democratic values and strengthen democratic institutions in the region. Thus, with this strategic interest President Bush advocated that the US interests would be better served by partnering with the nations of the region, like Japan, Australia and India that share common values.

However, due to lukewarm response from the three nations, the quadrilateral imitative during Bush administration did not take off. Although, Obama administration has argued that "more effective framework in Asia is needed that goes beyond bilateral agreements, occasional summits, and ad hoc arrangements, underscored this new policy orientation." However, President Obama, so far has not given enough indication on taking this quadrilateral idea forward. Moreover, President Obama is well aware that it needs China's support to steer the global governance process and resolve transnational issues.[14] Thus, it is unlikely that President Obama would advocate the formal setting up of quadrilateral alliance in near future.

Australia: From Quadrilateral to Asia-Pacific Community

Initially, Australian Prime Minister John Howard, along with the US and Japan overwhelmingly supported the idea of forming quadrilateral grouping with the inclusion of India. However, November 2007 elections was big setback to Howard administration, as his party lost the election and even he lost his own parliamentary seat from Bennelong. Thus, the election paved way for Labour Party leader Kevin Rudd to become the Prime Minister, who was not keen on taking the quadrilateral grouping forward. The reason for this response was the unpopularity of Bush administration in Australia due to unilateral policies, including in Iraq. It was also the verdict against Howard administration's overwhelming support to US policies such as deployment of specialist Australian Defence Force (ADF) in Afghanistan (2001) and Iraq (2003); support to controversial US National Missile Defence system (NMD); and opposing Kyoto Protocol.[15]

As a result, Kevin administration did not give any priority to quadrilateral grouping. At the same time, Australia did not want to antagonise China, the former is benefiting from exports and is seeking a Free Trade Agreement (FTA) with latter and feels it is in the interest of Australia to engage with China rather than to confront. This was also affirmed by the Australian Minister for

Defence Brendon Nelson in July 2007: "We do not wish to have formal quadrilateral strategic dialogue in defence and security matters... we do not want to do anything which... may otherwise cause concern in the region, principally China".[16]

Apart from this, Prime Minister Kevin, without appearing to be simply an American ally in the region was working to develop Australia's independent ties with Asian powers like China, India, Japan, Singapore and others. Interestingly, in June 2008 he even proposed the idea of 'Asia-Pacific Community"(APC).[17] This proposal is inclusive arrangements with all the countries including big powers like the US, Japan, India and Indonesia which are involved in evolving regional architecture of Asia. The APC was principally aimed at overcoming the compartmentalisation of existing regional institutions, creating an effective leadership, political, economic and security issues could be dealt with holistically rather than piecemeal. However, so far there is little regional backing for the creation of a new regional institution. Thus, Kevin administration was very unlikely to back quadrilateral groupings, at this juncture with the forthcoming federal elections.

Japan: Pro-active to lukewarm

Although, Prime Minister Abe was instrumental in forming the quadrilateral alliance, with his departure from the office, the successive Prime Ministers maintained restraint towards the alliance, due to domestic compulsions like the growing public pacifist sentiments towards Japan's overwhelming support to the unilateral policies of the US in Afghanistan and Iraq. Moreover, successive governments have worked on strengthening relations with China. Even the present Prime Minister Yukio Hatoyama has emphasised greater willingness to engage Beijing and rest of Asia to achieve Japan's strategic interest in the Asia-Pacific region. He is also keen on promoting the concept of East Asia Community (EAC), without US, which would please China. Moreover, Japan is well aware that its economic future is increasingly tied to China, as latter has already surpassed the US as its largest trading partner.[18] Thus, with Japan keen on promoting good relations with China the quadrilateral grouping has taken a back seat.

India: Principle acceptance to Non-committal

India shares many common values and strategic interest with the US, Japan and Australia. India is also concerned about China's increasing economic and military strength and its influence in the Asia-Pacific region in general and particularly in the South Asian region. However, from the beginning it has shown less interest in joining the quadrilateral group, due stiff opposition within India from the leftists and rightist parties for fear of India becoming the US 'Asian Israel", through joining any defence grouping with US. Moreover, India did not intend to "choose sides" and opposed any formal regional defense alliance, which target's China. India also, like Australia and Japan, was keen on strengthening its relations with China rather than antagonising Beijing. Thus, instead of joining this grouping India focussed on strengthening bilateral relations with the three countries through the Indo-US strategic partnership, India-Japan Action Plan 2009, Australia-India joint declaration on security cooperation signed in November 2009. Overall, India is balancing its approach and has been lukewarm in its response to quadrilateral initiative.

China's Unease

China has always expressed its displeasure towards the quadrilateral grouping, for example, in response to the May 2007 first informal meeting between the four in Manila, China's Foreign Affairs department sought clarification from each country as to what were the motives of floating such an idea. Following, the September 2007 Malabar naval exercise, China issued a formal diplomatic protest to Australia, India and Japan on forming a security alliance with the US against China. China also view this developments as a symbol of their potential inclination to contain China's expanding naval and military cooperation with Bangladesh, Myanmar and Sri Lanka in South Asia in general and in particular to send a clear signal to Beijing that the Malabar participants were ready and capable to balance rising Chinese offshore power if they perceived the need to do so.[19] Many of the Chinese analysts even dubbed the quadrilateral group as "Asian NATO", "Asian Arc of democracy" and US attempting to build anti-China axis in Asia.[20] Even Russia also conveyed its concerns saying Asia should avoid "exclusive groupings".[21] Thus, due to the stiff opposition from China and other nations, the quadrilateral initiative was put on hold.

Concluding Observations

There is a need for Quadrilateral grouping, since it can be a new initiative intended to shape a new international balance in response to the ongoing power shifts to Asia. It should not just be a security bloc, rather it should evolve common thinking on shared concern and values for the region. Moreover, the alliance should not contain an explicit element of containment [China] as this would be counterproductive for building the Asia-Pacific regional order and also would curtail the strategic interest of four countries in the long run. At the same time, this grouping should not duplicate the multilateral arrangements that already exist in the region like the ASEAN, EAS, APEC.

Apart from this, US should encourage the involvement of India, Japan and Australia in forming the alliance by convincing them the benefits of reviving and elevating a quad focussing on promoting democracy, counterterrorism, energy, maritime cooperation, economic and security issues in Asia. Moreover, through this grouping US could achieve its strategic interest in the Asia-Pacific region. At the same time, Japan and Australia instead of promoting EAC and APC respectively, which has little or no regional backing, should realise that their strategic interest would be met through Quadrilateral alliance.

India should better understand the strategic outlook of the US, Japan and Australia and then join the grouping if it happens in near future. India can use the Quadrilateral grouping to resolve some of the outstanding issues with the three countries. Although, India has always kept its strategic options open rather than avoiding being tied down in an alliance with any major power like the US. If India can join SCO to meet its energy requirement and achieve its strategic interests in Central Asian region, New Delhi should not shy away from joining the group to strengthen its influence in the Asia-Pacific region and also to curtail growing Chinese influence in the region.

In a nutshell, there is a need for quadrilateral alliance, although as of now it is on hold. However, it remains to be seen if geopolitical forces will push the arrangement forward.

NOTES

1. Richard N. Haass, "The Age of Nonpolarity: What will follow US Dominance", *Foreign Affairs,* Vol.87, No.3, May/June 2008, p.44.
2. Emma Chanlett-Avery and Bruce Vaughn, "Emerging trends in the Security Architecture in Asia: Bilateral and Multilateral ties among the US, Japan, Australia, and India", *CRS Report for Congress,* 7 January 2008, p.12.
3. Prime Minister Shinzo Abe had proposed the 'quad' idea in his book, *Toward a Beautiful Country*, published in July 2006. In this book he emphasized the strengthening of Japan-India relations. Brahma Chellaney, "The US-India-Japan-Australia Quadrilateral Initiative", *The Asian Age,* 2 June 2007.
4. *Ibid.*
5. Kitty Hawk, "Allies Complete Malabar Exercise", *US Navy Press Release,* 10 September 2007.
6. Armacost, Michael H. And Stapleton Roy, J. "American Overview: Asian Policy Challenges for the Next President", in *America's role in Asia: Asian and American views* (San Francisco: The Asia Foundation, San Francisco), pp. 73-100.
7. Satyajit Mohanty, " Indo-Japan relations and the Asian Security System", 25 July 2007. Available at www.ipcs.org/article/india/indo-japan-relations-and-the-asian-security-system-2340.html
8. Iskander Rehman, "Keeping the Dragon at Bay: India's counter-containment of China in Asia", *Asian Security,* Vol.5, No.2, 2009, p.122.
9. Lawrence S Prabhakar, "China's String of Pearls in Southern Asia-Indian Ocean: Implication for India and Taiwan" in M.J. Vinod, Yeong-Kuang Ger and S.Y. Surendra Kumar, *Security challenges in the Asia-Pacific Region* (New Delhi: Viva Books, 2009), p.44. Walter Ladwig III, " Delhi's pacific ambition: Naval Power, look east and

India's Emerging influence in the Asia Pacific", *Asian Security*, Vol.5 No.2, 2009, 87-113.

10 Kimberley Layton, " India-Australia ties: Times for more than Cricket", 22 April 2009, available at www.ipcs.org/article/india-the-world/india-australia-ties-time-for-more-than-cricket-2850.html also Rahula Mishra, " Australia's Force 20230 and India", June 2009, available at www.ipcs.org/article/india-the-world/australia8217s-force-2030-and-india-2881.html

11. *Ibid.*

12. Carlyle A. Thayer, "Kevin Rudd's multi-layered Asia Pacific Community initiative", June 22nd, 2009, available at www.eastasiaforum.org/2009/06/22/kevin-rudds-multi-layered-asia-pacific-community-initiative.

13. *CRS Report for Congress,* n. 2, p.2.

14. David M Lampton, "The US and China in the age of Obama: Looking each other Straight in the Eyes", *Journal of Contemporary China,* Vol. 18, No. 62 November 2009, pp. 703-727. Barack Obama, "Renewing American leadership", *Foreign Affairs, Vol.* 86, No. 4, 2007, p.12. William Tow and Beverley Loke, "Rules of engagement: American's Asia-Pacific Security Policy under an Obama Administration", *Australian Journal of International Affairs,* Vol. 64, No. 4, December 2009, pp. 443-457.

15. Purnendra Jain, "Japan-Australia security ties and the US: the Evolution of the Trilateral Dialogue Process and its Challenges," *Australian Journal of International Affairs,* Vol. 60, No. 4, December 2006, pp. 521-535.

16. Brendan Nelson, "There is nothing but Goodwill towards India", *The Hindu,* 23 July 2007, p. 11.

17. Bruce Vaughn, *Australia: Background and US Relations, CRS Report for Congress,* 8 August 2008, p. 15.

18. Martin Fackler, "US frets as Japan inches closer to China", *Deccan Herald,* 24 Feb 2010, p.11.

19. Xia, Liping," Ex Malabar: China not keen on a "Democratic" Alliance. *Opinion Asia,* 18 September 2007, available at www.opinionasia.com/Chinanotkeenonademocraticalliance

20. Iskander Rehaman, n. 8, p. 128.

21. Siddharth Varadarajan, "India, Japan say new Security ties not directed against China", *The Hindu,* 23 October 2008, p.10.

11

India, Australia and the ASEAN-driven Multilateralism: Negotiating a Common Agenda

Vibhanshu Shekhar

Introduction

An important pan-Asia-Pacific development reinforcing India-Australia relations is a trend towards institution-building and growth of ASEAN-driven regional and supra-regional multilateralism to identify and address areas of common concern, facilitate cooperation among member states and ensure peace and stability in the region. Both India and Australia have proved to be important stakeholders and contributors to the ASEAN-driven multilateralism in the Asia-Pacific. Three such regional frameworks are the ASEAN Regional Forum (ARF), East Asia Summit (EAS) and ASEAN Plus Defence Ministerial Meeting (ADMM+). The India-Australia Security Cooperation agreement emphasizes 'their common purpose in working together, and with other countries including through such regional fora as the East Asia Summit and ASEAN Regional Forum to achieve the objective of a prosperous, open and secure Asia'.

There are three important developments that have driven India and Australia to work together while participating in these multilateral institutions. First, fundamental changes have taken place in the politico-strategic landscape of the Asia-Pacific, effecting change in the nature and outlook of these institutions. Second, both these countries have, over the years, attached greater importance to the ASEAN cooperative frameworks, highlighting growing significance of these institutions in the politico-strategic calculations of member-states. Finally, the two countries have also realised the strategic necessity of working together in these institutions as they offer only hope for their multilateral engagement with East Asia.

In the light of these developments and growing strategic engagement between India and Australia, the paper deals with the following themes:

- evolving dimensions of the ASEAN-driven multilateral institutions;
- shared experiences of the two countries; and
- Potential areas of India-Australia cooperation within multilateral forums.

Understanding ASEAN-driven Multilateralism

Ever since ASEAN's formation in August 1967, its fundamental objectives have remained the same even though the number, scale and geographical canvas of operations has transformed significantly during the last four decades. First, ASEAN was meant to facilitate cooperation among the member states and after four decades of existence, it has emerged as the most efficient forum of cooperation within the non-developed world. Today, different countries and important global players deliberate over different issues of global and regional concerns in a number of official, ministerial or summit level meetings conducted periodically.

Second, ASEAN was formed as a conflict management initiative and remains so till today. What distinguishes today's ASEAN from its Cold War version is that the Association has undergone considerable expansion in terms of its zone and scale of operations. During the Cold War era, ASEAN was trying to manage conflicts between member-states and within Southeast Asia. Today, ASEAN is mandated to deliberate over any conflict or security-related issues occurring within the geopolitics of the Asia-Pacific. ASEAN Regional Forum has remained the main platform for doing so since 1995. Since 2005, East Asia Summit has also emerged as a summit-level platform discussing primarily non-traditional security issues – energy security, financial security, environmental security or climate change. Finally, ASEAN remains a grouping led by small powers and this often gets exhibited in its decisions and more so in the implementation of decisions. In other words, ASEAN continues to remain vulnerable to big-power domination and concomitant rivalries, especially when the stakeholders begin to push forth their strategic interests.

Notwithstanding these continuous threads, there are some structural shifts that have taken place in the region, leading to change in the priorities and responses of ASEAN. First and foremost, the nature of interactions has become much more complex, warranting a nuanced approach on behalf of ASEAN. For example, while ASEAN shares territorial disputes with China, the latter is the largest trading partner of the former. As China's power grows, the asymmetry of power in China-ASEAN relations grows wider, rendering ASEAN institutions vulnerable to the growing Chinese dominance. ASEAN has responded to China's rise by (a) involving other great powers in the management of regional affairs and (b) institutionalising great power relations through the ADMs, making them follow the rules of the game being decided unanimously under the ASEAN process. As ASEAN embarks on engaging the major players (China, India, Japan, Russia, USA), it has begun experiencing the heat of great power rivalries. The stakeholders can not just wait and watch the situation unfold. They have to play a more proactive role if they want ASEAN to serve their interests. Given the process of greater economic integration, the idea of collective vulnerability is taking deeper roots, again demanding collective responses that can be a complex process. Second, the body has seen sustained strategic withdrawal of the US, which tries to deal with ASEAN through its allies and other like-minded countries. Third, the region has witnessed the rise of two continental players, with the possibility of eclipsing ASEAN.

The nature and dynamics of ASEAN-driven multilateralism is an outcome of the above-mentioned continuities and changes. There are two important ASEAN-driven multilateral forums – ASEAN Regional Forum (ARF) and East Asia Summit - in which India and Australia have been participating together for several years now. Before discussing the overall contours of the participation of India and Australia in the ASEAN-driven multilateralism in these two forums, it is important to give a brief idea as to how these two bodies function. Since October 2010, India and Australia have shared another ASEAN platform – ADMM+ (ASEAN Plus Defence Ministerial Meetings). While EAS involves the participation of heads of the state, ARF engages Ministers of foreign relations; ADMM+ engages participation at the level of ministers of defence.

ASEAN Regional Forum

The ARF comprises 26 member states, from the South, Southeast and Northeast Asia as well as important players of the South and the Western Pacific.[1] Therefore, the ARF is larger and more diverse than ASEAN, encompassing divergent security approaches and threat perceptions. The geographical canvas of the ARF stretches from the Indian Ocean to the Pacific Ocean. The deliberations at the ARF have occurred at two levels – track-I (Ministerial Meetings) and track-II (Council for Security Cooperation in the Asia-Pacific).

The genesis of the ARF lies in the efforts to engage the regional powers, especially China, Japan and India, by making them stakeholders in regional security deliberations. The diminishing presence of the superpowers in Southeast Asia during the Post-Cold War era created a power vacuum that was filled by the regional powers, whose inter-relationships were equally hostile, such as the Sino-Japanese or Sino-Indian relations. The inclusion of regional players with their inimical equations in the ARF aimed at moderating the aggressive posturing of the big players by bringing them into the dialogue process. This simultaneously strengthened the strategic capacity of ASEAN to respond to the unilateral and confrontational approach of any power in the region.[2]

The ARF has emerged, over the years, as the sole cooperative framework to deliberate over common security issues in the Asia-Pacific. Though the grouping is mandated to discuss both traditional and non-traditional security issues, its normative and functional compulsions have confined its effective deliberations to the non-traditional security issues. The traditional security issues – North Korea, South China Sea have received nominal attention from the grouping. Moreover, the ARF deliberations, by and large, have remained at the preliminary level of Confidence Building Measures (CBMs), highlighting serious limitations in the functioning of the organisation. The failure of the ARF in taking the security deliberations to the next level of preventive diplomacy has occurred due to limitations imposed by the principle of ASEAN Way, the inviolability of state sovereignty closely related to security deliberations, long-standing strategic rivalries and mistrust among the member-states.

East Asia Summit (EAS)

Testifying to the changing contours of politico-strategic and economic engagement in the Asia-Pacific, the EAS has opened the prospect for wide-ranging politico-strategic and economic cooperation with the countries of Asia-Pacific at the highest political level. The EAS is deliberating the feasibility of a Comprehensive Economic Partnership in East Asia, proposed by Japan. The Expert Group has already submitted its report regarding the feasibility of the CEPEA at the third East Asia Summit, held in Singapore in November 2007. In furtherance of the process of economic integration, the EAS has formed the Economic Research Institute for ASEAN and East Asia (ERIA) in June 2008. The ERIA will concentrate on two structures of economic integration – the ASEAN Economic Community by 2015 and the East Asia Community. Thus, the institute will be able to facilitate the creation of what Surin Pitsuwan, the Secretary General of ASEAN, calls "the world's largest business space in a vibrant and more integrated East Asia."[3]

Energy security has emerged as an important agenda of cooperation at the EAS, and an area of strategic importance for India. During its second summit at Cebu, the Philippines, in January 2007, the EAS adopted a declaration on energy security with the objectives of increasing energy efficiency, mitigating greenhouse gas, reducing dependence on fossil fuels, and guaranteeing stable energy supply. The EAS has constituted three "Work Streams," addressing different aspects of multilateral cooperation on energy security. While Japan, Malaysia, and Thailand are piloting studies on energy efficiency and conservation, the Philippines and India have undertaken studies on the evaluation of the bio-fuel sector, and Singapore and Australia have investigated energy market integration within the EAS region.[4]

Besides economic integration and energy security, other issues such as climate change and revival of historical and cultural linkages have also figured prominently on the agenda of the EAS. The EAS member states have already agreed to facilitate the revival of the old Buddhist Nalanda University in the state of Bihar in India.

The EAS, since its inception, has found itself into the vortex of much more complex multilateral interrelationships with new players and their diverse priorities. The grouping has seen strong power posturing from two important global players – China and Japan with the potential consequence of polarizing Southeast and East Asian countries between those supporting the ASEAN+3 cooperative framework and those supporting the EAS framework. China, Malaysia, and Thailand seem to favour the former, while Japan, Singapore, Vietnam and Indonesia seem to prefer the latter process. On the eve of the fourth summit, China proposed dividing EAS members into core and secondary categories, and Chinese and Korean leaders refused to hold bilateral or trilateral talks with their Japanese counterparts.

The ascendancy of the ASEAN+3 framework may exclude non-East Asian countries – India, Australia and New Zealand from the process of East Asian economic integration and jeopardize their economic interests in East Asia. Therefore, the imminent challenge facing the supra-regional posturing of the Look East Policy is how to ensure the continued cooperation under the EAS. While the best possible option for India seems to be a multi-faceted approach of sustained engagement, multilateral activism and agenda-implementation at the EAS, the question arises as to whether the LEP has an appropriate policy framework or the requisite mechanisms to address the emerging complexity of engagement, as the frames of reference expand and given the strategic importance of the East Asian players in Asia. The LEP also needs to develop a viable agenda for cooperation involving all the member states of the EAS without antagonizing any member country, with an obvious reference to China.

ASEAN+ Defence Ministerial Meetings (ADMM+)

The representatives of 10 ASEAN countries and 8 major players in the Asia-Pacific – Australia, China, India, Japan, New Zealand, Russia, South Korea and USA – got together in Hanoi on 12 October 2010 in their bid to develop a regional architecture for an institutionalised and meaningful dialogue over security challenges. These countries were participating as members of ASEAN Plus Defence Ministerial Meeting (ADMM+), an ASEAN-driven newly-floated security initiative that met for the first time on 12 October 2010 in Hanoi. The forum follows the pattern of ASEAN's annual Defence Ministerial Meetings (ADMM), functioning since 2006.

The member states adopted a Joint Declaration, outlined areas of cooperation and came up with tentative proposals to work on. The thrust of the declaration remained on identifying important security threats rather than devising ways and means to combat them. In other words, the first meeting focused on creating a cooperative atmosphere and developing a consensus on prevailing security challenges with the objective of addressing them. However, no such mechanism could be discussed, indicating a similar pattern of gradual and contested evolution that another ASEAN security forum – an overly institutionalised and over-crowded ASEAN Regional Forum – has experienced. While the US identified maritime security and piracy as important security challenges, China laid stress on humanitarian aid and natural disasters and proposed to jointly chair with Vietnam an Expert Working Group to address the issues of humanitarian aid and natural disasters. India remained content with its call for peace and stability in the region.

The initiative is expected to be an emphatic diplomatic statement and an important face-saving exercise for the ASEAN-driven cooperative processes, which, otherwise, is giving way to an evolving spectre of great power politics, bilateral strategic partnerships, hedge formation, and growing clamour for strategic influence. The number of strategic partnerships has gone up considerably during the last five years. India alone has signed at least six bilateral strategic partnerships since 2005 – Australia, China, Indonesia, Japan, South Korea and Vietnam. Similarly, Indonesia has signed strategic partnerships with Australia, China, India, Japan, and USA. In this context, the ADMM+ appears a desperate ASEAN effort to salvage its role as a facilitator of regional security dialogue.

Before we discuss the evolving nature of relations in today's context, it is pertinent to examine and analyse as to how these two countries have interacted with ASEAN in the past. The inter-relationships can be discussed in terms of rationale for participation, long-term objectives, strategies of participation, and overall contours of their engagement with the ADMs.

India and Australia within ADMs: Drivers of Early Engagement

Australia became ASEAN's dialogue partner in 1974 and also is the first dialogue partner of ASEAN. Therefore, the two sides share the longest time-span of engagement. In contrast, India became ASEAN's full dialogue partner only in 1995. While Australia is the founding member of the ASEAN Regional Forum, India joined the forum in 1996, after two years of its formation.

While Australia's association with the ADM dates to Cold War strategic realities, India's association could be possible only after the dismantling of the Cold War alignment. India has viewed ASEAN as a launching pad for its diplomatic overtures in the eastern Asian hemisphere; Australia does not seem to attribute similar level of importance to ASEAN. Similarly, Australia also seems to have lost its economic importance more so after the rise of economic powerhouses like China and India. To quote John Ravenhill "...Australia's relative economic importance to the region – as a market, a source of investment or a source of development assistance – has declined significantly."[5]

The rationale for Australia's participation in the ADM has come from prevailing Cold War strategic alignment, in which both Australia and ASEAN found favours from similar mentor – USA. Moreover, Australia has viewed Southeast Asia of considerable strategic importance and any major negative change in the region can compromise Australia's security. In other words, Australia's strategic priorities for participation in the ADM emanates from its perceived external vulnerability. Similar perception has been reinforced with the rise of terrorism in the Muslim-majority country of Indonesia.

Table 1
Comparing Experiences of India and Australia

Issue Areas	*Australia*	*India*
Rationale	Cold-war Strategic Equations SEA very important for Australia's security economics an important driving force in the Post-Cold War era	stagnant South Asian regionalism; domestic economic challenges; and changed politico-strategic landscape in the aftermath of the Cold War.
Patterns of Security Engagement	ARF is the main forum NTS as the key issue area	ARF is the main forum NTS as the key issue area an

(Contd...)

Issue Areas	Australia	India
	troubled nature of engagement Thrust on maritime security and terrorism (after Bali bomb blast)	overly cautious approach. Thrust towards terrorism and maritime security
Methods and Strategies of Engagement	US-hyphenated and Western-alliance centric Howard Era – stress on bilateralism	ASEAN-centric Simultaneous pursuit of bilateral and multilateral approach
ASEAN's Perceptions of of India and Australia	A Western nation. An advanced economy and a US ally. An important source of external financial assistance	An Asian country with strong historical-cultural linkages. A'balancer' and an important player in the region. A huge market

Economic integration seems to be another important driving force of engagement with the ADM. While celebrating thirty years of ASEAN-Australia relations, the then Australian Foreign Minister, Alexander Downer identified economic/development cooperation as the basis of ASEAN-Australia relations. Moreover, the Australia-ASEAN economic relations have grown independent of the former's relations with the United States.[6] ASEAN is Australia's second largest trading partner and fourth largest export market. Australia's total bilateral trade in goods with ASEAN was more than AU$88 billion in 2008, with the volume of trade being bigger than Australia's bilateral trade with Japan, China or the United States.[7] The two sides have signed the Free Trade Agreement in February 2009 and this is the largest FTA Australia has ever signed. The agreement allows free trade not only in goods but also in services and investment.

The rationale for India's participation in the ADM comes from three sources – stagnation in South Asian regionalism and consequent desperation to wriggle out of moribund regionalism, domestic economic challenges and changed politico-strategic landscape in the aftermath of the Cold War. In the realm of economic cooperation, ADM has been seen as a means for India's larger interest in being a part of East Asian Economic Community. The logic of mutually beneficial economic cooperation pushed both the sides towards greater economic cooperation, which forms the most powerful driving force of the LEP. While ASEAN offered India a model for economic growth and a platform for engagement with the market economies of East Asia, the latter offered the former a vast opening market. To quote I K Gujral, who represented India's first participation in the ASEAN-PMC, "the minds of foreign ministers participating in the ASEAN-PMC meetings were riveted on the 250-300 million-strong Indian consumers and the attainment of seven per cent growth in 1995-96."[8] India has signed Comprehensive Economic Cooperation Agreement with ASEAN in August 2009. India-ASEAN bilateral trade stood at US$45 billion in 2008-09. In strategic terms, India aims at developing constituencies in the ASEAN region to protect its strategic interests and project its image as a benign power in the Asia-Pacific.

India and Australia Find Common Grounds in the 21st Century

The ADMs have provided India and Australia avenues to engage bilaterally, develop a shared understanding about the prevailing politico-strategic landscape in the Asia-Pacific, work together to strengthen these institutions, and push forth a meaningful agenda for cooperation among the member states. The track-I and track-II meetings of the ARF have enabled India and Australia to negotiate a common security agenda for multilateral deliberation concerning the entire region. While the ARF has offered an avenue for joint discussion primarily over non-traditional security issues, the EAS has facilitated joint deliberation at the highest level over the issues of economic integration, developing ways and means to overcome the 2008 global economic crisis, and evolving a common approach to issues of energy security and climate change. On the other hand, the ADMM+ provides a platform for the member states to share their security concerns and outline a common security agenda.

At the same time, these institutions have, of late, come under pressure from big-power rivalries and sustained Chinese diplomatic maneuverings to gain influence over the functioning and agenda of ASEAN-driven institutions. Given their high stakes in these cooperative frameworks, it is imperative that both India and Australia ensure (a) continued relevance and functioning of these institutions and (b) their independent and impartial performance. The Hanoi Declaration issued on the occasion of the commemoration of the fifth anniversary of the EAS of October 2010 reiterated "commitment to the principles, objectives and modalities of the EAS as established in the 2005 Kuala Lumpur Declaration, and continued support for ASEAN's central role in the EAS, including in developing, in close consultation with other EAS participants, the EAS agenda and priorities."[9]

Notwithstanding their divergent strategic priorities in the past, there has developed a common understanding between the two countries about the primacy of non-traditional security challenges threatening their maritime spaces and Sea-Lanes of Communications (SLOCs). The two countries have also been working towards developing a common understanding over the issues of climate change, disaster management, regional security and governance. The 2009 Joint Statement on India-Australia Foreign Ministers Framework Dialogue stressed upon the strategic necessity of joint efforts towards regional cooperation including under the aegis of the EAS (Joint Statement 2009). The idea of Comprehensive Economic Partnership in East Asia (CEPEA), under the EAS deliberation, promises to integrate the Indian and Australian economies. With the growing redundancy of the APEC and India's continued absence from its membership, the EAS offers the only avenue for both India and Australia to deliberate at the highest level with the East Asian countries (including Southeast and Northeast Asian) over the issues of security (energy and disaster management), economic integration, strategic engagement, confidence-building measures, and soft-power engagement within a single cooperative framework. In fact, the EAS provides both India and Australia the only overarching regional architecture for strategic engagement in the Asia-Pacific.

Institutionalising Great Power Politics in the Asia-Pacific

The region of Asia-Pacific, at the end of first decade of 21st century, stares at the possibility of an unstable structure of power relations marked by long-standing hostility, conflicting interests among the rising powers, and the possibility of aggression by one of the great powers. Any such situation does not portend well for the prospect of economic integration, stability and collective prosperity. The escalation of conflict in the South China Sea and China's growing aggression offer an example of instability and necessitate a coordinated approach towards collective management of regional strategic affairs.

ASEAN has begun to realise the rise of important players within the region and felt the heat from growing contestation for regional space. Given the long-standing hostility among these players, it becomes important for players to develop a modus operandi through which these powers could interact with each other. A few scholars view the centrality of ASEAN in the Asia-Pacific cooperative framework as reflective of a cooperative trend with no player willing to risk undermining ASEAN.[10] Therefore, ASEAN, in order to maintain the balance of influence and retain its centrality in the cooperative deliberations, has embarked on simultaneous engagement with important players like USA, China, India and Japan and begun setting up cooperative mechanisms to moderate the hostility among major powers in Asia.

Though the existing ASEAN structures are not powerful enough to dictate terms to the emerging great powers, it can certainly act as principal forum to institutionalise the relations among these players and facilitate regional cooperation and stability. Both India and Australia have emerged as responsible players in the strategic discourses of Asia-Pacific. They have, over the years, contributed significantly towards building peace and stability in the region and participated in the ASEAN deliberations over regional security issues. New Delhi and Canberra can work together towards promoting the ASEAN forums as the only mediating agency in the case of regional contestation. Such a practice can not only empower ASEAN towards effectively dealing with the regional issues but also develop an institutionalised framework of great power engagement in the region. India and Australia can work together in the EAS and ADMM+ towards facilitating engagement and CBMs among the conflicting parties.

Shared Stakes in the Maritime Governance in the Indian Ocean

Similarly, over the years, maritime security has emerged as an important area of concern within the region and therefore, forms an important agenda for deliberation at these forums. Both Australia and India view Southeast Asia as an immediate area of security and strategic concerns and are willing to work together in the forums over regional maritime security deliberations. The comprehensive nature of security, as identified by the ARF, has enabled the two countries to engage ASEAN over wide-ranging issues of security cooperation. These security issues primarily fall into non-traditional arena – maritime security, piracy, terrorism, environmental security, trafficking in drugs and human beings, food security, disaster management, pandemics, and similar other issues.

The region of Asia-Pacific has experienced growing nexus between maritime pirates, Islamic terrorists and land-based insurgent groups. A major impetus to piracy has come from arms trafficking in the region since it enables pirates to acquire advanced weapons and high-speed crafts to execute their activities. Both the Acehnese insurgents (GAM) in Indonesia and the Moro Insurgents (MNLF) in the Philippines are known to have been engaged in drugs-arms trafficking, abduction of ships and conducting small raids on the ships anchoring on shore. A Spanish navy, which was participating in the Operation Enduring Freedom to prevent escape of the Al-Qaeda forces by the sea, apprehended a merchant ship in the Indian Ocean in December 2002 carrying 15 Scud missiles on board.[11]

All the three forums – ARF, EAS and ADMM+ have deliberated over the prevailing challenges of maritime security and threats facing the peaceful navigation in the regional naval corridors. The membership of the ARF offered the two countries a forum during the 1990s and early years of 21st century to discuss the security challenges and develop a common agenda of threat perceptions and security cooperation both multilaterally with ASEAN as well as bilaterally. The two countries have also participated regularly in the meetings of the CSCAP, the track-II body of the ARF. Most of these initiatives have been in the arena of maritime security cooperation with small-scale bilateral naval exercises and goodwill visits of naval units. Both India and Australia have entered into different sets of maritime security cooperation – capacity-building, coordinated patrolling,[12] training of security personnel, and wide ranging naval exercises with countries in the Asia-Pacific. Australia has been engaged bilaterally with Indonesia, Japan and USA and multilaterally with ASEAN forums over maritime security cooperation. India has developed a wide range of cooperative activities both bilaterally as well as multilaterally. The Indian Minister for External Affairs, Natwar Singh, during interviews following the 11th ARF meet in July 2004, offered 'any help in principle,' whether directly undertaking the joint patrolling in and around the Straits of Malacca or strengthening the maritime capability of the littoral states in ensuring the safety of passage along the Strait.[13]

Countering Terrorism and Intelligence Sharing

While India has experienced the menace of terrorism for decades, the terrorist attack on the World Trade Center in September 2011 and deaths of more than 100 Australians in the Bali bomb blast in October 2002 woke up Australia to the challenge of terrorism. While India has been advocating concerted ASEAN efforts against terrorism, Australia has, since the Bali bomb blast, been an active participant in the ASEAN deliberations over various dimensions of terrorism.

India and Australia have been engaged in the annual, Inter-sessional official-level and non-official level deliberations as evident from a set of bilateral dialogues, and agreements with individual ASEAN countries primarily in the areas of security, defence cooperation and counter-terrorism.[14] The two countries had participated in the anti-terrorism meeting in Bali in 2004 that decided 'to assist regional countries in implementing the UN anti-terrorism conventions in order to strengthen the regional anti-terrorism legal framework.[15] The Bali meeting of 2004 also called upon the participating countries including India and Australia help build up the law-enforcement capacities of ASEAN countries in various ways including sharing of intelligence reports and vital information. The Chairman's Statement at the end of fifth EAS Summit in Hanoi in October 2010 "stressed the importance of continued bilateral and regional cooperative efforts, including through the Bali Process on People Smuggling, Trafficking in Persons and Related Transnational Crime, to address the impact of these and other transnational crimes."[16]

Sustaining the continued relevance of ADMs

Though the ADMs offer opportunities for strategic engagement, these institutions have, of late, come under pressure from big-power rivalries, threatening independent functioning of these institutions and possible domination by one player. India and Australia find themselves engaging each other at the ARF and EAS, whose conception and agenda lies in managing the big-power relations in East Asia. Small powers, led by ASEAN are seeking to ensure their strategic interests by making these institutions more and more representative and inclusive. In other words, ASEAN strategic overtures are experiencing challenges from big powers in maintaining the neutrality and inclusiveness of these cooperative frameworks. Finally, the big power rivalries and tensions manifest more in these institutions' agenda tabled. China is challenging the ASEAN consensus and pursuing an aggressive and revisionist foreign policy in the case of its immediate neighbourhood.

The rise of China and its efforts towards dominating the multilateral institutions poses a formidable challenge for both India and Australia to advance their multi-dimensional engagement within the regional cooperative framework. In this situation, the stakes for the two countries are high in the sustained and impartial functioning of the EAS. The EAS gains significance as it has been assigned to discuss the relevance and feasibility of Australia's proposed Asia-Pacific Community. For India, the EAS is the only platform to pursue a pan-East Asian economic integration. Similarly, with the growing stagnation of the APEC, EAS remains the only platform for Australia's economic integration with East Asia.

The increasingly dominant discourse of the rise of great powers in Asia and onset of the 'great game' in the Asia-Pacific seems to have put the ASEAN-driven cooperative discourse on the backburner. Apart from being the key interlocutor of regional cooperation, ASEAN is being viewed as the main prize for the winner of the great game that is unfolding in the eastern hemisphere. ASEAN, during the last two years, has failed to develop and put forth a united front against the Chinese aggression in the South China Sea, indicating at widening cracks within ASEAN that is so desperately trying to become a united community. The more ASEAN loses the momentum and the opportunities for leadership, more obvious would become the prevailing disunity within the region, affecting the grouping's overall cooperative vision. Such a situation can push the entire region of the Asia-Pacific towards an intense great power rivalry with no institution regulating their behaviour.

Given this crisis scenario, it is important for both India and Australia to sustain the ASEAN process and keep it relevant by rallying behind the regional forum and contributing to the processes of agenda setting and their implementation.

Conclusion

Both India and Australia have benefitted a lot in the new evolving structure based on great-power equations. Moreover, China has launched a calibrated approach to dominate the ASEAN-driven multilateral cooperative processes, causing concerns among other countries about China. China's diplomatic manoeuvrings to gain influence over the functioning and agenda of ASEAN-driven institutions (East Asia Summit and ASEAN Regional Forum) have invited resistance from countries like Japan and a few ASEAN countries. The rivalries among big powers manifest as a growing lack of consensus among the member-states about the agenda of cooperation, efforts to make these institutions exclusive, tendencies to dominate the agenda of cooperation and advocacy of strategic priorities that undermine the functioning and mandate of these institutions. India and Australia are stakeholders in the smooth functioning of the ADMs which alone would ensure a stable Asian Order.

NOTES

1. Members of the ARF are ten ASEAN countries, USA, Russia, China, Japan, South and North Korea, India, Bangladesh, Pakistan, Australia, New Zealand, Papua New Guinea, European Union, Canada, Timor Leste, and Sri Lanka. Sri Lanka became a member of the ARF in 2008.

2. Barry Buzan and Ole Waever, *Regions and Powers: The Structure of International Security*, Cambridge, Cambridge University Press, 2003, p. 161

3. "ASEAN and its East Asia Summit Partners Establish Own OECD-like Think Tank," *ASEAN Secretariat*, 04 June 2008, http://www.aseansec.org/21608.htm (accessed on 26 October 2008)

4. P.S. Suryanarayana, "East Asia Summit Explores Free Trade Area Prospects," *The Hindu*, 23 July 2008, http:// www.hindu.com/2008/07/23/stories/2008072357581400.htm (accessed on 27 January 2009)

5. John Ravenhill, "Adjusting to the ASEAN way: thirty years of Australia's relations with ASEAN," *The Pacific Review*, 11:2, 1998, p. 267

6. Anthony Milner, "Comments on Michael Richardson's article," *Australian Journal of International Affairs*, 59:3 (September 2005), p. 367.

7. "ASEAN–Australia-New Zealand Free Trade Agreement," Australian Government, Austrade, http://www. austrade.gov.au/ASEAN-Australia-New-Zealand-Free-Trade-Area/default.aspx (accessed on 18 April 2010)

8. I K Gujaral, "Lands of the Asian Miracle," *The Hindu,* 10 August 1996.

9. "Ha Noi Declaration on the Commemoration of the Fifth Anniversary of the East Asia Summit," *ASEAN Secretariat,* Fifth East Asia Summit, Hanoi, 30 October 2010, http://www.aseansec.org/25548.htm

10. Amitav Acharya, "Arguing about ASEAN: what do we disagree about?," *Cambridge Review of International Affairs,* vol. 22, no. 3, pp. 495; Amitav Acharya, "ASEAN at 40: Mid-Life Rejuvenation?," *Foreign Affairs,* 15 August 2007, http://www.foreignaffairs.com/articles/64249/amitav-acharya/asean-at-40-mid-life-rejuvenation

11. J.A. Roach, "Initiatives to Enhance Maritime Security at Sea," *Marine Policy,* vol. 28, 2004, p. 52.

12. India has entered into joint maritime patrolling agreement with Indonesia, Thailand, and Sri Lanka, covering the substantial maritime stretch of the Andaman Sea. See P S Suryanarayana, "India Signs Maritime Accord with Thailand," *The Hindu,* 21 May 2005, http://www.hindu.com/2005/05/21/stories/2005052104421200.htm (accessed on 26 January 26, 2009)

13. "Natwar Meets Megawati, Talks Terror with EU Team," *Indian Express*, 02 July 2004, http://www. indianexpress.com/oldstory.php?storyid=50194 (accessed on 17 January 2009)

14. Alexander Downer, "ASEAN Australia 30 years of Development Cooperation," Australian Government, AusAID, 16 April 2004, at http://www. ausaid.gov.au/media/release.cfm? BC=Speech&ID=2722 6020 6613 2143 6996(accessed on 18 April 2010).

15. Sandy Gordon, "Implications of the Growing Prevalence of Interregional crime for Cooperation in the Asia-Pacific Region," in William T. Tow and China Kin Wah (eds.) *ASEAN, India and Australia: Towards Closer Engagement in a New Asia* (Singapore: ISEAS, 2009), p. 312.

16. "Chairman's Statement of the East Asia Summit (EAS)," *ASEAN Secretariat,* fifth East Asia Summit, Hanoi, 30 October 2010, http://www.aseansec.org/25490.htm

12

Indo-Australian Relationship and Its Impact on Asia-Pacific

Sudhir Kumar Singh

The entire world has witnessed dramatic changes within international system in recent times. In the post-Cold War era, terror incidents, like 9/11 followed by several others in the recent past and the global economic recession have further aggravated the situation at the international level. Foreign policy in this era of globalization has been influenced by global incidents. Competition, Conflict and Cooperation [CCC] have become basic levers of the foreign policy. For example, the United States and China are largest trading partners, but they differ on political and strategic issues so is the case of China and India, and Japan and China. In the Asia-Pacific, China has grown up rapidly in recent decades and by all opinions is slated to accelerate its profile in the Asia-Pacific in particular and the rest of the globe in general. The thrust of new space by the Chinese has pushed the entire strategic framework of the Asia-Pacific as was the case of Europe during pre- and post- First World War. China's neighbor, India, is also growing very comfortably; in the face of all odds, it has sustained the annual growth rate of 8 percent since many years. This has further complicated the entire chess board of balance of power within Asia-Pacific.

The post-Cold War and further post-9/11 scenario have altered the traditional bi-lateral and multi-lateral relationships across the globe. Many old friends have become adversaries and many adversaries have become friends. But at the same time, many old friends remained friends and expanded the level of their friendship. Australia –India relation came into this category. The Asia-Pacific has become new power house of the world after the end of the cold war. As stated by gamut of pundits of the international politics, the 21st century will be the Asian century as the previous century was the European-American century.

Asia could not prove its importance till major Asian powers will not cooperate in a very coordinated manner. The present world system is dominated by uni-polar power that is USA. If the Asian powers have to challenge this monopoly then they have to prove it through their cooperation. The problem is Asian balance of power. This old theory of international relations has become extremely important even at the outset of 21st century. USA wished to put India and Japan against China due to the fact that both have had adverse relationship with China. China has been a source of threat to ASEAN countries. One of the important factors behind the formation of the ASEAN in 1967 was Chinese thereat. Even today when China holds important stakes into ASEAN affairs and has emerged as an important outside power within ASEAN, there are a gamut of thorny bilateral issues between China and -ASEAN.

Asia has the potential as the new power house of the international system in the 21st century. China wished to dominate Asia but at the same time wanted to establish multi-polar international system. India and Japan belong to the same category and wanted both Asia and the globe to be multi-lateral. This has emerged as a new struggle between important Asian giants. Besides India, China, Japan, South Korea and Indonesia, Australia is also an extended Asian country and events within Asia-Pacific have the capacity to shed more impact on Australia in comparison with the developments in the Western world.

The Asia-Pacific region has emerged as the new power house of the world, but according to the *Asian Development Bank Report*

[2008], there were constitutes around 670 million poor people. Needless to say that these people are languishing under chronic poverty and long back it has been established that poverty is the root cause of all contemporary global problems ranging from terrorism to global warming. Being the custodian of the international regime of human rights, Australia must take an initiative to eradicate chronic poverty from Asia-Pacific and of course India must be an important partner of Australia in this endeavor. Both are practicing democracies and they are committed to the focal agenda of participatory governance. Poverty is the biggest violator of human rights and without the promotion and protection of human rights a democratic regime could not be categorized as a genuine democratic regime therefore it is the moral duty of both countries to take some concrete steps in this direction. They of course could seek cooperation from common minded countries like Japan, South Korea and any other countries, who wished to contribute in this greater service to the humanity.

There are a gamut of bilateral issues between India and Australia, which could be of common interest for Asia-Pacific as well. The most severe among them have been the tentacles of terror. he tentacles of terror, which have shown their ugly face again in Russia in the last week of March 2010, aggravated the threat to the mankind. Despite the US-led NATO attack on Afghanistan to eliminate the perpetuator of terror, Pakistan and Afghanistan still remain the breeding ground of international terrorism. This ongoing saga of terror has posed a severe threat for the survival of humanity therefore being the harbinger of these cardinal human values, India and Australia must contribute their best for the reconstruction of Afghanistan. In due process of Afghan war, it has been vindicated that Pakistan will not permit to stabilize Afghanistan due to fact that a strong Afghanistan has always opposed Pakistani design within Southwest Asia therefore despite their cooperation with the U.S led operation they have sustained their tacit support to the Taliban and Al-Qaeda and it has been proved by US agencies that Quetta has been used as the headquarters of the Taliban government's capital in exile. Terror is a common threat for India and Australia. Needless to say that Al-Qaeda has its regional outlets in Southeast Asia, which caused collateral damages to Australian interests in recent past and vowed to launch more attacks in foreseeable future. India has been a victim of the terror network since many decades and the fact of the matter is the epi-centre of international terrorism still located in Pakistan.

With the return of the Taliban regime in Kabul, the Southeast Asia-based off-shoots of the Al-Qaeda will be acting with a new devastating zeal, insofar as Australia is concerned. This danger will be on India too due to geographical proximity. International terrorism will also be strengthened. Therefore, more collaborative cooperation is required between both countries on this front to ensure prevention of counter terror efforts. These efforts will be not only mutually beneficial but will stabilize the Asia-Pacific and the entire globe as well.

Beside terror, Maritime security has been one of the concerns for both India and Australia. India in recent years has done well to contain piracy and this need to be sustainable. Piracy is not a problem for India and Australia only but it is an issue of common concern for Asia-Pacific. India's expanding maritime interests in coming decades and the rapid economic progress needs energy from a variety of sources. India will be number three energy consumer within 15 years and that complicates the entire contours of maritime security. Australia is also equally concerned for the smooth passage of goods from the Indian Ocean and other sea lanes. With the growing pace of development an energy hungry India is emerging and that did not confine to the Indian Ocean, South China Sea and the Upper reaches of the Pacific, but also included Australia and the South Pacific. Therefore, there is a convergence of interests between the two countries, which is bound to cement in foreseeable future. There is need for India-Australia to seek cooperation from other countries within the region for a better and safe movement of goods through the Indian Ocean. There are hardly any divergences of maritime interests between India and Southeast Asia. There is ample scope for cooperation between India and Southeast Asia. Since last few years the Chinese are getting assertive to covertly declare South China Sea as their regional lake. In September 2010, Japan and China had a virtual clash for dominance over an Island in the South China Sea. Such incidents are quite common between many Southeast Asian countries and China and in recent past these events have increased. That has prompted Vietnam which fought a long and deadly battle against the United States in the 196s and 1970s to forge close relationship with it. After 15 years of diplomatic relationship, the U.S Secretary of State and Defense has visited Hanoi.[1] Southeast Asia and its nearby sea lanes are equally important for India and Australia and also make boundaries between India and Australia. These lanes have additionally been important for international trade and their combined effort will of course yield adequate results in this direction and it would be conducive for international trade and an effective containment of piracy.

Global warming has emerged as an issue of concern for the humanity. It has posed a grave threat for the survival of humanity. Although, Australian population is only equal to that of the city of Delhi, Australia has a vast landmass, much bigger than that of India and Australia can contribute positively for environmental security. India has a huge population of more than 1 billion people and emerged as the fifth global energy consumer. Its economy is expanding therefore it needs to take care of the safety of environment and together both countries could do better. Environmental security was a major issue in 2010 general election of Australia and new Australian Prime Minister, Julia Gillard has promised to ensure environmental security.

The new architecture of power within Asia-Pacific is emerging. In this process many traditional players have to lose some power, while some new players are supposed to acquire new acumen in the chessboard of this emerging power game. Long back during the Peloponnesian War, Thucydides [c. 471- 400 BC], the great Athenian historian, regarded in the West as the founder of international relations theory, identified the root cause of the war between Sparta and Athens as their struggle for power. He argued, "what made war inevitable was the growth of Athenian power and the fear which this caused in Sparta. In the first stage of the war, Sparta, the predominant power, decided to wage war against Athens; while in the second stage, Athens, the rising power, was determined to conquer Sparta.[2] Of course, time and context has changed but the real struggle of power still holds the same dimension. The new balance of power in Asia-Pacific is all set to reshape existing power architecture. However, the theory of balance of power, according to its proponents, has come into being with the theory of Prisoner's Dilemma. Balance of power has been one of the most debated concepts of the international relations. The balance of power is a kind of compromise among states which finds order preferable to absolute chaos, even though it is a system that favors the stronger and more prosperous states at the expense of the weaker. Great powers play the dominant role in balance of power system because of their preponderant military force and their control of key technologies.[3] The Cold War era just after the end of the Second World War is a classic example of balance of power sustained by the United States and the Soviet Union. In the post-Cold War era even the prevalence of the anarchic international environment has created a fear psychosis. Military build-ups and their competition by rival powers have left everyone in the international system insecure therefore all countries are trapped in a dilemma, called the Security Dilemma.[4]

In Asia-Pacific this situation is prevailing even after the end of the cold war because of the fact that emerging countries are trying to dominate the entire continent. Probably it has happened first time that India, Japan and China have become dominant players at the same time. One wanted a multi-polar world but uni-polar Asia and rest two wanted both world and Asia multi-polar. It is pertinent to mention here that present uni-polar power of the world namely the United States wants to sustain uni-polar world but multi-polar Asia and here lies the seed of the concept of Prisoner's Dilemma and Balance of Power. The balance of power and prisoner's dilemma seems to be born together due to its interdependency. The representative proponent of new realism,

Prof. Kenneth Waltz, once said, "Rational countries are living in the state of anarchy and the security dilemma would be suspicious of and hostile to each other because of their tense relations, although that was not their original idea."[5] We have witnessed the frequency of conflicts even after the end of the cold war in Asia in particular and rest of the globe in general. In such an international environment, it is natural that countries would use the "Balance of Power" to protect their own security. This would then make the "Security Dilemma" a regular phenomenon in international politics.

Strategic cooperation between both countries is also demand of the hour. The balance of power within Asia-Pacific has been under transformation since last decades due to gamut of reasons. China wanted to grab the opportunity to its advantage but it is not in the interest of Asia-Pacific as well as India-Australia. Although the Kevin Rudd-led Labor government was a bit inclined towards China but the changes of leadership in Australia probably contribute positively in this direction. The convergence of interests between India and Australia will find that if multi-polarity was established in the Asia-Pacific region then only the real peace and prosperity would prevail not only within their region but also into all parts of the globe. In contrast, the U.S will be able to play the role of headmaster. The stability of Asia-Pacific is the key to the global stability as was the case of 20th century Europe. Therefore, stability in the Asia-Pacific should be an issue of common concern to India and Australia. Of course, the United States, majority of Southeast Asian countries and other important players within Asia-Pacific will contribute to achieve this goal. Russia still holds much currency in the balance of power game within Asia-Pacific and will be happy to contribute more in this regard. The stability of Asia-Pacific, therefore, a common interest for India and Australia and needless to say that it will ensure the decline of low-intensity conflicts and even bigger conflicts within the region and it will surely stabilize the global balance of power. It is pertinent to mention here that this stabilization will be of great help for the survival and well being of the humanity.

Besides these issues of common concern for India and Australia, there are many areas, where increased cooperation between India and Australia could strengthen the security and prosperity within the Asia-Pacific region. Both countries have excellent trade relations and doing business of around $ 19 billion dollar and it is increasing. But, there are ample opportunities to increase the level of cooperation between both countries not only in the above-mentioned areas but in human development sector, health sector, science and technology sectors and the list goes on. This will create better environment between both countries and additionally facilitate better peace and prosperity in Asia-Pacific region in particular and the globe in general. One more important area needs attention here and this is engagement of skilled manpower. It is an open secret that Australia has only 22 million people but occupies more territory than that of India. For the sustainability of the pace of development, Australia needs skilled manpower in large number. India has a huge population and despite the fact that in world poverty index India occupies 67th position which is even below that of Sudan but a sizable portion of Indian population is rich and educated also. New ventures of education are mushrooming in India in a massive manner and producing huge skilled man power. Indian economy is growing very rapidly since last many years and expected to maintain the momentum in foreseeable future also. But, despite this positive picture, Indian economy is unable to accommodate all skilled man power. Australia needs more skilled man power. Closer cooperation between both countries has become all the more urgent in view of a new development that is certain to boost Australia, s economic performance over the next few decades. The discovery of three huge gas and oil fields off the coasts of South Australia, Western Australia and Queensland has further emboldened the Indian engagement in the development of Australia given the fact that India is energy starved country and needs the supply from diverse sources. India also needs other minerals to sustain its pace of sustainable development. To sustain a rapidly expanding economy, Australia will also need to significantly enlarge its skilled manpower pool, attract investment in a number of areas and, in turn, engage in developmental activities abroad. Australia could use Indian managerial and technological talent. Indian Diaspora will be additional use for this purpose. Despite last year attacks against the Indian Diaspora it is an open secret that Indians never created any problem to the Australian system and worked hard for the smooth development of the country.

Only one single issue has been an irritant between India and Australia and that is the negation of Uranium supply to India for the fear of nuclear proliferation by Australia. First of all, Australia has every right to take its own decisions being an independent country but on one issue two decisions could not be legitimized. Australia could not legitimize its supply of Uranium to China, because China has emerged as the biggest nuclear proliferator and due to growing tussle for balance of power on Asian and global theater China is bound to sustain this tempo. Australia is supplying Uranium to China, which is sweeping supply of Uranium and nuclear technology to Pakistan and North Korea under the carpet. It has been accepted by the international agencies. After the 123 Nuclear Treaty with the United States in 2008, there is long queue to supply Uranium to India by Uranium rich countries like Kazakhstan, Mongolia and Canada and list goes on. Australia needs to rethink on this issue. I think that the new government of Prime Minister Julia Gillard will take some positive decisions on this issue. India needs Australian Uranium to sustain its overall development by diversifying its sources of energy supplies. Australia has been a consistent supporter of peace and opponent of nuclear proliferation and it has been on the top of Australian agenda to ensure international peace. It has been felt by gamut of international experts that the Taliban would grab power in Kabul after the United States withdrawal from Afghanistan in July 2011. Extremist forces will try to take over Pakistan and needless to say that if it will happen, it will be devastating for the entire world. Weapons of mass destruction [WMD] will come into the hands of terror network and that will lead the world towards unimaginable holocaust. India is extremely concerned about this hypothetical fallout and being a champion of peace, Australia also needs to cooperate with India and other like-minded countries to prevent this possibility. Needless to say that it is very tough task and requires concrete efforts from all like-minded countries. Through this cooperation, Australia will be able to real global peace. The 21st century is known for its enlightenment. It is a century, where humanity is supposed to avail the largest peace of history but we are witnessing gamut of violence in Asia-Pacific. The prevention of nuclear terrorism will be a great service to the humanity.

Both India and Australia, despite drastic changes into the contours of international politics, have shared interests and we are aware of the fact that since Kautilyan times that commonality of interest is the basic agenda for the formulation of foreign policy. In the Asia-Pacific these interests are converging therefore they must cooperate with new vision. If stability was not established in the Asia-Pacific in the 21st Century, India and Australia will be one of the biggest sufferers; therefore, it is their duty to look into the matter and convert this area as an abode of peace and prosperity. It has been said that the 21st century is an era of Enlightened Modernism. At least within Asia-Pacific, it is the moral duty of both countries to achieve this egalitarian goal.

Given these issues in the minds of knowledgeable people of both countries, the call for deepening cooperation is emerging from different quarters. These opinions stressed the need for deepening cooperation between both countries. In an article published in *The Sunday Morning Herald* [April 2-4, 2010] , Richard Woolcott, a former Secretary of the Department of Foreign Affairs and Trade [Australia], urged the two countries to " move well beyond the three Cs: Curry, Cricket and the Commonwealth". After lauding India's growth rate and its vibrant democracy, he emphasized the complementarity between India and Australia in many aspects, including economy, services and renewable and clean energy technology.

One serious grievance of Australia has been that since the 1986 visit of Indian Prime Minister, Rajiv Gandhi, no Indian Prime Minister has ever visited Australia. In the meantime, many

Australian Prime Ministers have already visited India. Indian Prime Minister must visit Australia immediately to give a new twist to this extremely important bilateral relation. During the Nehruvian era of Indian foreign policy, much harm had been done to the Indian interests vis-à-vis Australian due to unnecessary obsession to idealism. Since former Prime Minister Narasimha Rao had initiated Look East Policy and after him, Prime Minister, Atal Bihari Vajpayee gave this mantra of realistic Indian foreign policy a new twist and after that the UPA-1 and UPA-2 regimes are bound to sustain the tempo. Therefore an Indian Prime Ministerial visit to Australia will cement the bilateral relationships into new horizons of deepening stage. Any excuses in this regard probably will not assuage Australian grievances. The changing contours of international politics have pushed both India and Australia into the same boat. There are varieties of convergences between both countries with nominal divergences therefore they must mitigate nominal divergences and take the bilateral relationship to a new high.

NOTES

1. Shared Concern About China Aligns U.S. and Vietnam, Seth Mydans, *New York Times*, New York, 10 October 2010.
2. Qing Simei, *From Allies to Enemies; Vision of Identity, and U.S - China Diplomacy, 1945- 1960,* Harvard University Press, Cambridge, 2007, p. 297.
3. Griffiths, Martin & Terry O Callaghan, *Key Concepts in International Relations,* Routledge, London, 2004, p.13.
4. Herz, John, H, "Idealist Internationalism and Security Dilemma", *World Politics,* Volume 2, 1950, pp.157-158.
5. Waltz, Kenneth, *Theories of International Politics,* Addison Wesley, New York, 1979, p.3.

13

Regional Integration or Cooperation: India, Australia and Japan

Prabhakar H.S.

I. New Growth Paradigm in Asia-Pacific

The Asia-Pacific Economic Cooperation (APEC) is a gigantic economic bloc that accounts for half of global gross domestic product. Led by APEC as the center of growth, the global financial crisis has finally got out of the worst. APEC forum ended its two-day summit meeting in Singapore last November where leaders of Pacific Rim economies have hammered out a vision for strengthening their unity to realize sustainable growth in the region in the post-financial crisis era. The most significant point at summit meeting was that the joint declaration stipulates that the APEC leaders will draw up a comprehensive long-term economic growth strategy next year, when Japan chairs APEC meetings. The declaration also stressed that the leaders will maintain economic stimulus policies until a durable economic recovery has clearly taken hold.

Asia More Reliant on U.S.

Nevertheless, prospects for a full-fledged economic recovery remain uncertain. The Asia-Pacific economies, therefore, expressed their resolve to strengthen cooperation and serve as an engine to drive the global economy after overcoming the crisis. The "new growth paradigm" envisages future growth that is compatible with global climate change efforts, and balanced growth. Asian countries allowed the financial crisis to worsen by remaining heavily dependent on exports to the United States. Also, economic disparities have widened in the region. Japanese Prime Minister Yukio Hatoyama emphasized his proposal of making global-warming countermeasures part of the region's growth strategy. At the summit meeting, the leaders also agreed on the importance of seeking a political agreement on a post-Kyoto Protocol framework to tackle global warming. What kind of new growth strategy will APEC, which includes the United States and China—the largest carbon dioxide emitters—as its members, come up with? The leadership of Japan, the next APEC chair, will be severely tested on this point.

A Step Forward

The joint declaration also rejects protectionism and stipulates that APEC leaders will continue to explore ways to build a free trade area in the Asia-Pacific that covers APEC. The declaration is a step forward for APEC that reflects the stance of U.S. President Barack Obama of putting importance on Asia. In the Asia-Pacific region, various ideas for economic cooperation, including Hatoyama's East Asian community concept exist. An important thing is to promote open regional cooperation that includes the United States. The trade and investment liberalization that APEC agreed upon needs implementation to this end. Concrete progress requires to be made by the end of 2010, a year targeted by APEC's more developed members to achieve the liberalization. Besides, it is important that APEC play a leading role in settling the stalled Doha Round of free trade negotiations under the World Trade Organization by the end of next year.

Asia to help Global Stability

There is no "Asian way" for resolving global challenges. Given

Asia's growing influence, the world may have much to gain from an emerging Asian way. Asian approach is pragmatism - Asians constantly adapt and change. Earlier, Asians put a premium on protecting their sovereignty and were wary of any multilateral approaches that could dilute it. Nevertheless, in response to global challenges as for example, financial crises and climate change — the vast majority of Asian countries understand that collective action does not erode but instead protects sovereignty. Despite losing faith in the International Monetary Fund after the region's financial crisis in 1997, they agreed to contribute billions to the IMF after the recent global financial meltdown.There has also been another significant shift in Asian attitudes. The discussion in Asia is increasingly about outputs: how to create institutions that are more effective. At the same time, the Asians remain ready to accept continuing American leadership and domination of global institutions. Nor do they challenge the United States-led security umbrella for the Asia-Pacific region.

The inevitable question is: Can Asians lead in meeting global challenges? Both China and India are already making a major contribution to global stability and order by taking better care of more than 2 billion people. Truly, if a majority of Asians continue to improve their livelihoods, the world would certainly a better place. There are both positive and negative aspects of the Asian approach to the challenges of global governance. The positive aspects include respect for diversity and an emphasis on consensus-building over conflict, practical solutions over lofty principles and gradualism over abrupt change. On the other hand, the desire to avoid confrontation can prevent meaningful agreements from being reached in a reasonable time frame, and the appearance of consensus may hide politics at work. The positive aspects of Asian way suggest the possibility of more inclusive decision-making in the institutions of global governance. The problem in such an approach is that decisions may not be taken, thereby failing to resolve fundamental political challenges.

A few areas in which Asia can contribute to solving some key global challenges:

- *Peace and Security:* Asia includes many new naval powers, such as China and India, which could help bolster the security of sea lanes by creating partnerships with traditional naval powers such as the U.S. Various Asian countries joined efforts to combat piracy off the coast of Somalia. China is developing a deployable police capacity that may provide an important new tool in peace operations in fragile states.
- *Climate Change:* Asia needs to build up innovative markets that help technology transfer. East Asia - China, Japan and Korea - has become leading producer of green technology. Asian governments are in a position to take the lead in developing alternative energy sources.
- *Financial Regulation:* Asian countries may take more leadership in regulating financial markets. China, questioning the wisdom of putting the fate of the world economy in the US dollar, has proposed the creation of a global currency. Progress has been made on the Chiang Mai Initiative — a multilateral currency swap arrangement among the 10 ASEAN members, China, Japan and South Korea — and the possibility of an Asian Monetary Fund remains still.
- *Health:* Asian countries' experience in dealing with SARS, bird flu, H1N1 and other diseases needs careful attention — for both positive and negative lessons —that might help develop a new global consensus on handling pandemics.
- *Social Enterprises:* Asia is a leader in social entrepreneurship. The successes of social businesses such as Grameen Bank impacts social objectives that can be fused with revenue-generating practices.

In brief, there is an absence of systematic Asian approach for meeting global challenges. In response to each challenge, Asians respond pragmatically. Pragmatism may offer a constructive way gradually.

Japan outlines East Asia Community Concept

JPM Yukio Hatoyama at APEC summit highlighted four key areas of cooperation in his concept for an East Asian community — regional prosperity, the environment, protecting human life and maritime safety. Hatoyama indicated the U.S. is a potential member of his envisaged regional grouping, "The United States has been playing and will continue to play an important role in ensuring the peace and prosperity of Asia, including Japan." Japan will speed up negotiations for economic partnership agreements with South Korea, India and Australia, and study the possibilities of talks with other countries as a means to pursuing prosperity in the region.

Hatoyama proposed expanding maritime cooperation in Southeast Asia, such as antipiracy operations in the Strait of Malacca, to other regions as part of efforts to build a "sea of 'yu-ai' (fraternity)," noting that "most regional commerce depends on sea routes.""The concept behind this initiative for an East Asian community stems from the philosophy of yu-ai". "Within yu-ai, people respect the freedom and human dignity of others just as they respect their own freedom and human dignity. In other words, yu-ai means not only the independence of people but also their coexistence. The developing countries must take advantage of advanced energy-saving technologies, water purification techniques and other environment-focused technologies owned by Japanese companies as they aim to reduce greenhouse gas emissions while pursuing sustainable growth to achieve a "green Asia."

Japan will make a "proactive contribution" to encourage governments and other institutions to register their human and material assets for disaster relief, which would allow the region to conduct more prompt and effective rescue and relief activities in response to disasters.

In addition, Hatoyama cited nuclear disarmament, nuclear nonproliferation, urban issues, social security and cultural exchange as potential fields of regional cooperation. As a framework of future regional cooperation, China envisions a grouping of 13 countries — Japan, China and South Korea plus the 10 Association of Southeast Asian Nations members of Brunei, Cambodia, Indonesia, Laos, Malaysia, Myanmar, the Philippines, Singapore, Thailand and Vietnam. Japan envisages a wider grouping including Australia, India, New Zealand and possibly the United States.(*The Japan Times:* Nov. 16, 2009).

APEC as it stands

The positive role played by Asian nations in helping recovery from the global economic crisis indicates APEC's potential. The usual rhetoric — a commitment to free trade, a rejection of protectionism, a recognition of the need for a long-term growth strategy respects the diversity of APEC's members. Echoing recent G20 statements, the group pledged to continue economic stimulus packages until there is a durable and sustainable recovery. And, like the G20, the assembled leaders acknowledged that "growth as usual" is no longer an answer. "We need a fresh growth paradigm. We need a fresh model of economic integration."The APEC group will continue to explore the prospects and problems of an Asia Pacific free trade area. In theory, that remains the APEC goal. In reality, the differences among the 21 APEC member economies make progress toward the objective of a fitful and sometimes painful process. This list of complaints should look familiar. The APEC meeting also provides an opportunity for regional leaders to meet with trans-Pacific counterparts. A substantial number of bilateral meetings occurs on the sidelines of the forum. This familiarization process cannot be quantified, but it does pay dividends.

Similarly, little noticed among many observers has been progress on technical issues that have been pressed or even championed by APEC. Reducing trade transaction costs is not headline-grabbing initiative, but it matters greatly to business and to the region's economic prospects. This is just one example of the "micro-level" action that APEC is taking that has real consequences for the region. The challenge for the future is building upon these smaller initiatives and integrating them into the group's broader vision. Success in that effort rests on the shoulders of

Japan and the United States. That is only fitting since, as the two leading economies of the world, those two countries have a special responsibility to use their power, influence and experience to lead the region forward. But it is especially true since Tokyo hosts the APEC summit in 2010 and the U.S. will host the following year. If these two countries truly believe in APEC and its potential, they will seize this opportunity to move the forum forward in the next two years, to overcome the persistent criticisms and realize its potential.

It is impossible to ignore India though India still finds it difficult to fully perceive itself as a world power. One of the indirect consequences of the rise of China and India and their privileged relationship with the West, however, has been the deepening of Japan's identity worries. "Japan represented the "Asian West" hitherto. But now, the emergence of Chinese-style and Indian-style modernity is considerably disturbing Japan. After all, if China is America's main economic partner in Asia, and if India is America's main diplomatic partner, one wonders what major role will be available for Japan to play in Asia-pacific regional forums? As Japan's biggest trade partner China offers opportunities for Japanese enterprises, and is economically crucial to Japan. The two together wish to coexist under conditions of mutual prosperity and work to resolve bilateral problems in a practical way. Australia and India are there with plenty of plain expectations.

II. Regional Integration or Cooperation: Japan, Australia and India

JFDI in Australia - A wave of Japanese investment in Australia is being driven by Japan's economic stagnation and the need for its corporation to seek fresh growth strategies and a secure supply of food and energy. *The key focus of foreign investment has been China in the past two years*, but direct investment from Japan to Australia hit $36 billion in 2008, up more than 50 per on 2006 levels, and is predicted to keep growing. The figure eclipses the long-term average of $3.3 bn of yearly direct investment from Japan, as well as the 2008 total of Chinese direct investment in Australia of $3bn.

Japan's response to ageing crisis - An ageing population, coupled with a declining birth rate, is an unprecedented challenge for Japanese policymakers. The issues created by this situation can be readily identified in the administration of Japan's pension system. It is widely recognized that record management for Japanese pensions has been, moderately speaking, incomplete, and more strictly speaking, defective. Surprisingly, 50 million pension numbers still remain to be identified.

'Stand up' (Tachigare) Party – The next couple of years will be crucial for the realization of genuine Japanese democracy. More than that, if the DPJ-Minshuto leaders succeed in carrying out their aim of creating a cabinet-centered government, this will be a grand example for others - one of the very few positive turns of fate in the political life of Japan. But the obstacles to achieving this are formidable. Not only domestic forces but also Washington will seek to torpedo the plans for a truly independent Japan that can stand on its own feet in the world. Understanding those obstacles well could help Japanese citizens contribute to the chances for a good outcome.

A new political party to be launched will be named Tachiagare Nippon (Stand Up, Japan), former trade minister Takeo Hiranuma, an independent House of Representatives member who will head the party, announced on 7 April 2010. Creation of a new party obviously represents a sense of crisis among the founding members toward political gridlock caused by the two major parties—the Democratic Party of Japan (DPJ) and the Liberal Democratic Party. The new party put forth three political goals—"defeat of the DPJ," "resurgence of Japan" and "realignment of political parties." It criticized the DPJ, saying Japan would be ruined if the party stayed in power. At the same time, they expressed dissatisfaction with the LDP, complaining that the party lacked determination to regain power. Thus, they stressed that the new party would take an "anti-DPJ, non-LDP" stance in its political activities.

To achieve political realignment, the new party must lead policy debate by presenting its visions of a future Japan that could serve as the basis for realignment, and concrete measures to achieve that goal.

Pledges to deepen Security pact with US – Japan will seek to further deepen the security alliance with the United States this year, the 50th anniversary of the bilateral security pact, and actively promote a worldwide movement for the abolition of nuclear weapons, the Foreign Ministry said on 7 April 2010 in its annual report on diplomacy. The Diplomatic Blue Book 2010 says it is "an important task" to strengthen the Japan-U.S. security arrangement when there remain "uncertain elements surrounding Japan," adding the alliance has "effectively served as a basic framework to secure the stability and development of the Asia-Pacific region in the postwar period."

III. India-Japan Relations

With trade and investment ties being the prime focus in Japan's relations with leading economies in East and South-East Asia, the relationship with India paradoxically has been a story of performance falling below potential level. The Hatoyama Government's support will be important in the successful implementation of ongoing projects such as the Delhi-Mumbai Industrial Corridor and the Dedicated Freight Corridor. The 2009 August electoral verdict in Japan turned as much on change in domestic and foreign policy as the US electoral verdict last year, yet the interest evinced in India in what the new government in Tokyo may signify for our relationship with the world's second largest economy has been remains meagre.

Change Driver: Over the years, the unrealized potential of India-Japan relations has been the theme of much discussion, with the establishment of a "Strategic and Global Partnership" between the two countries in December 2006. Annual summits and a structure of multiple channels of dialogue are common and regular now. With the change of Government in Japan, and the DPJ in power for the first time, there is certain uncertainty as to how India-Japan relations will move in the immediate future.

The question is whether the new trend in the relationship with India under the last three LDP (Liberal Democratic Party) Governments will be sustained and, if so, to what extent under a DPJ-led government. There is unlikely to be any significant change as the new Government would be more disposed to leave well alone the "Roadmap for New Dimensions to the Strategic and Global Partnership" that has already made some strides through the exchanges of prime ministerial visits in the last three years. The short answer to the question is that the next India-Japan summit, which the Prime Minister, Mr Yukio Hatoyama, is due to attend in India in 2010, will give a clear indication on how Japan under his Government views the relationship with India.

Growing Ties: With trade and investment ties assuming the prime space in Japan's relationship with leading countries in East and South-East Asia, the relationship with India is falling far short of potential. Ms Yoriko Kawaguchi, Japan's former Foreign Minister, has mentioned two reasons by way of explanation. India is not geographically close to Japan, unlike China, Korea and other countries in East Asia. "Complementarity in cultures is another issue in that South-East Asia is much closer to Japan, which explains the high Japanese investments there."

For another, in East Asia, Japanese companies have 'production, information and tradition networks', which are difficult to create in India, according to her. She mentions a specific instance: average tariff in China is 4.5 per cent but in India it is about 19 per cent. With such disparity in the cost of importing inputs it is difficult for Japanese manufacturers to invest in India. Ms Kawaguchi, however, terms China as a huge opportunity for Japanese companies, which supply inputs for China's high-value manufacturing sector, thereby developing a relationship based on interlocking interests. This scheme of things has been changing and contextual conditions are more favourable for India-Japan trade and investment ties today than even in 2005. Strategically India is important for Japan and that Japanese companies had not only discovered India, but were incorporating India as part of their international network.

In conjunction with the growth of the inter-governmental dialogue, Japanese corporate presence has since acquired rising visibility in India what with investments by such Japanese majors as Honda, Toyota and Nissan (not to speak of Suzuki) and such notable acquisitions as Matsushita Electric, Daiichi Sankyo and DoCoMo. The target for the two-way trade by 2010-11 is $20 billion, while in terms of Japanese overseas development assistance, India is the largest recipient of all countries.

Flagship Projects: The most significant Japanese involvement with the Indian economy is in terms of the implementation of the flagship infrastructure projects of the Delhi-Mumbai Industrial Corridor (DMIC) and the Dedicated Freight Corridor (DFC) linking the two poles of the country's development. Modelled on the famed Tokyo-Kyoto Osaka Corridor in its aim of developing the entire region along the 1,483-km transportation link, the DMIC project plans to cover 20 per cent of the Indian population in a time-frame of 11 years.

On the Indian side, the implementation has been predictably subjected to delays for a variety of reasons coupled with cost escalation, but the Japanese Government, business and industry also have their work cut out for them in this colossal project, offering as it does vast opportunities for global investment. As for the DFC, centre-piece of the country's infrastructure development under the Eleventh and Twelfth Five-Year Plans, discussions are already under way with the Japan Bank for International Cooperation for credit funding of the project.

DPJ's Perspectives: The economic reforms and the increasing foreign direct investments have, by and large, persuaded the Japanese companies about the attractiveness of India as a market and investment destination. What remains as a lacuna with the previous LDP Government and the present DPJ-led Government, is the political will to partner with India, inspired by a larger vision of Asia wherein India-Japan relationship will serve to promote Japan's economic interests and security in a multi-polar world.

Not much is also known about Prime Minister Hatoyama's and the DPJ's perspectives on Japan's relations with India in an Asian neighbourhood where both China and India will figure prominently in the years to come. And what has been known so far does not quite point to the possibility of a re-orientation of Japan's policy towards India at the political and economic levels. In an article that he wrote in the *New York Times* on August 27, 2009, three days before the elections, Mr Hatoyama spoke of the east Asian region embodying the potential of an East Asian Community as Japan's "basic sphere of being" and perceived the country as caught between the US as the world's dominant power and China, which is seeking to become dominant; there was no reference to India either as an economic partner or in the context of building "new structures for international co-operation". It is to be hoped that in time and with a more proactive diplomacy on India's part, the change that the Hatoyama Government seeks for Japan will also include new possibilities in relations with India.

Japan keen to Strengthen Economic Ties with India

Innovative Investment Strategy: With the global meltdown lengthening its dark shadows on the capital market and financial institutions showing diffidence to lend, the Government has to take innovative investment strategy to keep the investment flow steady until economies recover. This would help developing countries overcome bottlenecks to raise capital to fund their crucial projects, particularly in the infrastructure sector, said a senior executive of the Japan External Trade Organization (JETRO).

Investment Mechanism: A viable investment mechanism that helped in overcoming short-term debacles without disturbing the role of private sector should be evolved, said Mr. Tomaharu Washio, Special Advisor, Strategic Research, JETRO. The process of development should not be allowed to be stunted by such short-term hurdles, particularly when the free flow of private capital was difficult to get..

Mr. Washio, who is here in connection with the 18th International Engineering & Technology Fair organized by

Confederation of Indian Industry, said Japan was keen to strengthen its economic ties with India.

Growth Pangs: Due to recessionary pressures following its structural reforms and the impact of deceleration of US economy, Japan was keen to seek investment opportunities in India. He said India's resilience in withstanding the global economic shock, caused by the US financial sector collapse, encouraged Japan to rely on its market.

DMIC Project: He referred to the major Indo-Japanese project– the $90 billion Delhi-Mumbai Industrial Corridor (DMIC) consisting of five components of an integrated India-Japan Enclave in Haryana, Free Trade Warehouse Zone project in Greater Noida, Captive Power plant Neemrana and DMIC Human Resources Training project — and said key promoters such Mistsui, Hitachi, Sony and NYK Logistics were keen to see the quicker implementation of the proposal.

A few observers have recently suggested Japan is tilting toward China under the Hatoyama administration. While China-Japan relations have improved, the United States will continue to remain at the core of Japanese foreign policy. A dominant pattern of Japan's international relations has been its tendency to ally with a great power, usually the strongest power in the international system- China during the Sino-centric Order, Great Britain during the imperial period, Germany during World War II, and the United States in the post-war period.

Japanese Companies Keen to Invest More in India

Japanese corporations, scouting for partners to expand their overseas investments, are inclined to give an impetus to India as an investment destination. In a gradual shift from their earlier trading pattern, which was focussed on the US and Europe, Japanese companies expect India to emerge as the third most important trading partner after the US and China, in the next three years.

Sharing the latest findings of a survey by the Japanese External Trade Organization (Jetro), Mr Toshiki Takahashi, Director of the International Economic Research Division (Overseas Research Department), Jetro, said the increasing interest in India is its large market and the macro-economic strength that have helped it minimize the impact of the financial crisis. Mr Takahashi said Japanese corporations were keen to further expand their investments in India, which not only was a huge market but also had the potential to become a cost-effective production hub.

Mergers and Acquisitions: Japan's increasing interest since 2005 is reflected in recent mergers and acquisitions, such as of Matsushita Electric Works in electricals, Daiichi Sankyo in Ranbaxy Laboratories, and NTT DoCoMo's investment in Tata Teleservices. Takahashi said despite the global economic crisis, India figured strongly in the Japanese corporations' outlook for investment in the next three years with 50.23 per cent of the surveyed planning to expand their business overseas, with either new investments or expansion of existing bases. This figure exceeded those planning to expand domestic operations.

An overwhelming majority, whose performance had been affected by the financial crisis cited falling demand, rising costs in the both the manufacturing and non-manufacturing sectors and forex losses as the reasons for shifting their focus of investment. There is yet another trend manifesting in an overall declining interest in expanding sales and production functions in China, with some exceptions such as expansion in sale functions in material industries including wood, textiles, in addition to the food and beverages and precision equipment industries. Although interest in expanding sales in China was declining, stronger interest for expanding the activity was seen in India, Brazil and Russia.

IV. Reality Check in Asia

The desire of Japan's new government to 'rebalance' its foreign policy between East and West and the subsequent tensions between Japan and the US could be portents of a shift in the regional balance of power. Propelled by a global recession that was seen to be 'made in USA,' and the striking contrast of China's resilience and rising confidence, there is a growing sense of a fundamental transition in the way the world moves. This compelling idea does not capture the dynamics of contemporary Asia. The Obama administration talks about a new commitment to Asia, but it is distracted by wars elsewhere and absorbed by bruising political fights at home. Its capacity for action is limited by rising debt and dependence on other nations whose interests often differ from those of the U.S.

China clearly is the beneficiary of these constraints, which is eager to pursue its place of prominence in Asia. The JPM Hatoyama has declared that he seeks to "rebalance" relations with the U.S. and forge a new relationship with Asia as a whole, and China in particular. The implication of this shift is evident in visible tensions with Washington, triggered by delays in the relocation of U.S. Marine Corps Air Station Futenma in Okinawa Prefecture, which is seen as part of a more general devaluing of the alliance as a whole. The visit of Democratic Party of Japan kingpin Ozawa Ichiro to Beijing with several hundred businessmen and politicians contrasts with antagonism between Tokyo and Washington. Hatoyama's call for an East Asian community that excludes the U.S. completes the case for a shift in the global balance of power opens advantage to Beijing.

The Changing World: Asia is assuming a more prominent role in the global economy. Hitherto, its political influence has lagged. The creation of an East Asian community is one expression of that desire. Certainly China is playing and will continue to play a key role in that process while Japan is still debating its place in the region and the world, and that debate has taken on new intensity in the wake of changes since the end of the Cold War. China is rising, but there are real limits to its influence, strength and allure. Economic growth is creating unprecedented strains in Chinese society and it is not clear how the political system will cope. China is a big presence, but Asian governments have little faith or confidence in Beijing. Beijing is a stalwart defender of the principle of noninterference in domestic affairs, but it has shown little inclination to provide the international public goods — security and stability — that have made Asian prosperity possible.

Japan is debating national identity — but that discussion has been going on since the Meiji Restoration. Governments in Tokyo have always been tugged between East and West, and compromises have been made, modified and discarded since the isolationism of the Edo period was abandoned. That is exactly what any country should do as internal and external circumstances change. While rapprochement between Tokyo and Beijing is a good thing — the region's two leading powers are seen to be on good terms and no regional community is possible without them. Yet, there are observable basic conflicts of interest, values and perspective that limit diplomatic maneuver. Despite the new government in Japan, the two countries display periodic spats over disputed territory in the East China Sea.

Japan's call for respect and equality in the US-Japan relationship is not new. Every Tokyo government has remained the 'junior partner'. Public opinion polls in Japan support for the alliance is at high level. This DPJ government, like other governments in the region, looks to the US to provide regional security and stability. Washington's power may be diminished, but it continues to remain an integral part of the Asian order. It is a trusted 'great power' in the region. Washington remains a key partner as Asia as it passes through a transformative period.

REFERENCES

The Australian, 08 April 2010.

East Asia Forum, 06 April 2010.

The Japan Times, 8 April 2010.

The Japan Times, 07 April 2010.

The New York Times, 27August 2009.

The Hindu, Bangalore, 18 May 2009.

The Hindu Business Line (Bangalore), 25 February 2010.

The Yomiuri Shimbun/The Daily Yomiuri, 16 November 2009.

The Japan Times, 4 March 2010.

APEC goes through the motions, *The Japan Times*, 16 November 2009.

The Japan Times, 18 November 2009.

Mieko Kawashima, "Hatoyama unveils Asia-focused foreign policy", *The Daily Yomiuri*, 16 November 2009

Yoshinari Kurose, "Obama takes realistic approach to Asia", *The Daily Yomiuri*, 16 November 2009.

"Japan - the indispensable power in East Asia", *East Asia Forum*, February 2010.

Dominique Moisi, "Recognizing confident India as indispensable", (http://www.project-syndicate.org/) *The Japan Times*, 22 December 2009.

"A look at the Asia-Pacific Economic Cooperation forum Pragmatic Asia can bolster global stability", *The Japan Times*, 23 February 2010.

Kyodo News, 11 April 2010.

Kishore Mahbubani and Simon Chesyterman, "Pragmatic Asia can bolster global stability", *The Japan Times*, 4 March 2010.

Iio Jun, "What will the change of government bring to Japanese politics", *Social science Journal Newsletter*, No 42, March 2010.

Maeda Yukio, "The change of government and public opinion: September 2005 to August 2009", *Social science Journal Newsletter*, No 42, March 2010.

Uekami Takayoshi, "Electoral Manifestos of the Democratic Party of Japan", *Social science Journal Newsletter*, No 42, March 2010.

14

Insinuation of a Bilateral Free Trade Agreement between India and Australia: Some Evidence from an Empirical Model

Nabeel Mancheri

This paper explores the bilateral trade, trade barriers and the effect of a possible Free Trade Agreement (FTA) between India and Australia assuming a hypothetical membership of FTA. Despite recent official talks and significant public interest on this issue, there has been no consensus about the economic impact of the closer regional trade integration. India and Australia are undertaking negotiations over "new-age" FTA or CEPA. The purpose of this paper is to evaluate the impact of the FTAs on the welfare implications of the trade agreement by examining macroeconomic and trade performance, exports, and the trade creation and trade diversion effects on India and Australia. FTAs can have significant economic impacts on their member and non-member countries. In particular, the economic impacts are likely to be greater when FTAs/EPAs are more comprehensive, involving not only trade liberalization but also liberalization of trade in services and investment, trade facilitation measures such as simplified customs clearance and mutual recognition of standards, and technical assistance.

Several studies have analyzed the trade enhancing impact of preferential trading arrangements. These studies predict the additional bilateral trade that would be a consequence of the economic integration of a set of economies. There are two basic approaches to the empirical assessment of FTAs. The first, known as the "gravity model" approach, uses a cross-section of bilateral trade data and attempts to estimate a 'normal' trade pattern. If order can be found in the deviations from that pattern, this technique can provide useful information on trade effects of FTAs (in particular if the cross sections are available for several time periods). Because this approach requires the application of statistical techniques to existing data, it is usually used ex-post – to confirm the presence of trade creation/diversion after agreements are put in place.

For situations where analysis prior to the fact is required, the most common used technique in recent years has been simulation with a Computable General Equilibrium (CGE) model. This approach is quite different. It takes cross-sectional data from a single base period, not only for trade but also production, and consumption, and imposes a detailed theoretical structure on the interactions between different data elements. An earlier major study by the World Bank which ran into several volumes using this technique examined in depth the trade liberalisation experience of developing countries. They found that liberalisation conferred significant benefits and, what was more surprising to the researchers, that the costs of adjustment were very small, even in the short term.

By relying on the simulation approach that combines data and prospective scenarios in a structured manner to analyze the economic effects of policy changes due to the formation of a FTA, CGE models have emerged as an important tool for shedding light on these issues. The CGE models used have varied somewhat in their underlying economic structure, behavior of agents and focus, but while the theoretical structure varies, commonly these models build on the Global Trade Analysis Project (GTAP) database. The primary focus of such policy scenarios has been on the removal of price distortions against imports that arise from existing trade barriers (in particular merchandise tariffs). Most studies have used the standard GTAP model with constant returns to scale in production, perfect competition, and the Armington assumption (or some variant of GTAP) while a few have adopted CGE models with firm-level imperfect competition (Francois J F and G Wignaraja, 2008). The simulation approach uses a static CGE model (for example, Brown, Deardorff and Stern, 1992; Scollay and Gilbert, 2001; and Urata and Kiyota, 2003), or a dynamic intertemporal general equilibrium model (for example, McKibbin, 1998; and McKibbin, Lee and Cheong, 2004). The models specify economic structures and behaviour of agents in detail and, using the framework, simulate the economic effects of existing or proposed FTAs. Simulations based on the general equilibrium models usually find substantial potential gains from trade liberalisation between members of an FTA.

For example, Brown, Deardorff and Stern (1992) estimate that NAFTA has increased intra-region trade by 8.0 per cent from the baseline, and has led to a welfare gain of 0.1 per cent of GDP for the United States and 5.0 per cent of GDP for Mexico. Scollay and Gilbert (2001) estimate that a Japan-Korea-China FTA will generate welfare gains of 0.25 per cent of GDP for Japan, 0.80 per cent of GDP for Korea, and 2.1 per cent of GDP for China. Urata and Kiyota (2003) expect that an East Asian FTA including China, Japan, Asian NIEs and ASEAN will produce welfare gains ranged from the lowest 0.19 per cent of GDP for Japan to the highest 12.5 per cent of GDP for Thailand. McKibbin, Lee and Cheong (2004), show that gains for Korea and Japan from a bilateral FTA will amount to about 0.1–0.2 per cent of GDP per year for both countries. Robinson and Thierfelder (1999) review theoretical and empirical models of RTAs and summarise 'a few robust conclusions' from empirical surveys of CGE model analysis. They suggest that empirical evidence of proliferating FTAs strongly supports positive welfare effect of FTAs on members measured in terms of real GDP or equivalent variation and net trade-creation effect.

Emanuel Ornelas (2005) evaluates the impact of FTAs on the world trading system by using an oligopolistic-political-economy model where the external tariffs of FTA members, as well as the decision to form FTAs, are endogenously determined. In this context, the study finds that FTAs are primarily beneficial to the multilateral trading system. This conclusion is based, first, upon the finding that FTAs induce their member governments to lower their external tariffs, and to do so deeply enough to enhance trade even between FTA members and non-members. While this ensures gains for the latter, in general FTA members may not gain. However, thatgovernments will endorse only welfare-improving arrangements, in spite of their political motivations; as a result, FTA members benefit from ratified arrangements as well.

Bonda Eric W et al. (2004), provide new insights on the strategic aspects and welfare effects of FTAs. They use a simple three country general-equilibrium trade model to analyze how the formation of an FTA between two countries affects the tariff and welfare levels of all trade partners and the results indicate that the formation of an FTA improves the terms of trade and welfare of nonmember countries because it creates an incentive for members to reduce their external tariffs. However, for member states, there are two opposing effects. In equilibrium, their terms of trade vis-a-vis ROW deteriorate and this is welfare-reducing. At the same time, the liberalization of internal trade causes intra-union trade to expand and this is welfare-improving. They have shown that, as long as member countries are sufficiently large, the latter effect will dominate and the formation of an FTA will benefit both members.

The main elements of the prospective India- Australia FTA involve bilateral liberalization and facilitation of trade through reduction of tariff and non-tariff barriers as well as the mutual recognition of national standards, streamlining customs procedures, facilitation of increased services trade, as well as establishment of an exemplary framework for foreign investment. These "new age" FTAs also envision increased collaboration on intellectual property, education and training, media and broadcasting and tourism. This trade agreement is particularly significant, since it is viewed by many as providing a possible template for future FTAs in the region.

Trade Relationship between India and Australia

The Australia – India trade and economic relationship has improved over recent years, fuelled by the many complementarities between the two economies as India progressively liberalises its domestic economy and moves towards a more international orientation. Over the past five years, bilateral trade in goods and services has increased by 24 per cent annually to AS$ 22 billion in 2010.

In 2009-10, India's exports to Australia stood at just US$1.38 billion, while imports amounted US$12.4 billion, translating into a trade deficit of about US$11 billion for New Delhi. While considering their relative importance to each other, India's share of export to Australia was 0.78 % of its total export as against the import share of 3.5% of its total imports from rest of the world making Australia as India's one of most important source for energy and commodities. How important is India to Australia for her imports compare to her rest of the trading partners, Australia exported about 8.1% of her total exports to India and imported around 0.9% from India of its total import demand. There are many opportunities, but both countries are not taking advantage of them. Australia and India have a huge potential of increasing the trade and investment and on negotiation of the proposed FTA is great step towards this realization. The latest country-wise trade data for the financial year 2009-10 shows Australia as India's eighth largest goods trade partner and fourth largest export market. Australia accounted for about 3 per cent of India's total goods trade. India's trade with Australia, however, is much less than its trade with its top three partners; China ($29.9 billion), UAE

($28.4 billion) and the US ($25.1 billion). During 2008-09 Australia's share in India's total trade was 2.6 per cent.

The section below examines the bilateral flow of commodities between India and Australia in 2009. The commodities are classified on the basis of standard international trade classification (SITC 3) data available at UN Comtrade database.

Table 1
India's Exports and Imports from Australia in 2009

(in US$ million)

	Commodities, SITC 1 Digit level	*Exports*	*Imports*
0.	Food and Live Animals	104.108	187.975
1.	Beverages and Tobacco	13.272	1.457
2.	Crude materials, inedible, except fuel	72.828	829.527
3.	Mineral Fuels, lubricants and related materials	38.417	3849.552
4.	Animal and vegetable oils, fats and waxes	2.519	7.350
5.	Chemicals and related products, n.e.s	177.920	150.388
6.	Manufactured goods, classified chiefly by materials	381. 322	394.695
7.	Machinery and transport equipment	283.042	151.172
8.	Miscellaneous manufactured articles	330.895	57.626
9.	Commodities and Transactions not classified elsewhere in the SITC	5.869	6387.303
	Total	1410.197	12017.049

Source: UN Comtrade database

The Table 1 represents India's bilateral trade of major commodities with Australia, the merchandise trade disintegrated with SITC 1 digit level for the year 2009.[1] According to India's Ministry of Commerce data, petroleum products have overtaken the jewellery and gemstones sector to become the top export product as India's top export product to the world after 2007. This is due to the rapid development of domestic refining capacity. In 1996, India imported both crude and refined petrol (around 2/3 crude and 1/3 refined) and exported only negligible quantities. In 2010 its imports of crude petrol have more than tripled (in quantity), its imports of refined petrol have considerably declined, and refined petrol has become a key export. It is yet unclear whether this export boom is sustainable or it was due to an incipient excess domestic refining capacity. This trend is evident in India's increasing import of crude from Australia also which was equal to USD 3.84 billion in 2009.

The major commodity items India exported to Australia included manufactured goods (SITC 6), worth of USD 381.32 million, chiefly classified by materials such as leather, leather manufactures, n.e.s., and dressed fur skins, rubber manufactures, n.e.s.; cork and wood manufactures (excluding furniture), paper, paperboard and articles of paper pulp, of paper or of paperboard, textile yarn, fabrics, made-up articles, n.e.s., and related products, non-metallic mineral manufactures, n.e.s. iron and steel, non-ferrous metals, manufactures of metals, n.e.s. The next important item of exports were miscellaneous manufactured articles (SITC 8), worth of USD330.89 million which include prefabricated buildings; sanitary, plumbing, heating and lighting fixtures and fittings, n.e.s. furniture, and parts thereof; bedding, mattresses, mattress supports, cushions and similar stuffed furnishings, travel goods, handbags and similar containers, articles of apparel and clothing accessories, footwear, professional, scientific and controlling instruments and apparatus, n.e.s. and photographic apparatus, equipment and supplies and optical goods, n.e.s.; watches and clocks followed by machinery and transport equipment (SITC 7) worth of US$ 283.04 million a share of around 29 per cent, such as power-generating machinery and equipment, machinery specialized for particular industries, metalworking machinery, general industrial machinery and equipment, and machine parts.

The major items India imported from Australia include commodities and transactions not classified elsewhere (SITC 9) equal to USD 6.387 billion, the items basically consist of postal packages not classified according to kind special transactions and commodities not classified according to kind coin (other than gold coin), gold, armored fighting vehicles, war firearm, ammunition and parts. The other major items of imports included mineral fuels, lubricants and related materials (SITC 3) worth of US$ 3.849 billion, which comprises the major commodities such as, coal, coke and briquettes, petroleum, petroleum products and related materials, gas, natural and manufactured; and electric current etc followed by crude materials, inedible, except fuel (SITC 2) worth of USD 829 million and manufactured goods (SITC 6) equal to US$ 394.69 million. Besides the three major items, viz., coal, gold and copper, India also imported from Australia other items like, fertilisers, manganese, wool, aluminium, vegetables and lead.

It is interesting to note that the bilateral trade relationship between Australia and India is to a significant extent characterised by India's imports from Australia of raw materials and intermediate products which are used by India to produce final goods for export, a part of which in turn is imported from India by Australia.

It is hoped that the two countries will strive for mutually beneficial and sustainable economic growth by cultivating stronger levels of bilateral economic exchange. The Australian business community has displayed sharply increased interest in India in recent years. In fact, Australian companies that had set up business in India have remarkably increased. Moreover, it is estimated that total direct investment amount by Australian companies will increase greatly. The signing of "strategic and global partnership" agreement as well as a variety of undertakings, and the start of negotiations on (Comprehensive) Economic Partnership Agreement (EPA/ CEPA) reflect a deeply shared interest on the part of both countries to seek an even-stronger bilateral relationship. In the interest of cultivating mutually beneficial economic ties, it is critically important that those negotiations lead to the early conclusion of CEPA/ EPA. The conclusion of EPA/CEPA will effectively remove or reduce tariff as well as non-tariff barriers will increase both exports and imports. Since a stable and peaceful regional and international environment provides necessary climate for continued growth in trade and economic activity, Australia is encouraged by and supportive of India's growing engagement with the East Asian region. India matters to Australia because the country is the major driver of the global economy.

India's Bilateral Trade Share with Australia

The following table explains India's export share with Australia in terms of Australia's total imports as well as India's import share with Australia in terms of India's total imports as the commodities classified at SITC one digit level. Such an analysis helps to understand the relative importance of Australia as a market for Indian goods and the same way it shows how much India is dependent on Australia for its major import items in terms of India's total imports from rest of the world.

Table 2
India's Bilateral Trade Share with Australia

SITC One- Digit Summary[2]
Unit: Percent

Commodity	*India's Export Share to Australia in terms of Australia's Total Importss*	*India's Import Share from Australia in Terms of India's Total Imports*
SITC 0	1.86	7.22
SITC 1	0.63	1.92
SITC 2	3.62	10.1
SITC 3	0.014	3.55
SITC 4	0.54	0.004
SITC 5	0.695	0.37
SITC 6	2.09	1.05
SITC 7	0.32	0.32
SITC 8	0.91	0.48
SITC 9	0.11	14.6
Total	0.69	3.51

All shares are denoted in terms of importer's or demander's viewpoint.

For commodity classifications at the SITC one digit level, please refer footnote 2.

Source: Calculated using data from the *UN Comtrade database*

The top 10 exporting sectors of India to the world constituted about 40 per cent of total exports of goods. Precious stones such as diamonds remain the leading export sector and constitute 13 per cent of total merchandise exports. The sectors which recorded a noticeable increase in their shares were iron ore and concentrates, and jewellery. Clearly, India's leading exporting sectors are highly labour intensive with low capital intensity. India ranks among the top 10 exporters of clothing, leather and textile. The similar situation is reflected in India's bilateral trade with Australia.

India is not a significant source of imports for Australia. What Australia imports from India are easily available to her from rest of her trading partners, pointing to the inefficiency of India's trade specialization and incompetence to penetrate to the Australian market? The major commodities Australia imported from India in 2007 constitute rotating electric plant & parts worth of AusD 154 million, pearls & gems of 107 million, jewellery for 67 million, made-up textile articles for 53 million. These commodities are classified in a much wider way. If we look at the SITC 1 digit level, the majority of items, Australia imports from India include manufactured goods classified chiefly by materials including textile and cloths (SITC 6) worth of USD 368 million, machinery and transport equipment (SITC 7) for about 210 USD million, miscellaneous manufactured articles (SITC8) worth of 184 USD million which basically include prefabricated buildings; sanitary, plumbing, heating and lighting fixtures and fittings, n.e.s. furniture, and parts thereof; bedding, mattresses, mattress supports, cushions and similar stuffed furnishings, travel goods, handbags and similar containers, articles of apparel and clothing accessories and footwear. Interestingly Australia imports USD 111 million worth of food and live animals from India as India imports USD 288 million worth of same commodities from Australia, however, at a more disintegrated level nature commodities traded may have some differences.

The share of each commodity that Australia imports from India to her total import of that particular commodity is very meager. India's export of crude materials, inedible, except fuel

(SITC 2) make 3.62 % of Australian total import of the same commodities from rest of the world. The other important items for which Australia depends on India are manufactured goods classified chiefly by materials (SITC 6), represent 2.09 %, food and live animals (SITC 0) make up 1.86% of her total import of these commodities. Commodities those make up less than 1% that Australia imports from India include miscellaneous manufactured articles (SITC 8) equal to 0.91%, chemicals and related products (SITC 5) equal to 0.69%, beverages and tobacco (SITC 1) equal 0.63% and SITC 4 equal to 0.54% of Australia's total imports.

Obviously the Table 2 depicts that what are the sectors that Australia has a comparative advantage in trading. The foremost item that India imports from Australia is SITC 9, which basically constitutes Postal packages (not classified according to kind), Special transactions and commodities (not classified according to kind), Coin (other than gold coin, not being legal tender and Gold (non-monetary, excluding gold ores and concentrates), which make up about 14.62% of the total import of the same commodity from rest of the world. In this category, non-monetary gold was far and away the bulk, by value, of Australia's merchandise exports to India, worth some $A 4022 million in 2007-8. The rest include crude materials, inedible, except fuels (SITC 2) accounting for 10.15%; basic copper ores and concentrates, food and live animals (SITC 0) equal to 7.22%; mineral fuels, lubricants and related materials (SITC 3) equal to 3.55 %; followed by manufactured goods (SITC 6) chiefly composed of wool making up 1.05 % of India's total imports. The structure of merchandise imports has remained stable over the years with fuels and mining products representing around 40% of the total bill. Manufactured goods represent around 50% and agricultural and food products only 10% of India's import from rest of the world.

Barriers to Trade and Prospects of Bilateral FTA between India and Australia

Trade barriers play a central role in models of international specialization and trade. Much of the theory concerns the effects of barriers on trade, and trade costs figure prominently in recent work that extends our understanding of the nature of specialization. Goto (2001) found that by liberalizing the economy, the welfare of Asian developing economies would improve substantially within an Asian trading bloc. A gravity model of bilateral trade involving 11 trading blocs, mostly in the Asia Pacific region, found that the impacts of preferential trade agreements vary remarkably across the region (Clarete et al. 2002). Trade liberalization in the present analysis assumes the partial/complete elimination of import tariffs and export subsidies (taxes) for the countries involved in an FTA. Using the simulation results of the major studies in the area this study also attempts to discuss agriculture trade liberalization by examining not only scenarios of full trade liberalization in all sectors but also those of partial trade liberalization in the agriculture sector as well as those excluding the agriculture sector from trade liberalization.

A study in 2008 by ADB shows that the benefits of regional integration outweigh its costs. The following figure illustrates the major variables in which the ADB study outlined the benefits and costs and the relative importance of these variables.

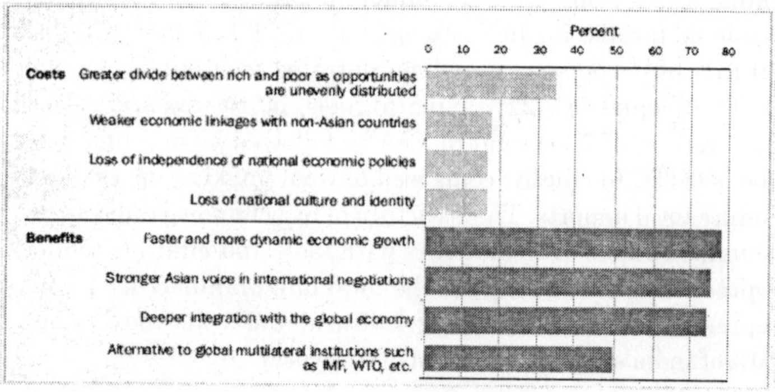

Figure 1: The Benefits and Costs of Regional Integration

(Asian opinion leaders' replies to survey questionnaire, percent of respondents answering "high" or "very high") *Source: ADB, 2008*

The Figure shows that the advantages of closer economic relations within Asia outweigh the costs. Their approach is pragmatic: they favor a step-by-step approach to integration and believe that regionalism provides opportunities for "win-win" outcomes throughout the region. Economic integration is viewed as benefiting these countries through faster economic growth, deeper integration with the world economy, and a stronger Asian voice in global economic forums. The potential costs of integration—such as a greater economic divide between rich and poor and the loss of some autonomy in national economic policy making—are judged to be substantially smaller than its benefits.

Table 3
Import-Weighted Average Bilateral Applied Tariff Rates for all Merchandise Trade for India and Australia

Importers :	*India*	*Australia*
India	*	5.6
Australia	26.5	*
RoW	21.8	4.3

Source: GTAP Version 6 database

As with other such regional trade agreements, the FTAs between India and Australia envision bilateral elimination of tariffs (Joint Study Group, 2006a, 2000b). Table 3 reports estimated import-weighted average bilateral tariffs levied by India and Australia on one another's exports. The tariff estimates are based on average applied rates for the year 2001 reported in Global Trade Analysis Project (GTAP) database version 6. For instance, India's tariffs imposed on imports from Australia exceed 20 percent. In scenarios of full trade liberalization in all sectors, all tariffs are removed. More specifically, when trade is fully liberalized between India, and Australia with a significant amount of trade, tariffs are removed.

Table 4
Import-Weighted Average Bilateral Applied Tariff Rates

Sectoral import tariff	*India*	*Australia*
Agri& food	50.2	2.8
Fishery& forestry	6.8	0.1
Mining	16.2	4.9
Textile& apparel	26.6	17.0
Wood& paper	22.0	3.6
Mineral products	28.8	3.0
Iron& steel	33.6	3.6
General machinery	25.4	3.5
Electronic machinery	15.1	0.8
Transport equipment	27.4	12.9
Other manufacturing	33.8	5.2
Manufacturing total	24.8	5.4
Total	21.8	4.3

Source: Adapted from REITI, 2009 based on GTAP version 6

Table 4 shows import-weighted sectoral average tariff rates in India and Australia which are calculated by using sectoral import values at domestic prices and world prices. As the table shows, average tariffs for all sectors are particularly high in India with a tariff rate of 25 percent, comparatively with Australia at 4.3 percent. At the sectoral level, clearly, the agriculture and food sector is protected by high tariffs for India. On the other hand, tariffs in manufacturing sectors on average are already less than six percent except 25 percent for India. Some of the manufacturing sectors, however, have relatively high tariffs. A typical high sector tariff is the textile and apparel sector: tariffs are 26.6% for India, 17% for Australia.

The transport equipment sector is another high tariff sector; India with a tariff rate of 27 percent, and Australia with 13 percent.

India's tariff rates are higher for the sectors such as wood and paper with 22%, mineral products 28.8%, steel and iron 33.6% and other manufacturing 33.8% other than the above mentioned sectors. Australia's tariff reductions over the 1970s, 80s and 90s have been one of the major unilateral liberalisations in the world. The starting point, as Garnaut puts it is that 'for two decades until the mid-1980s, Australia and New Zealand had the most protected manufacturing sectors among the members of the OECD (Garnaut, R. 2002). One would expect that there is considerable room for trade liberalization in these countries/sectors.

Table 5
Value of Import Taxes between India and Australia

Commodities	*Tariff rates*	
	India	*Australia*
Agriculture	38.27	0.0031
Mining & Extraction	328.45	0.084
Processed Food	14.38	0.257
Labor-Intensive Manufactures	30.8	39.29
Capital-Intensive Manufactures	497.51	4.28

Adapted from the *GTAP Database 7* (http://www.gtap.agecon.purdue.edu/databases/v7/v7_sampledata.asp?Version=7.0)

The above Table shows that the value of import taxes levied by India and Australia on commodities imported from each other's market on the basis of GTAP version 7 commodity aggregations. The value is positively related with the value of commodities traded. India collects high import taxes on capital intensive manufacturing and mining and extraction commodities such as coal, oil and gas importing from Australia. Australia has high import tax on labour intensive manufacturing items originating from India.

India's imports from Australia mainly concentrated on food and agricultural items and mining and crude materials. Bilateral imports of meat and other food products are modest, but face a very high average tariff. It is clear from this table why food and agriculture represent a very sensitive part of these agreements for all three countries. Given the very high tariffs facing these products imported, it is quite likely that agriculture will be left out of the final FTA agreement – or perhaps it will be implemented in a gradual manner. Of course, textiles and apparel products and leather goods also face non-negligible tariffs so that substantial expansion of imports from India to Australia is expected under the FTAs. Clearly this trading relationship involves a great deal of intra-industry trade that should receive a substantial boost from any reduction in non-tariff trade costs.

These, together with agriculture, are the key sectors for the FTAs. But, in the space of a generation, Australia's tariff walls were dismantled with the average level of industry protection, as measured by the effective rate of assistance, falling from over 30 per cent to under 5 per cent between 1970 and 2001 (Leigh, A. 2002). Effective rates of assistance have remained at a little under 5 per cent since. Major tariff reform ended in 1991 but further reductions to Australia's more highly protected car and textile industries were announced in 1997 by the Howard government. The intention was to achieve tariffs of 10 per cent for cars, textiles and footwear and 15 per cent for clothing by 2005. Car tariffs are expected to be 5 per cent by 2010 and an average (across 1000 tariff lines) of 5.23 per cent for textiles, clothing and footwear

A study in 2009 by the Centre for International Economics (CIE), Canberra, calculated that the welfare reducing effect of global tariff increases by ten percent.

Table 6

Impact of Raising Global Tariffs by 10 per cent

(Per cent deviation from baseline)

Regions	*Impact of raising global tariff*				
	Import %	*Export* %	*Investment* %	*Consumption* %	*GDP* %
India	-1.45	-1.75	-0.27	-0.06	-0.15
Australia	-0.59	-0.43	-0.30	-0.11	-0.13
RoW	-1.10	-1.05	-0.53	-0.21	-0.28

Source: Adapted from CIE, 2009, based on GTAP simulation

The Table shows that an increase in global tariff by 10 percent will impact India's exports and imports more than the exports and imports of Australia by a reduction of 1.45% and 1.75% respectively from the baseline scenario. This demonstrates that the reduction or elimination of trade barriers within the region is of course important in establishing FTAs. Since the trade has already grown dramatically between India and Australia, FTAs are expected to be comprehensive; they cover not only trade liberalization but also other contents such as trade facilitation, including the simplification of customs clearance procedures and mutual recognition of standards, and technical assistance and technology transfers. A tariff reduction of an FTA has a wide variety of economic impacts on the member countries of the agreement, as well as the rest of the world. The effects encompass welfare, production, exports and imports in both real and nominal terms.

In addition to the above effects, researchers have identified the effects on economic growth of trade liberalization under an FTA. The tariff reduction may provide an incentive: (i) to mobilize inputs and to improve their quality; (ii) to increase the efficiency of management through the increased pressure of competition (the "competition enhancing" effect); and (iii) to enhance technological innovation. Most of these effects are hypothetical, and empirical studies on the growth function have tested them by the panel data estimates.

The strongest arguments for FTAs relate to their dynamic effects, which are cumulative and pervasive. If FTAs can reduce the transaction costs of trading and investment, they can create a production base of unparalleled scale and diversity. Regional production and trade networks are the principal drivers and beneficiaries of this process. By boosting FDI inflows, FTAs could promote technology transfer and make it easier to adopt trade- and investment-facilitating measures, such as harmonized customs classifications and procedures, compatible product standards, and best practices in accounting and management— all of which bolster efficiency and attract investment. The traditional objection to FTAs focuses on static trade effects. While

FTAs remove discrimination among partner countries (and thus create trade), they discriminate in favor of members at the expense of non members (and thus divert trade to less productive suppliers located within the FTA). This worsens an economy's terms of trade, since it implies purchasing imports from a higher-cost source. It also worsens the terms of trade of efficient outside producers, since they are left with smaller markets for their products. Are, then, FTAs building or stumbling blocks to global free trade? It depends on the context and structure of each FTA.

Gains from Different FTA Scenarios Involving India and Australia

To examine potential trade flows as a result of tariff removal by India and Australia, the study uses 100 per cent tariff shocks on imports from each other are simulated. The outcomes of the simulations are reported on macro variables such as welfare, output, exports and imports. Projections of welfare gains from consolidating FTAs in Asia are discussed in Kawai and Wignaraja (2008), Kazutomo Abe (2007) and Mitsuyo Ando (2009). Using a global computable general equilibrium model they show that welfare gains for Asia increase with wider agreements (such as those that are ASEAN+3 or EAS-wide) in comparison with ASEAN+1-type FTAs or bilateral FTAs. Substantial additional research confirms this. Harrigan et al (2007), note that large trade areas minimize trade diversion and that creating hub-and-spoke system that "fails to connect the spokes" is very costly. Kawai and Wignaraja (2008) make a strong case for a single East Asian FTA to reduce the costs associated with overlapping ROORs and other inefficiencies. They find that an EAS arrangement would generate the largest gains, while costs to non members from trade diversion would be small. This section illustrates the welfare gains accruing to India and Australia under various FTA scenarios. Since the availability of data is limited and purchasing the databases and the software packages for simulation is beyond the means of the researcher, the section mostly depends on the secondary data and simulation results derived for both courtiers under various scenarios by other researchers. The present assessments of the economic impacts of free trade agreements (FTAs) relating to India and Australia, the analysis relies on simulation with a computable general equilibrium model. The impacts of various combinations of FTAs are assessed to draw policy implications.

Simulation Results Based on Static GTAP

Trade among various countries and trade blocs have been growing rapidly in recent years following reductions in tariff barriers as a result of domestic reforms, WTO commitments and FTA engagement. The trade statistics analysed in the above section shows a great potential for further expansion in case of bilateral trade between India and Australia. This section attempts to investigate further the potential trade flows among these countries as a result of proposed FTAs. The results in this study are based on hypothetical tariff simulations, using a computable general equilibrium model called the GTAP model. Hypothetical tariff simulations have been undertaken to explore the rationale for deeper integration among India and Australia. The simulation results for increase in exports of India to Australia as well as to Japan, China and rest of the world are presented in Table 7 at a disaggregated commodity level.

Table 7
Bilateral Exports of Commodity i from India to Japan, Australia, China and Rest of the World

(% change)

Commodities	*Japan*	*Australia*	*China*	*ROW*
Grain Crops	74.39	33.18	20.16	0.86
MeatLstk	36.84	22.31	63.26	3.02
Extraction	6.1	1.28	2.17	-2.09
Proc. Food	11.19	4.5	40.47	3.36
Text Wapp	13.47	13.67	21.37	6.25
Light. Manuf's	16.40	7.02	45.24	5.63
Heavy Manuf's	15.27	7.37	49.47	6.48
Services	8.18	5.89	4.99	5.86
Total	12.86	10.53	22.75	5.39

Author's simulation on the basis of *GTAP standard ver. 6*

The figures of India's exports to Australia indicate an increase in exports of food grain crop sector by 33.18 percent, meat and live stock by 22.31 percent, extraction by 1. 28 percent, processed food by 4.5 percent, textile and wearing apparel by 13.67 percent, light manufacturing by 7.02 percent, heavy manufacturing items by 7.37 percent and services by 5.89 percent which shows the proposed FTA between India and Australia having considerable positive effects on India's exports to Australia on items such as grain crops, meat and live stock, textile and wearing apparels, and light and heavy manufacturing, and less impact on services, extraction and processed food items. The simulation result also indicates great potential in India's export to China. The figure reveals an increase in India's exports of grain crop sector by 20. 16 percent, meat and live stock by 63.26 percent, processed food by 40.47 percent, textile and wearing apparels by 21.37 percent, light manufacturing items by 45.24 percent, heavy manufacturing items by 49.47 percent and service sector exports by 4.99 percent. India's overall exports to China rose by 22.75 percent which is highest gain for any single country market.

Table 8

Bilateral Exports of Commodity i from Australia to India, Japan, China and Rest of the World

(% change)

Commodities	*India*	*Japan*	*China*	*ROW*
GrainCrops	33.48	14.13	42.66	2.14
MeatLstk	53.57	63.73	67.83	-5.35
Extraction	39.37	29.04	44.35	-7.58
ProcFood	20.07	25.06	54.28	-2.17
TextWapp	8.97	-1.17	37.17	-8.78
LightMnfc	26.23	0.62	46.96	-7.14
HeavyMnfc	16.62	0.96	17.38	-6.59
Services	-5.19	-2.79	-3.32	-6.24
Total	13.43	3.66	15.96	-6.72

Author's simulation on the basis of *GTAP standard ver, 6*

Examining the bilateral export flows from Australia to India, Japan, China and rest of the world as a result of free trade, exports of Australia to India increased by 13.43 percent. Of which, the simulation results reveal an increase in exports of grain crop sector by 33.48 percent, meat and live stock by 53.57 percent, extraction by 39.37 percent, processed food by 20.07 percent, textile and wearing apparel by 8.97 percent, light manufacturing items by 26.23 percent and heavy manufacturing by 16.62 percent. However, service exports were expected to decline by -5.19 percent. The exports of Australia to Japan indicate an increase in exports of grain crops by 14.13 percent, meat and live stock by 63.73 percent, extraction by 29.04 percent, processed food by 25.06 percent, light manufacturing by 0.62 percent and heavy manufacturing items by 0.96 percent. Exports of services and textile to Japan are expected to register negative growth of -1.17 and 2.79 respectively. Total exports of Australia to Japan increases by 3.66 percent. Exports of Australia to China are expected to increase by 15.96 percent a little bigger than the exports to India. Exports of Australia to China indicate an increase in exports of grain crops by 42.66 percent, meat and livestock by 67.83 percent, extraction by 44.35 percent, processed food by 54.28 percent, textile and wearing apparel by 37.17 percent, light manufacturing by 46.96 percent and heavy manufacturing items by 17.38 percent. Exports of services to China are expected to come down by -3.32 percent. As far as Australia's to the rest of the world are concerned, results indicate a decline by -6.72 percent.

Results indicate that the transactions involving processed food items and textile and wearing apparel and light manufacturing contributes a major part to productive gains particularly in Indian market. Results indicate highest increase in global exports of India followed by Australia. The study indicates a sharp increase in Indian exports to Japan, Australia as well as China. Gains in Indian exports are concentrated in grain crops, meat and live stock, processed food towards Japan and China, textile and wearing apparel towards all three countries. As a result of FTA, India's exports of light manufacturing and heavy manufacturing items are expected to grow towards Japan and China. The simulation results also indicate that India's services exports are growing at moderate rate towards these countries.

As far as Australia's exports under the FTAs are concerned, it gains mostly with its export to India and China where the total exports increases by 13.43 percent and 15.96 percent respectively where as exports to Japan increases moderately with 3.66 percent. Australia will gain mostly in exports of grain crops, meat and live stock, extraction and processed food. Changes in the trade by India and Australia will probably induce changes in their border prices with consequent effects on welfare through the change of their terms of trade. If imports of the FTA members from the rest of the world decrease, then the terms of trade of the members of the FTA are likely to improve, and vice versa. The terms of trade effects are supposed to have ambiguous results in general, because an FTA may or may not bring expansion of intra-regional trade and contraction of external trade. Researchers have identified many of the effects of an FTA other than the static efficiency improvement. An important one is the location effect. There is a concern that regional integration may be associated with increased inequality between the regions. In a perfectly competitive environment, regional integration reduces intra-FTA factor price differences, as was proven in the "factor price equalization theorem". As long as the countries' endowments lie inside the same cone of diversification, integration will equalize factor prices, in the long run.

Conclusion

It is evident from the above analysis that both countries have different comparative advantages and the developing economies like India would gain in labor-intensive sectors from bilateral or regional trade liberalization and in case of Australia, the country would gain in agriculture sector as well as mining and extraction and there would be productivity gain in Manufacturing sector. However, the impact of a regional FTA may more likely be determined by trade structures and the degree of import liberalization by sectors. In fact, estimating the impact of bilateral FTAs between, India and Australia have revealed that changes in sectoral trade balance, production and welfare gains would vary according to the FTAs and partners since each FTA has different rules and regulations. As it has already been noted, regional integration can be a potent aggregate growth stimulus for Asia. Although country-specific outcomes vary, combined regional tariff reductions and extensive improvements in trade efficiency can achieve substantial improvements in real incomes. Moreover, this trade and income growth represents diversification and new market development that can promote wider regional benefits and greater sustainability.

The study reveals that tariff liberalization has positive effects on all major countries in the region, with no or nominal negative effect on rest of the world. The present study predicts change in positive direction and therefore need to explore greater cooperation like the EU in Asian region. In a place of shallow integration process these countries need to start considering ways to deepen either economic integration to compete in global world order. Although this process has started in East Asia, which has achieved a high degree "de facto" market-based integration through establishment of cross border production net work and now backed by institutional frame works like swap agreements and other monetary initiative like Chiang Mai Initiative and free trade agreements, India and Australia are yet to join these initiatives along with East Asian countries. Efforts towards multinational free trade framework building in Asia have evolved with Japan, China, India, South Korea and Australia each pursuing bilateral FTAs as well as with ASEAN.

To optimize gains, these countries should enhance the economic, trade and investment cooperation beyond just goods trade. In addition to the liberal trade, these countries should also liberalize and promote trade in services, promotion of mutual recognition of professions, establish a transparent and predictable mechanism for currency and financial crisis and facilitative investment regime. The present research illustrates that commitment of India and Australia along with Japan, China and ASEAN are crucial for Asian regionalism if the goal is to maximise welfare of the people in the region. The countries should speed up their bilateral negotiation for a comprehensive FTA, followed by joint negotiation with other countries for an FTA engagement such as ASEAN plus six. However, James (2006) finds that Asian FTAs generally lack consistency. How can such regional FTAs be configured? While even a system of bilateral FTAs may have positive welfare effects, economic analysis and intuition both suggest that wider arrangements would bring far larger gains than bilateral or disparate FTAs. An expansion of the area covered by an FTA can also mitigate the harmful "noodle-bowl effect" caused by a tangled web of agreements with overlapping ROORs and varying coverage, not least of services and investment-related provisions.

Economic relations between India and Australia are characterized by the mutually complimentary nature of manufactured products, natural resources and services, and it will likely move towards new complimentary relations. Partnerships are promoted in the areas of capital markets, energy, biotechnology, information technology (IT), healthcare, nursing, science, research and development. All of this underlines Australia's accelerating integration into the economic activities of Asia and the enormous potential to expand economic ties across the region. The present level of intense trade relations as explained in the paper shows an absolute advantage for India and Australia in signing the FTAs. Following are the few results that generally derived from the above analysis and expected to strengthen the bilateral trade and investment relations, such as economic growth and domestic and international liberalisation in these countries. Opportunity for sectors existing and potential, range across: agribusiness (reflecting increasing demand in India), natural resources and mining (in particular, new technologies and services focused around safety, environment, communications and training, as well as manufacturing and processing of value-added mineral products), increasing diversification and productivity of Indian manufacturing sector through technology transfer, merger and acquisition, share holdings of Indian companies with its Australian counterparts.

The traditional trading relationship, based on the strategic raw materials trade, remains important, but a new relationship built on human capital and people-to-people business will be more important in the coming decades. There are different sorts of challenges in these new markets – in the form of institutional and regulatory systems to be negotiated. And there is need for a new framework of arrangements between the two countries to support the growth of the new trade relationship.

It is naive to expect that an Australia- India FTA will be an easy negotiation or produce a good outcome. A recent report by the ADB is critical of the proliferation of bilateral trade agreements in the Asian region and their potential to divert trade, marginalise peripheral countries with small markets and polarise the region more generally in the long term. Bilateral FTAs can create wider liberalisation and economic integration, as noticed in the Australia-US FTA; they can also include limited liberalisation and significant exemptions. In the same way the proposed India – Australia free trade agreement may lead to a similar kind of outcome.

NOTES

1. For more information on commodity classification at SITC 2 digit level on UN Comtrade, visit Website at http://comtrade.un.org/db/mr/rfCommoditiesList.aspx Scollay, R. and J. Gilbert (2001), New Subregional Trading Arrangements in the Asia-Pacific, Washington, DC: Institute for International Economics.Urata, S. and K Kiyota (2003), "The Impact of an East Asia FTA on Foreign Trade in East Asia", NBER Working Paper Series 10173, National Bureau of Economic Research.
2. SITC one digit summary based on Rev. 3 of UN Comtrade. 0. Food and Live Animals, 1. Beverages and Tobacco, 2. Crude materials, inedible, except fuel, 3. Mineral Fuels, lubricants and related materials, 4. Animal and vegetable oils, fats and waxes, 5.

Chemicals and related products, n.e.s 6. Manufactured goods, classified chiefly by materials, 7. machinery and transport equipment, 8. Miscellaneous manufactured articles, 9. Commodities and Transactions not classified elsewhere in the SITC.

REFERENCES

ABARE (Australian Bureau of Agricultural and Resource Economics) (2008), *Australian Commodity Statistics 2003*, Commonwealth of Australia, Canberra.

ABS (2009), *International Investment Position, Australia: Supplementary Country Statistics*, cat. no. 5352.0, Canberra.

ABS (Australian Bureau of statistics) (2009), *Australian System of National Accounts 2001-08*, cat. no. 5352.0, Canberra.

ABS (Australian Bureau of Statistics) (2009), *Balance of Payments and International Investment Position, Australia*, cat. no. 5302.0, Canberra.

ADB (2006), "Free Trade Agreements in Asia: The Way Ahead", Technical Assistance Report, Project Number: 40117, October.

ADB (2008), "Emerging Asian Regionalism A Partnership for Shared Prosperity" *ERD Working Paper*. Manila.

Asian Development Bank (2002), *Asian Development Outlook* , 2002, Oxford University Press, Manila.p.161.

Bonda Eric W et al, (2004), "A Strategic and Welfare Theoretic Analysis of Free Trade Areas", *Journal of International Economics*, (64): 1–27.

Brown, D., A. V. Deardorff and R. M. Stern (1992), "A North American Free Trade Agreement: Analytical Issues and Computational Assessment", *The World Economy*, 15 (1): 11–29.

CIE (2009), "Benefits of Trade and Trade Liberalization", Centre for International Economics, Canberra.

Clarete, R., Edmonds, C. and Wallack, J.S. (2002), "Asian Regionalism and its Effects on Trade in the 1980s and 1990s", Economics and Research Department Working Paper 30, ADB, Manila.

Deardorff, Alan and Stern, Robert (1994), "Multilateral Trade Negotiations and Preferential Trading Arrangements", in Alan Deardorff and Robert Stern (eds.) *Analytical and Negotiating Issues in the Global Trading System*, Ann Arbor: Michigan University Press.

Emanuel Ornelas (2005), "Endogenous Free Trade Agreements and the Multilateral Trading System", *Journal of International Economics,* (67): 471–497.

Emanuel, Ornelas (2008), "Feasible multilateralism and the effects of regionalism", *Journal of International Economics,* (74): 202–224.

Francois J F and Ganeshan Wignaraja (2008), "Economic Implications of Asian Integration", *Global Economy Journal,* 8 (3): Article 1

Garnaut, R (2002), "Australia: A Case Study of Unilateral Trade Liberalization', in Bhagwati, J (eds.) Going Alone: The Case for Relaxed Reciprocity in Freeing Trade, Massachusetts Institute of Technology.

GTAP Database (2010), sample data, online: (https://www.gtap.agecon.purdue.edu/databases/v7/v7_sampledata.asp?Version=7.0)

Goto, J. (2001), "FTAs and Their Economic Implications with Reference to Asia", Paper presented to Capacity Building Workshop on Trade Policy Issues organized by Asian Development Bank Institute and Ministry of Foreign Affairs, Singapore, 16–24 April.

James, W. E (2006), "Rules of Origin in Emerging Asia-Pacific Preferential Trade Agreements: Will PTAs Promote Trade and Development?" Asia- Pacific Research and Training Network on Trade, ARTNet Working Paper Series No. 19, August.

Kawasaki (2003), "The Impact of Free Trade Agreements in Asia", RIETI Discussion Paper Series 03- E- 018.

Kazutomo Abe (2007), "Assessing the Economic Impacts of Free Trade Agreements: A Computable Equilibrium Model Approach", RIETI Discussion Paper Series 07-E -053, RIETI, Tokyo.

Leigh, A (2002), "Trade Liberalisation and the Australian Labour Party", *Australian Journal of Politics and History,* 48 (4)

McKibbin, W. J. (1998), "Regional and Multilateral Trade Liberalization: The Effects on Trade, Investment and Welfare", in P. Drysdale and D. Vines (eds.) Europe, East Asia and APEC: A Shared Global Agenda? Cambridge: Cambridge University Press, 195–220.

McKibbin, W. J., J.-W. Lee and I. Cheong (2004), "A Dynamic Analysis of a Korea-Japan Free Trade Area: Simulations with the G-Cubed Asia-Pacific Model", *International Economic Journal,* (18): 3–32.

Mitsuyo Ando (2009), "Impacts of FTAs in East Asia: CGE Simulation Analysis", RIETI Discussion Paper Series 09-E -037. RIETI, Tokyo.

Robinson, S. and K. Thierfelder (1999), "Trade Liberalization and Regional Integration: The Search for Large Numbers", TMD Discussion Paper No. 34, Trade and Macroeconomic Division, International Food Policy Research Institute.

Scollay, R and J Gilbert (2000), "Measuring the Gains from APEC Trade Liberalization: An Overview of CGE Assessments", *World Economy*, (23):175–197.

15

Indian Diaspora in Australia and their Contribution to Australian Society and Economy

Chandrakant Yatanoor

Introduction

India and Australia are both multiparty democracies, with shared colonial heritage, history and language, common democratic traditions, similar legal, financial and Government structures and common interests as Indian Ocean littoral States, and both are members of the Commonwealth of Nations, founder members of the United Nations and members of the Indian Ocean Rim – Association for Regional Cooperation (IOR-ARC), ASEAN Regional Forum (ARF) and dialogue partners with ASEAN. With the increasing prominence of the Asia-Pacific region in global geo-politics and economics, Indo-Australian relations assume much more significance. Both are the liberal countries of the Indian Ocean region and in varying degrees regional maritime powers with the security of the nation constituting a vital factor in their respective national security agendas. These two countries of continental size also have agricultural economies with a developing industrial base and share common concerns about global trading partners, disarmament, intellectual property, globalisation, environment, state sponsored terrorism and Weapons of Mass Destruction. However, both countries defend their national and security needs differently and took different paths during the cold war period. India's policy of NAM was considered as imprudent by Australia. The main thrust of the Western alliance was to contain Communism, whereas, India was concerned with forces of colonialism and imperialism. Australia's preoccupation with its fear of Communism and the cold war made it to ignore India. India considered Australia as a client state of the United States, whereas Australia treated India as an ally of the USSR.

India's booming economy and its vast resource, product and services hungry market have been progressively attracting developed nations interest. Thus, in spite of the strong stand Australia took following the nuclear tests in May 1998, relations have normalised and grown in leaps and bounds since then. The other reasons for the growing interest of Australia in our nation include India's enormous English-speaking workforce that provides cheaper outsourcing opportunities to Australian businesses, the fact that India is one of the top sources of post-graduate students in Australia and the ready market for Australia's abundant resources in the large and growing Indian economy. Potential for Indo-Australian cooperation exists in infrastructure development including roads, ports, airports and railways; power sector; mining; oil and natural gas including LNG; biotechnology; drugs and pharmaceuticals; information technology; water management, soil conservation and waste disposal; food processing and agribusiness; film and television; processing of gems and jewellery; tourism; and education. The Commonwealth Games 2010 in New Delhi also provides a significant opportunity for sporting business including infrastructure development, venue management, etc.

Indian Diaspora's Contribution to Australia

The Indian Diaspora today constitutes an important, and in some respects unique, force in world culture. The origins of the modern Indian Diaspora lie mainly in the subjugation of India by the British and its incorporation into the British empire. Indians were taken over as indentured labour to far-flung parts of the empire in the nineteenth-century, a circumstance to which the modern Indian populations of Australia, Fiji, Mauritius, Guyana, Trinidad, Surinam, Malaysia, South Africa, Sri Lanka, and other places attest in their own peculiar ways. Over two million Indian men fought on behalf of the empire in numerous wars, including the Boer War and the two World Wars, and some stayed back to claim the land on which they had fought as their own. As if in emulation of their ancestors, many Gujarati traders once again left for East Africa in large numbers in the early part of the twentieth century. Finally, in the post-World War II period, the dispersal of Indian labour and professionals has been a nearly world-wide phenomenon. Indians, and other South Asians, provided the labour that helped in the reconstruction of war-torn Europe, particularly the United Kingdom and the Netherlands, and in more recent years unskilled labour from South Asia has been the main force in the transformation of the physical landscape of much of the Asia Pacific and Middle East. Meanwhile, in countries such as the United States, Canada, and Australia, Indians have made their presence visibly felt in the professions.[1]

So, Australia has one of the fastest growing Indian communities in the world, numbering some 240,000. "Australia's Indian community has made their mark in the professional fields of IT, education, engineering and medicine as well as a significant number becoming successful entrepreneurs across a range of industries. And non-resident Indians tend to maintain strong banking affiliations with India, so there's a real demand from the Indian community in Australia for access to Indian financial services. The first Indians that arrived in Australia were predominantly Punjabis from the Punjab region in north-western India; religiously they were predominantly Sikhs and Muslims. Between 1860 and 1901, more Indians arrived and worked as agricultural labourers, hawkers and domestic help. A number of Indians also worked in the gold fields. Migration from India was curtailed after the Australian Government introduced the

Immigration Restriction Act 1901, but following India's independence from Britain in 1947, the number of Anglo-Indians and Indian-born British citizens immigrating to Australia increased. At the 2006 Census 147,106 Australian residents declared that they were born in India, of which 79,025 held Australian citizenship. The states with the largest Indian-born residents were New South Wales (57,156), Victoria (52,853) and Western Australia (15,157). 64,968 declared they were Hindu and 49,975 declared they were Christian. Other minorities include Muslims and Sikhs. 243,722 Australian residents declared that they had Indian ancestry, either alone or in combination with another ancestry. In 2009 there were an additional 90,000 Indian Students studying at Australian tertiary institutions.[2]

Indian migration to Australia is very recent compared to Indian migration to other parts of the world like USA, UK, Africa etc. It is said that the first Indian had come to Australia as part of Captain Cook's ship, the first settlers in Australia. Before Roads and road transport was developed, many Indians had come to Australia to run Camel trains. These brave Indians were called Afghans and kept the communication and supply line open between Melbourne and the center of Australia. They would transport goods and mail over Camel backs in the desert. More Indians came to Australia more than fifty years ago while both Australia and India were British colonies. These enterprising Sikhs came to work on the Banana Plantations in Southern Queensland. Today, a large number of them live in the town of Wolgoolga (roughly half way between Sydney and Brisbane on the highway) and own their own Banana Farms and are quite rich. Their riches have come by hard work. There are two Sikh temples in Wolgoolga. One of them even has a Museum on Sikhism.

A large number of British and Anglo-Indians, who were born in India, migrated to Australia after 1947. These British citizens decided to settle in Australia in large numbers but are still counted as 'Indian Nationals' in the Census. You will be surprised to find that a full blooded Australian looking old man will whisper to you in Hindi or Urdu. The third wave of Indians came about 30 years ago, just after Australia abandoned its "Whites Only" policy. Yes, this is a little known fact that Australia until recently was a 'whites only' country. With the abolition of this policy, many Teachers and Doctors had gone to settle in Australia. Another big influx began with the IT revolution. Large number of Indian Computer Software professionals started arriving in Australia from 1976 onwards. Today, it is hard to go to an IT shop and not find a few Indians working there. When a military 'coup' took place in Fiji, almost a decade ago and Indians were prosecuted there, many of them came to Australia. Australia and New Zealand provided refuge to these Fiji Indians. Today, there is a large Fiji Indian population in Australia who call Australia their home. These Fiji Indians have changed the face of Indian Australia. While earlier Indian migration was that of educated professionals, these new Fiji Indians were more dynamic and business going. Their arrival has increased the services enjoyed by all Indians. Now Indians can buy Sarees and Gold Jewellery. There are Indian night clubs and off course, Indian cinema can be seen on weekends.

The current wave of Indian migration is that of Engineers, tool makers from India, Gujrati business families from Africa and second level relatives of settled Indians. Most Gujrati families go into business. Engineers and Tool Makers, most of them, find a dead end of job. Being as enterprising as many Indians are, they either go back to College and study programming to secure a decent and stable job. Others are venturing into their own businesses. A new wave of Indian immigrants has hit Australia. Starved of government funding, Australian education institutes are desperately recruiting full fee paying overseas students. Many universities have permanent representatives stationed in India and other Asian countries. Their efforts have been rewarded and a new influx of Indian students is entering Australia. It is estimated that Canberra University which is one of about two dozen universities is recruiting about 500 students every year for the last five or six years. Many regional universities like University of Ballarratt have opened campus in Sydney to cater to these foreign students. Many of these students have paid large sums of fees and are looking for work to support themselves. This has started the transformation of the working class. In 1986 a flux of non-skilled Indian immigrants meant that you could see white Australians being replaced by Indians in cleaning jobs. In 1998 we have started seeing the replacement of counter staff and chefs at McDonalds and other places by young, bright and attentive Indian students. I guess the plight of Indian students in Australia is that of Indian student migration to USA during the 1970's. We will see many of these young boys becoming future millionaires in Australia in the years to come.

Australia has commended the growing Indian Diaspora in the country for its contribution in enhancing bilateral links. In a joint statement issued following the fifth Australia-India Foreign Ministers Framework Dialogue held on 22 June, 2008 at Canberra, the Australian Foreign Minister, Mr. Smith said that the "Indian Diaspora in Australia is making a tangible contribution to enhancing bilateral links"[3]. Recognising the diverse and expanding people-to-people links underpinning this bilateral relationship, Smith and India's then External Affairs Minister, Mr. Pranab Mukherjee called for more youth exchanges in various fields, including young professionals, to build up people-to-people connections and take the bilateral partnership forward over the coming decades. Australia agreed to a proposal for sending a group of Australian Youth Ambassadors to India in the near future. India has become the third largest source of international immigrants and second largest source of skilled migrants and international students to Australia. Young Indians are helping strengthen the Australian economy with 15,865 professionals seeking permanent residence under the skilled migration programme during 2006-2007. According to the 2006 Census conducted by the Australian Bureau of Statistics, there were 234,720 people of Indian origin in Australia.[4]

Australia has become an attractive destination for Indian students. Estimates indicate the presence of nearly 70,000 students in various Universities all over Australia. Unfazed by the attacks on Indian students Down Under, over 20,000 Indians have migrated under Australia's permanent skilled visa category beating Chinese who stood at over 13,000 during 2008-09. According to official figures released recently, overseas workers who were sponsored by employers comprised 33 per cent of the 2008-09 skill stream compared to 22 per cent in 2007-08 and 17 per cent in 2006-07. Across all permanent skilled visa categories, top three occupations for successful applicants were accountancy (6,238), computing professionals (3,879) and registered nurses (3,355) and top three nations under the skill stream were the United Kingdom (23,178), India (20,105) and China (13,927). Australian Minister for Immigration and Citizenship, Chris Evans said that changes introduced in January 2009 including the Critical Skills List (CSL) of high value occupations and prioritizing employer-sponsored or state/territory-sponsored skilled migration visa grants were having a significant impact.

Attack on Indian Students

The recent attacks on Indian students studying in Australia have attracted global attention. This rabid cultural and racial menace has attracted worldwide condemnation. One Sravan Kumar Theerthala was hit with petrol bottles by some unidentified teens while he was reading book in his house at Melbourne. Baljinder Singh, another student from India studying in Melbourne, was robbed and stabbed in his abdomen. Both are struggling for life in hospitals. In a separate incident, four students were attacked and burgled by racist elements in Australia. One Suketu Modi, a businessman from Surat, was attacked in train by a group of students when he had gone there for IT business. According to student's organisations, these racist attacks have been taking place in Australia for quite some time; most of them went unreported. According to a report, about 20 racial attacks on Indians have taken place in a single month of May 2009 in Sydney alone. Australia, interestingly, is not the only country where rabid faces of racism have been raising heads. Such dastardly incidents have been taking place in countries like UK, Germany, France and some African and Gulf countries. This incident has raised a very perturbing question, which every one of us would like to ponder about and like to find consolable if not acceptable answers.

Another disturbing incident occurred recently on Sunday, 3rd January, 2010, an Indian youth Nitin Garg, stabbed to death in Australia is the first case of casualty in a series of vicious attacks on the Indian community members, prompting a strong reaction from India which warned such incidents could have a bearing on bilateral ties.[5] Nitin Garg, who migrated from Punjab and had permanent residency in Australia, was stabbed in the abdomen in a park while on his way to Hungry Jack's restaurant, where he was working as part time employee. He staggered in to the restaurant and pleaded for help before collapsing. Mr. Garg, who had on a previous occasion been beaten up by a group at the Newport railway station, was taken to the Royal Melbourne Hospital, where he was declared died. The fatal stabbing of 21-year-old Nitin Garg and the recovery of the burnt body of a Punjabi youth and the attack on 29-year old Jaspreet Singh, who was set ablaze by a group of four men in a suburb of Essendon in Northwest Melbourne on 9th January 2010, have re-ignited the debate about the safety of Indian students in Australia. Coming in the wake of a spate of attacks on Indian students over the past year, they are certainly disturbing.

Regrettably, the official reaction in Australia, at the federal as well as the state level, has been less than satisfactory–a reaction wrapped around denial. Australian officials have busied themselves in discounting the possibility that racism could be a significant cause for Indian students being targeted. At a time when precious young lives have been lost and emotions are running high, it is poor consolation and bad diplomacy to tell that the number of attacks has been exaggerated or that the Indian students are soft targets because they live or work in rough neighborhoods. This kind of insensitivity was reflected in acting Foreign Minister Simon Crean's remark that such incidents happen not only in Melbourne but also in "Delhi and Mumbai."[6]

It is possible that many of the attacks on Indian students in the Melbourne area are opportunistic rather than racial. But virtually ruling out racial motivation in advance of a proper police investigation of two brutal murders against a distressing background of attacks suggests that the authorities are making light of a serious problem. The Australian government needs to address, at the highest political level, the growing feeling among Indian students that their concerns about racial violence are not being addressed sincerely. This is against the background of a rise over the last few years in the number of attacks against the Indian community, as evidenced by the Victoria police's own data. Not surprisingly, visa applications from Indian students-who constitute the second largest foreign student contingent in Australia, after Chinese students- have shown a 46 per cent decline. This will certainly worry a nation where the higher education industry has emerged as the third largest export, valued close to $14 billion. Australia has built its reputation as an attractive educational destination by offering a variety of courses, good value for money and the promise of a friendly environment. Australian government needs to be firmly reminded that efforts to tackle an unacceptable series of attacks on young Indians can be undermined by a stance of defensiveness, denial, and insensitivity.[7]

Reasons of such attacks

It is too simplistic a proposition to categorically brand them as acts of criminal or opportunistic activities as uttered by the Australian High Commissioner and DCP Melbourne, John McCarthy. The former has, however, not denied that some racist elements might have been involved in what he called shameful criminal acts. If not the global society, Indian civil society must quest reasons behind it; after all why Indians are being attacked everywhere? It seems that the existence of these vestigial racial elements even in cultural, plural societies does have other hidden reasons apart from ostensible causes. Chagrin does not prevail in Australia; and even Australian media lamented only after vociferous diplomatic and societal protests at home.

Economic

India has written stories of astounding success in economic fields; thanks to flooded brilliant young brains in the fields of science and technology, management and other frontier areas.

Our IITs, IIMs, and plethora of business and other schools have produced best brains in the world. The campus selections by Multinational Corporations and Transnational Corporations over a couple of decades have been a matter of concern to the students of those countries, which have been destinations of our 'smart English speaking IT-BPO guys' for obvious reasons. Many of them feel that their job opportunities are being eaten up by Indians. Many guys working in MNCs and TNCs in countries like the US, the UK, Australia, Germany and a host of other such developed countries have faced similar acts of discrimination. Many such incidents go unreported for simple reason; as the victims have to run from pillar to post once FIR is registered. Student community particularly does not like to be involved in legal wrangles because they think that they have come here not to fight legal battle but to complete their studies and make careers. They are also tormented by the lackadaisical, callous and sometimes, ignorant attitude of police. For instance, in Australia, the police would not act till the matter was blown out of their capacity to hold. According to Forbes; about US$ 13 billion is spent by Indian students abroad annually. Australia alone has a US$ 15.5 billion business with foreign students and as many as 1 lakh Indian students study in Australia at present. According to an estimate about 8.3 lakh Indian students are studying in countries like the US, the UK, Russia, France, Australia, etc. Needless to say, those going abroad for higher studies belong to affluent class of the society. The number of High Net Income (HNI) individuals in India has swelled for some years. Like many other areas, the lopsided development in the field of education has created a dangerous in-equilibrium. The affluence of these students studying abroad or working guys, who earn handsome salaries in MNCs, betrays in their lifestyles and attracts opportunistic activities by teens, who have been already suffering from a sense of inferiority complexes. These complexes find expression in such opportunistic acts blended with racism.

Sociological and educational

With the passage of time, the colonies have gained independence from colonial powers. The European countries are finding their erstwhile colonies rubbing shoulders in gatherings at International forums. The sense of hatred unconsciously precipitates in their mind and find expression in such abhorable acts of racial attacks. History has taught us to be proud of our past. Their past had been excellent but future is full of intense competition which extra-individualistic. In the present global financial regime, every one, may it be individual or nation has to find a place for itself not on the basis of its past but on the basis of its present. The economic hegemony of the US is all set to nosedive. The American Tsardom in financial market is likely to be over. The global financial crisis (GFC) has bashed the US, the pain of which is still emanating. Asian giant China has purchased US$ 1.3 trillion worth US Treasury Bills. A sense of chagrin prevails in USA, what a travesty; once lender has become a borrower. The Chinese export juggernaut into the US has changed the entire economic power structure. Protectionist measures taken by the USA and host of developed nations have these social and psychological dimensions also. The sense of frustration is obvious in younger minds because their economic future is not as secure as it had been decades ago.

Ethical and moral

There is no denying the fact that economic development in India has changed our lifestyles and cultural traits to a great extent. Still then, our social, family, and religious ethos, which have deep roots, have not eroded to the extent of disappearance. Religious tolerance and non-violence are still way of our lives. When our boys go abroad we preach them to be adherent to these ethos. In spite of spate of attacks, students in Australia decided to take out a peace march rather than taking to streets. Normally such incidents meet violent backlashes. But the kind of restraint, which has been showed by Indians in Australia and abroad, is suggestive of the fact that ethos of non-violence and Satyagraha are still alive in our soul and the teachings of Mahatma Gandhi are inculcated in our way of life. These characteristics of ours have been taken by many nations as timidity and cowardice. After all, what explains when two teens attacked four students and went un-retaliated, physically they could have not only been overpowered but thrashed also. Progress and affluence of students studying abroad do manifest in their lifestyles, which tempt these racist elements to attack that serves twin purpose; on the one hand they snatch something from them and on the other it satiates their hidden desire of inferiority complex.

Role of Embassies

The role of embassies in this regard has particularly been callous. According to reports available in public domain, hundreds of such attacks have taken place on Indian students in different parts of the world. When the students approach the authorities in embassies, they are treated with callous and cool attitude. This has emboldened the morale of such lumpen elements, who indulge in acts of such vandalism and at the same time, it leaves students at the mercy of their fate. In this case also, the Indian Embassy could take up the issue only after matter was reported in Indian media and the prime minister and External Affairs Minister talked to Kelvin Rudd and Julia Gillard in strongest possible diplomatic over tone and conveyed their frowning over the issue. This approach of our diplomatic babus needs to be changed.

To sum up, we can say that these incidents are rooted in sociological, economic, historical and ethical soil of developed cultural, pluralistic societies. The lasting and amicable solution therefore can only be found in the roots and not in stems. The concerned governments have to deal such incidents very much carefully and firmly. One of the Indian students Mr. Gaurav, who has been living in Melbourne since six years, said that Melbourne has seen a major jump in the street violence in the past couple of years especially at night. He has advised the fellow students to take some precautions while they are going out of their rooms, for example: [8]

- Walking away from a dispute or a brawl doesn't make you a coward but it makes you sensible
- Don't take anything personally and just walk away if you have any situation and just be calm

- Stay away from people who indulge in binge drinking
- Always call 000 if you think there is emergency
- Try to use buses when you travel late in the night as they are safer than trains.

REFERENCES

1. "Migration: permanent additions to Australia's population". *4102.0 - Australian Social Trends, 2007* and *Australian Bureau of Statistics,* 7 August 2007.
2. *Ibid.*
3. *The Hindu,* 23 June 2008.
4. *Australian Bureau of Statistics 2006.*
5. *The Hindu,* 4 January 2010.
6. *The Hindu,* 6 January 2010.
7. *Ibid.*
8. *Business Line,* 28 May 2009

16

Attacks on Indian Students and Supply of Uranium: Issues in India-Australia Bilateral Relationship

M. Prayaga

India in conformity with her age-old traditions, culture and philosophy has been at once professing and practising the policy of cooperation, peace and friendship with its neighbours and distant friends. Certain basic linkages of historical legacy and geographical location provided the supportive environment for an active growth of the relations between India and Australia, the two littoral states of Indian Ocean. The contacts between India and Australia under the common British colonial rule contributed to the growth of the relations even after India attained Independence. India has been striving to get its economic, political and cultural ties with this island-continent-nation strengthened. However, because of their affiliations to two ideologically divergent blocs, India and Australia had suffered from certain misconceptions and misunderstandings during the Cold War era. The break up of the Soviet Union led to the redefining of the relations between India and Australia by way of developing mutual understanding. Following the termination of the end of Cold War, India's opening of economy showed remarkable resilience in recovering from the crisis. Further, India's Look East Policy, an externally-oriented foreign policy, contributed to the expansion of its relations with Australia, especially in the trade and strategic spheres. In the fast changing globalized world, both the nations recognized their individual economic potential and its importance for mutual cooperation. Events have been heading towards consolidation and establishment of strategic partnership between the two. Against this background, this paper will focus on recent Australia's changing perceptions of India mainly in the context of a spate of attacks on Indian students in Australia and Canberra's adamant uranium policy towards India.

Impressive Economic Relations

The growing economic interactions between India and Australia and the efforts of the Joint Ministerial Commission (JMC), Joint Business Council (JBC) and Trade and Economic Framework Agreement gave a new impetus to the bilateral trade. The bilateral trade of India and Australia which was A$ 10.12 billion in 2006, crawled to A$ 10.92 billion in 2007 and reached A$18.02 billion in 2010. Australia's exports to India were A$ 16.17 billion as against Indian exports of A$ 1.84 billion in 2010 (Table-1). In the process, India becomes 4th largest export destination and 6th largest services trading partner of Australia.

Table-1
India-Australia Trade in Goods, 2005 – 2010

(in billion A$)

	2005-06	*2006 - 07*	*2007 - 08*	*2008 – 09*	*2009 - 10*
Total trade	10.12	10.75	10.92	17.53	18.02
India's Exports	1.28	1.46	1.60	2.	1.84
India's Imports	8.84	9.29	9.32	15.42	16.17

Source: http://www.hcindia-au.org/bilateral_economic_relation.html

India's imports include three major products, namely, coal, gold and copper ores, accounting for 86 per cent of India's imports from Australia. Other Australian export-commodities to India are wool, vegetables, silver, platinum and telecommunication equipments. On other hand, India's exports largely consist of precious and semi-precious stones, floor coverings, textile, agricultural products and medicaments. India at present ranks the 21st largest exporter to Australia.

No doubt, the statistics indicate the sustainable partnership of both the countries in economic cooperation. India's exports are far below Australian exports resulting in India's escalating trade imbalance with Australia, being the largest that India had with any of its trading partners.[1] The imbalance in India-Australia trade is hardly surprising. Coal imports, alone accounting for more than 45 per cent of India's total imports from Australia, testify to India's dependence on Australia for meeting its energy demands.[2] Taking advantage of Australian trade restrictions and tariffs which are low, Indian companies are indeed to increase export of goods and services to narrow down the trade gap.

Australia is gradually increasing its economic presence and visibility in India through investments in infrastructure, energy and telecommunications. Many Australian companies have established their offices in India.[#] The total value of the Australian investments in India during the period from April 2000 to September 2008 was Rs 9.98 billion (US$ 226.02 million).[3] Indian companies have also made their presence felt in Australia. The IT majors including Infosys, TCS, HCL, Polaris Software Lab Ltd, Birlasoft, NIIT and Wipro, have set up shops in Australia. Some famous Indian companies made investments in collaboration with Australian firms in coal and oil sectors.[+] The Taj Group of Hotels acquired "Blue" Hotel in Sydney. RIL Australia Pty Limited (RILA), a subsidiary of Reliance Industries Limited, has a Joint Venture agreement with Uranium Exploration Australia Limited to participate in the Australian energy sector including uranium exploration and mining. Mahindra & Mahindra Limited established a new venture called Mahindra Automotive Australia (MAU) in Australia.[4]

The Bilateral Investment Promotion Agreement (BIPA), signed between India and Australia in 2000, provides for more investment flows on both sides. The total Australian investments in India reached A$ 4,798 million in 2010 comprising 755 FDI investments. Further, the service exports also form a key sector in bilateral trade relations. Australian export of services to India in 2010 yielded A $ 3,154 million, of which A$ 2,667 million being from education. India's service exports to Australia earned only A$ 660 million mainly through travel and information technology.[5]

Belittled Expectations of Kevin Rudd's Labour Government

It was Gareth Evans, who claimed that "Australia was part of Asia," and even produced a new map of the region – 'East Asian hemisphere,' which included Australia along with East and Southeast Asian nations.[6] Evans who served as Foreign Minister in Hawke and Keating governments, initiated the process of revitalizing India-Australia relations. In the context of termination of Cold War and India's economic reforms and its Look East Policy, Australia too enthusiastically geared up its mechanism to enhance its bilateral partnership. Though availed the credit of having launched 'India-Australia New Horizons' campaign in New Delhi itself, Howard government's strident reaction to India's nuclear explosions in 1998 reenacted the old rhythm of estrangement in India-Australia relations. Cognizant of the bonhomie in the Indo-US relationship, Australia reconciled to the imperatives of restoring the bilateral relationship; yet it almost remained adamant in its refusal to supply uranium to India.

It was about this time that the Kevin Rudd's Labour government, which succeeded the Howard's Liberal Party government in November 2007 elections, was expected to engage Asia for economic prosperity and strategic integration. Political strategists also felt that nearly 8 years of his stay in China as an Australian diplomat and his being a fluent speaker in Mandarin would entitle him to be a good friend of the Asian region. His predecessors – Howard, Keating and Bob Hawke who had also followed the policy of engaging East Asia – started changing the contours of Australia's foreign policy towards Asia. However, Rudd's long association with and his inclination towards China led many to surmise that his policies would be pro-China. As Australia has become largest trading partner of China, Beijing became a natural choice that included along with the US and some European countries in his 18-day overseas visit in 2008. That he was apathetic about India was clear from his itinerary wherein India did not figure. What is more, Rudd took a firm decision not to sell uranium to India and the same was publicly announced. [7] Further, Rudd in his speech on 31 March 2008 at Brookings Institution of Washington DC, indicated his preference for China in the six-power group and certainly not India.[8]

After completing two years in office, Rudd finally undertook a two-day mission to India in November 2009 following the APEC Summit in Sydney. During his visit, the two issues that loomed large were the repeated incidents of attacks on Indian students in Australia and Australia's decision to deny uranium supply to India. Rudd's visit was in succession to the Australian ministers and officials who tried to address the damage done to the international student sector, particularly Indian students. His visit became indispensable for bringing back India-Australia relations on track. Policy makers in Australia expected that his visit would focus on the long ignored economic and strategic relations with India. Rory Medcalf, Lowy Institute Program Director, says, "Canberra has neglected the subcontinent but the feeling has been mutual". Kevin Rudd therefore availed himself of his visit to forge multilateral relations with India. Indian Prime Minister Manmohan Singh welcomed Rudd's move to convene a 1.5 track conference in Sydney in December 2009 to consider further Australia's Asia-Pacific Community initiative. In a joint statement Rudd reiterated Australia's support for a permanent seat for India on the UNSC.[9] During his visit, both decided to elevate the relationship to the level of 'Strategic Partnership'. As part of forging the relations,

Joint Declaration on Security Cooperation was also signed to ensure more collaboration in security issues such as *defence, disarmament,* maritime security and combating international terrorism.

Australia's Education: Indian Students

Rudd's visit attracted large attention of Indian media on the grave issues of non-supply of uranium and violent attacks on Indian students in Australia. While the barring of uranium supply reverberated at high level discussions, the news of assaults on Indian students have hit the headlines in the powerful Indian media. The reason offered was that the Indian students have been gaining ground in Australian foreign education-related industry.

The successful expansion of globalization and the emergence of rapidly developing Indian economy provide ample opportunities for Australia to turn as an export market for services, as a source of investment and human capital. The factors like gradual surge of the middle-class and the growth of affordability in India have encouraged Indian students to choose Australia for their overseas education, besides the US and the UK. Australia also became a destination for transnational students in improving their educational qualifications, skills and job opportunities which are credited globally. Educational services which are becoming a major export sector for Australia were worth an estimated A$ 13.7 billion in 2007-08. According to AEI, education services remain Australia's third largest export, behind coal and iron ore (A$46 billion and A$30.2 billion respectively) and the largest services export industry ahead of personal travel services (A$11.7 billion).[10] China and India, which have become the source countries for overseas students in Australia, together accounted for 267,000 enrolments in 2009 and contributed as much as A$ 5.1 billion to service exports.[11]

Some internal and external factors contributed to the growth of overseas students in Australia: the abandonment of the most controversial 'Australia's Whites only policy' and the policy pursued by the Australian universities to come out of the consequent financial crunch in 1998, which was to open admissions to full-fee paying overseas students and the opening of the representative offices in India. Their efforts were rewarded with a steady growth of Indian students in Australian universities as well as in private institutions, mostly in vocational colleges. Canberra University along with 12 more Universities started recruiting 500 students annually. It was further strengthened by many regional Universities like the University of Ballarratt which have opened a campus in Sydney to cater to the needs of many foreign students.

During 2003-2009, the enrolment of the Chinese students increased on an average of 16 per cent per year to 146,000 in 2009; at about the same time, the enrolment of Indian students increased by 46 per cent on average to 121,000 in 2009. Indian students chose Vocational Education and Training (VET) for their career and formed majority in the enrolment twice the number in Higher Education in 2008 (Table-2). The number of VET enrolments by Indian students has grown very rapidly from 2,223 in 2002 to 52,236 in 2008 and reached the level of 75,000 in 2009. Higher Education makes up 24 per cent of the enrolments by Indian students.[12]

Table-2
Overseas Student Enrolments by Selected Sector by Top 10 Nationalities, 2002 and 2008

Nationality	*2002*	*2008*	*2002*	*2008*
	Higher Education		*VET*	
China	16,073	52,663	5,786	25,823
India	8,834	27,482	2,223	52,236
Malaysia	13,514	15,633	—	—
Singapore	10,399	7,473	—	—
Indonesia	11,362	7,430	5,160	5,247
Hong Kong	8,280	7,265	5,659	4,229
Korea (South)	3,661	6,301	4,650	9,358
Thailand	4,879	4,233	3,694	8,621
Viet Nam	1,729	3,880	—	—
Other	36,610	49,599	19,804	42,950
Total	115,341	181,959	53,673	174,638

Source: Australian Universities' Review, Vol. 52, No. 1, 2010.

However, a spate of violent attacks has posed number of questions as to why the Indian students alone have become target of the attacks and as to the involvement of any racist motives behind these otherwise inexplicable attacks launched against Indian students only. A probe into these issues is likely to give some of the possible reasons for the unwelcome episodes.

True, some Indian students entertain the hope of obtaining permanent residency in Australia. Many of these students who have paid large sums of fee naturally search for jobs to support themselves through earnings. This has led to the 'transformation of the working class' in Australia. Indian students quickly opted for small part-time jobs. This resulted in the "replacement of counter staff and chefs at McDonalds and other places by young, bright and attentive Indian students."[13] In 1999, the Australian government introduced a suite of reforms by way of facilitating the overseas students' trials to obtain permanent residence on completion of their courses. Many Indian students undertook to venture Masters programmes in Information Technology and Accountancy courses in order to obtain permanent residency in Australia. Almost three quarters of the Indian students graduating from university programmes got permanent residency in 2004-2005.[14] In 2005, Australian government tightened the migration requirements by mandating higher levels of English proficiency and professional experience. Besides, the number of points was also increased for international graduates to obtain permanent residency. It somehow dampened the admissions at the universities, whereas private colleges took advantage of the situation to offer enrolment to overseas students in vocational courses which catered almost exclusively to the international students seeking fast and easy qualifications in support of migration applications. In 2008, nearly 14,400 Indian students got admission in private colleges of which more than a quarter of students got themselves enrolled in 'food, hospitality and personal services' courses. Enrolment in migration-oriented programmes in private colleges had grown continuously, though they took no note of the demand for the occupations concerned,[15] and this confounded the problem of unemployment.

There were several cases of attacks on taxi drivers in Australia. High number of professional taxi drivers is Indians who work on day shifts. With the rise of student part-time workers, some students are driven to choose taxi driving and odd jobs such as working in restaurants till the late night hours. Taxi drivers are fated to drunkard passengers, unruly citizens, drug addicts and other anti-social elements. Odd jobs till the wee-hours normally take place in the isolated parks which can be considered highly crime-prone. [16] Of all the international students in Australia, most of the attacks were on Indian students. In the course of probing, some research studies suggested that the Indian students are more likely to be living in outer suburbs (out backs) where lodging is inexpensive. This necessitated their travelling late on trains more often, especially in areas where street violence is more common. Another reason pertains to the question of gender. As assaults against strangers on and around public transport are generally perpetrated by young men on other young men, the vast majority of Indian students are males whereas East and Southeast Asian students are evenly split by gender. As a result, one would expect a greater rate of assaults against Indian students.[17]

On 29 April 2008, an Indian student working as taxi driver in Melbourne became a victim to his own passenger. Certain cases of robbery have been mostly going unreported. A year later, in May and June, attacks on taxi drivers were slowly shifted to a series of serious assaults on Indian students in Melbourne and Sydney at bus and railway stations where some students were critically injured and laid on death bed. In a furious reaction, number of street protests were staged and attracted the media spotlight in Australia and in India. Media in India projected these incidents as inhuman as well as "racist attacks". Some allusions have given scope to label the happenings as allegations of racism. Trevor Carter, the Victorian police commander, said, "there is an element of (racism), but the purpose is to steal property from people." A far-Right Australian website "urged a racial holy war against Indian students". Besides this, the race riots in 2005 shook Sydney when a "mob of 5,000 White youths, egged on by

White supremacists and neo-Nazis, rampaged through a beach suburb, attacking people of Middle-Eastern background."[18] Peter Spolc and Murray Lee, who worked on the dimensions of racism on Indian students and on the background of the attacks, while accusing the violent attacks on Indian students, believed that:

> In the simplest terms, the scoop on Indian students as victims of racist crime became international news because the global media market is perpetually hungry for racist sensationalism, and once that media cat was out of the bag, no amount of rational examination of the matter could put it back in. [19]

However, in India the reactions over these incidents were very high. Amitabh Bachchan, famous Indian film star, besides turning down the honorary doctorate from Queensland University of Technology, announced that:

> I mean no disrespect to the Institution that honors me, but under the present circumstances, where citizens of my own country are subjected to such acts of inhuman horror, my conscience does not permit me to accept this decoration from a country that perpetrates such indignity to my fellow countrymen. [20]

China also joined India in demanding better protection for its international students who were also in large number pursing their studies in Australia. Since these concerns would damage the image of Australia in education sector, the Prime Minister and Foreign Minister both responded swiftly and expressed their "abhorrence at the attacks." Prime Minister Kevin Rudd was quick to condemn the attacks saying, "It is appalling in every sense. Any act of violence, any decent human being just responds with horror at the sorts of attack which have occurred recently." [21] He further added: "Indian students are welcome guests in Australia. They are important for the Australian economy and we want them to stay amicably in a cordial manner."[22] Rudd took additional measures to repose faith in Indian public by deputing high profile visits of Australian leaders Julia Gillard (Deputy Prime

Minister and Minister for Education, Employment and Workplace Relations), Stephen Smith (Foreign Minister) and John Brumby (Premier of Victoria State) to convey that Australia is a safe educational destination for Indian students. Kevin Rudd, while in New Delhi in November 2009, sought to address the concerns about violent attacks on Indian students. Australian government has taken several transparent measures like bringing perpetrators of attacks to the justice to ensure safety for the overseas students in the states of Victoria, New South Wales, South Australia and Queensland. Stephen Smith, Minister for Foreign Affairs, in his Ministerial Statement reported that, in the Victoria state, where majority of Indian students are studying in Australia, the government launched an International Student Care Service, which "is a new 24-hour service where international students can get greater access to accommodation, counseling, legal services, emergency and welfare assistance."[23]

In addition to the Australian government's reassuring measures, Indian student representatives appealed to John Brumby to enhance the police personnel in "International Student High Risk Zones," at train and bus stations to stop the attacks on students. A.R. Rahman, the Indian Oscar Award winner for film music, visited Australia in January 2010, and performed the concert with a catchy phrase "Long live the India-Australia Relationship" in the Sydney Festival. Some Indians even started web forums to cultivate harmony among Indians and Australians. Murthy, Director, Dhanush Infotech, who started a web forum while appealing to the government for stern action on those who were found guilty, also advises "Indian students to realize the situation and lead their life at Australia without any hassle."[24] While the Indian students' enrolment registered a downturn to 50 per cent immediately after the attacks, the aspiring Indian students enrolment slowly climbed following the assurances of improved environment, which include the streamline of the private educational colleges to provide safety and quality of education to the overseas students. S.M. Krishna, Minister of External Affairs, who visited Australia in January 2011, felt quite satisfied with the improved conditions of students and remarked that, "Indian students were now feeling confident and secure despite the fact that the number of enrolments had dropped by almost half." [25]

On the whole, the enlarged interactions and deliberations on the students' issue, which was somewhat grim at one stage, have further deepened the mutual trust and relationship.

India's Energy Security and Australia's Uranium

The dawn of 21st century has begun witnessing the emergence of China and India as global economic players. Accordingly, the growing energy requirements for the sustainable development of their economies drove them to rely heavily on energy imports. It is estimated that India's energy consumption will increase to 50 per cent by 2015. At present, the significant energy resource for India is coal. India is importing 70 per cent of crude oil required for its domestic consumption. Its booming economy needs more energy for its industries as well as ~~to~~ many villages which are not connected with national electricity grid. As Sascha Muller-Kraenner, a German scholar, felt, "Energy poverty has become a growing problem for the population of the largest democracy in the world."[26] India has signed number of oil and gas supply contracts with other countries in Central Asia and Southeast Asia. Besides, India focuses on enhanced nuclear energy to meet its future energy requirements. Therefore, India signed two far-reaching nuclear agreements for nuclear technological cooperation with the US and France.

For its nuclear energy production, India needs uranium from Australia's vast reserves accounting for 40 per cent of the world known deposits. India hoped that the signing of the Indo-US civil nuclear deal would allay the worries of Australia in the sale of uranium to India. But, Australia's policy has been not to sell uranium to the non-parties of Nuclear Non-proliferation Treaty (NPT). However, John Howard's government in August 2007 overturned the ban on Australian uranium sales to India and finalized the deal. Howard stated that the deal "is based on the condition the uranium is used for peaceful purpose and India signing safeguard agreements with Australia and the UN's nuclear watchdog."[27] He added: "Assisting India to meet her rapidly growing energy needs using low emission energy sources such as nuclear power will make a huge contribution to reducing global greenhouse emissions."[28] Kevin Rudd, who opposed the deal when he was the opposition party leader, reversed this policy and announced Australia would not sell uranium to India in January 2008 three months after he became the Prime Minister of Australia.

Since then, the sale of uranium became a point of heated discussion between the two nations. India repeatedly requested Australia for revoking a ban on the supply of uranium. However, Australia, already a key supplier of other resources such as coal to India, is well positioned to meet India's energy demands. This was demonstrated in August 2008, with the conclusion of the US $ 20 billion deal between Exxonmobil and India's Petronet to supply Australian Liquefied Natural Gas to India from 2014 from the Gorgon project in Western Australia, which is the first long-term gas contract between the two countries. [29] India has become one of the leading energy customers of Australia.

However, Canberra remained steadfast in its policy of not selling uranium to NPT non-signatories. Indian External Affairs Minister, S.M. Krishna, raised the issue with his counterpart Kevin Rudd, the incumbent Australian Foreign Minister, during his visit in January 2011. Rudd acknowledged India's clean record on nuclear proliferation, but continued to maintain "it was Australia's national policy not to sell the yellow metal to NPT non-signatories."[30] While the Indian leaders persist in their request for the supply of uranium, there are some Australians also arguing in support of the sale of uranium to India. Sandy Gordon, specialist on Indian studies, favours the sale of uranium to India, as nuclear energy is clean energy, which will help India to emit low carbon into the environment, without prejudice to Australia's national interests and international nuclear mechanisms.[31]

As the relations between the two countries have been upgraded to that of "Strategic Partnership," there are innumerable opportunities for boosting trade and other areas for cooperation. The two sides created 'Australia-India Strategic Research Fund' an equal funding scheme worth of US $ 130 million to promote innovative research in marine science, agriculture, water management and nanotechnology. India and Australia are also working together under five Action Plans in the areas of mines, coal, renewable energy, petroleum and natural gas and power. Peter Drysdale, Australian Emeritus Professor of Economics, noted, "India and Australia are on the cusp of an historic opportunity for sharing a new, much more important relationship in the future than we have shared in the past." As India and Australia are building a broad range of collaborative projects in science and technology, New Delhi can also learn many things from Australia for the betterment of its people. particularly in land and water management, agricultural economics (cropping, dairying, livestock ranching), mineral prospecting, industrial development, environmental management, urban planning, social and economic infrastructural facilities.[32]

Conclusion

The long standing and matured relations between India and Australia being complementary in nature could play a key role in strengthening trade, economic, strategic and people-to-people ties. Though attacks on the Indian students and the sale of uranium issue came to the fore in the recent period, they did not adversely affect the process of closer links between the two being forged. From Indian perspective, Australia continued to be important on two counts, for supply of much needed resources and for India's integration in multilateral forums in the Asia-Pacific region. For Australia the emerging India could serve as a potential catalyst to get integrated with South Asia, as Canberra has become an observer in the South Asian Association for Regional Cooperation. Australia's fourth biggest migrant communities, Indian Diaspora, with their professional skills, are bound to put both the economies on high growth trajectory.

NOTES

\# Chief among the Australian companies in India are: Telstra (telecommunications); BHP Billiton (mining); Rio Tinto (mining); MIM Holdings (mining); Snowy Mountains Engineering Corporation (infrastructure development); Argyle diamonds (technical support office for diamond sales); P & O (development of container ports); Orica Limited (joint venture with Imperial Chemical Industries); Lucent Technologies (IT); ANZ (IT); Accor (Hotel Chain); Boral Ltd; and Qantas (Airlines).

± India's Oswal Group (Ammonia plant at Karratha, State of Western Australia); Sterlite Industries (two copper mines in the State of Tasmania); Aditya Birla Group (copper mines at Nifty, Western Australia); Gujarat NRE Coke (coal mines in New South Wales) are a few to reached an agreement with Linc Energy's Queensland, to get a stake in Galilee Basin coal deposits worth upto A$ 3 billion over 20 years. Bharat Petro Resources Ltd (BPRL) and Norwest Energy agreed to a 'farm-in' (exploration and investment agreement) in two of Norwest's Perth Basin permits (EP413 and TP/15). BPRL will invest nearly $10 million towards drilling and testing programs to evaluate the shale gas potential in the region. Tata Steel has visible presence in Brisbane.

REFERENCES

1. Nabeel Mancheri, " India-Australia: Skepticism beyond the economics," http://www.eastasiaforum.org/2011/02/16/india-australia-skepticism-prevails-beyond-economics/
2. Amitendu Palit, "India's trade deficits with China and Australia," *East Asia Forum*, 8 September 2010 , http://www.eastasiaforum.org/2010/09/08/indias-trade-deficits-with-china-and-australia/
3. "Bilateral Economic Relations," http://www.hcindia-au.org/bilateral_economic_relation.html
4. http://www.hcindia-au.org/bilateral_economic_relation.html
5. Fact sheet, *Department of Foreign Affairs and Trade*, 2010.
6. Purnendra Jain, "Australia's Asian Dilemma," *Global Asia*, Vol.3, No.3, Fall 2008, p.88.
7. B. Raman, "Kevin Rudd: All the Way With China," Paper No. 2680, 24 April 2008, http://www.southasiaanalysis.org/%5Cpapers27%5Cpaper2680.html

8. *Ibid.*
9. Joint Statement, Meeting Between The Prime Minister Of India, Dr Manmohan Singh, and the Prime Minister of Australia, Mr Kevin Rudd, New Delhi 12 November 2009, http://www.hcindia-au.org/pdf/joint_statement.pdf
10. Bob Birrell & T Fred Smith "Export earnings from the overseas student industry: how much?," *Australian Universities' Review,* vol. 52, no. 1, 2010, p.4.
11. "Expanding links with China and India," ABS *Australia Social Trends,* September 2009, p.3,http://www.ausstats.abs.gov.au/ausstats/subscriber.nsf/LookupAttach/4102.0Publication 24.09.092/$File/41020_ChinaIndia.pdf
12. Grame Hugo and Gauranga Lal Dasvarma, "Recent Developments in Indian Migration to Australia (with Special Reference to Academics)," in D. Gopal and Alan Mayne (eds.), *Cultural Diversity, Governance and Policy: India-Australia,* New Delhi, 2009, pp.213-215; see also ***Ibid***, p.4.
13. "Indian arrival in Australia," http://www.sikh.com.au/inaus/index.html?arrival.html~ bottomaus
14. Bob Birrell, "Implications of Low English Standards among Overseas Students at Australian Universities, *People and Place,* Monash University, Vol. 14, No. 4, 2006, p.58.
15. Christopher Ziguras, "Indian students in Australia: how did it come this?," http://globalhighered.wordpress.com/2009/08/11/indian-students-in-australia-how-did-it-come-to-this/
16. "Australia offers a truly harmonious experience for Indian students," http://www.pravasitoday.com/australia-offers-a-truly-harmonious-experience-for-indian-students%E2%80%99
17. Christopher Ziguras, n.15.
18. Bonnie Malkin, "Australia must protest foreign students from attacks, say China and India", *The Telegraph*, 4 June 2009.
19. Peter Spolc and Murray Lee, "Indian students in Australia: victims of crime, racism or the media?, http://proceedings.com.au/isana2009/PDF/paper_Spolc.pdf
20. http://www.anigalla.net/70mm/post/Amitabh-Bachchan-Rejects-Australias-Queensland-University-of-Technology-Doctorate.aspx
21. http://www.embraceaustralia.com/truth-behind-indian-student-attacks-in-australia-5823.htm

22. "Australian PM Kevin Rudd Says 'Indian Students are Welcome Guests to Australia," http://www.india-server.com/news/australian-pm-kevin-rudd-syas-indian-15789.html
23. "Ministerial Statement on the Australia-India Relationship," 9 February 2010, http://www.foreignminister.gov.au/speeches/2010/100209_australia_india.html
24. "Australia offers a truly harmonious experience for Indian students," n.16.
25. "Australia snubs India, refuses to lift ban on Uranium sale," http://www.expressindia.com/latest-news/Australia-snubs-India-refuses-to-lift-ban-on-Uranium-sale/739923/
26. Sascha Muller-Kraenner, *Energy Security,* London, 2007, p.59.
27. "Howard defends Australia-India nuclear deal," http//nebuchadnezzarwoolyd.blogspot. com/2007/08/ howard-defends-australia-india nuclear.html Error! Hyperlink reference not valid.
28. Ruth David, *"Australian Prime Minister Defends Nuclear Deal With India,"* http://www.forbes.com/2007/08/17/australia-india-nuclear-markets-equity-cx_rd_0817markets03.html
29. "India, Australia sign $20.5 bn gas deal," http://www.thaindian.com/newsportal/tag/ gorgon-project.
30. "Australia snubs India, refuses to lift ban on Uranium sale," n.25.
31. Sandy Gordon, *Implications of the Sale of Australian Uranium to India,* Working Paper No.410, Strategic and Defence Studies Centre, Australia National University, Canberra, September 2008, pp.2-8.
32. Y. Yagama Reddy, *India and Australia: Towards Realization of Prospects of Cooperation,* Centre for Southeast Asian and Pacific Studies, S.V. University, Tirupati, 2009, p.60.